THE
AMERICAN
TERRORISTS

THE AMERICAN TERRORISTS

The Untold True Story of a Real Telepath

BOO MARX

authorHOUSE®

AuthorHouse™
1663 Liberty Drive
Bloomington, IN 47403
www.authorhouse.com
Phone: 1 (800) 839-8640

Published by AuthorHouse 11/11/2016

ISBN: 978-1-4969-3124-5 (sc)
ISBN: 978-1-4969-3620-2 (e)

Print information available on the last page.

SPECIAL DEDICATION

I would like to thank all of those who helped me through these very trying times of this true story. Special thanks to those of MSNBC, especially Rachel Maddow. I would also like to thank Ainsley Earhardt of FOX News, San Diego California. Thanks for your support.

I would also like to thank Regis Philbin. It was nice of you and Ainsley to lend your open ears. I greatly appreciate it. You gave me more hope and will than you can possibly imagine. Thank you once again.

Jessica Alba, it was so nice talking to you. I have something to say to you someday that is a secret of my own and the coolest ever. You're the best.

I want to thank President Obama. I have to say, "What a weird way to meet one another." I gave it all I had mentally and even though it took a while for my act to come together I have finally succeeded. I'm even using a new tooth paste these days thanks to you.

Once again, thank you everyone for your support.

Finally, I would like to thank my parents, Patrick and Deborah; I love you both dearly. You've been the best parents anyone could ask for. I know you never fully understood what I was going through and even called me delusional at times, but when you read this story you will understand. This truly is a true story.

When I was six years old, I used to stay up at night listing to the oldies but goodies station on an old AM, FM radio my parents lent me. On one particular night late in the evening, I had turned off the radio before going to bed. But it seemed as if the music wanted to continue to play. Reaching down for the controls, I made sure the radio was off. And it was. The problem was I could still hear the oldies but goodies station. It was playing in my head. Faint, but still there. Making sure I wasn't hearing things, I turned the radio back on. What do you know? The music in my head matched exactly what was playing on the radio. A gentleman was singing, "That girl with her red dress on." Amazed, I began turning the radio on and off. Each time the radio was off, the music continuously played in my ears. It seemed I had the ability to hear radio waves.

For many hours on this same night I lie silently in my bed listing to the radio without it actually being on. I don't know what time it was, but I had eventually fallen asleep waking in the morning only to find I was no longer able to hear the radio waves.

For the last thirty years of my life, my ability to hear radio frequencies has randomly come and gone. The older I have become, the more frequent its presence has made its way into my life. Now, I hear the radio playing in my ears a few times a day.

What is even more amazing came four years after the night I discovered I could hear radio waves. I became telepathic at the age of ten.

In 2006, I decided to prove my gift to the world. I put myself into the public eye as a real telepath. In the process of putting myself out there, I was discovered by an Elite military force. This force was sent to my hometown to train me for a special agency.

Just before I was to leave home with this force, a dramatic change for the worse had occurred. This force decided to kill me instead.

I was tortured, raped, and brainwashed by this force for a period exceeding seven years.

They now call me Boo.

CHAPTER 1

The story I am about to reveal is very unbelievable, but true. It is of a commander of an Elite Force who tried killing me because I had discovered too many secrets in this world. With the help of the commander's soldiers, his tyrant behavior leads his teams to the rape of over 5,000 American civilians. Some of whom were children. Ladies and gentleman, meet the American Terrorists.

Seven years ago, I was discovered in a small town in Colorado as a real telepath. Prior to being discovered, I had many problems with alcohol abuse. My issues had landed me in prison for many years where I learned to be a better person in life as well as a more productive member in society. I can only let you imagine the hardships I went through which lead to a self-destructive pattern in life. Let me tell you, I put myself in many horrible situations throughout my journey.

In 2003, my abuse sent me to the Colorado Department of Corrections, the state penitentiary. I had been arrested for multiple DUI offenses, cultivation of marijuana, and criminal impersonation. I am not proud of my actions, instead I feel remorseful to say the least. This is why I changed my life and began to live by the golden rule; do onto others as you would want them to do unto you. I now keep this value as I live my life.

While incarcerated, I spent three years in Eastern Colorado living in an old correctional facility. The prison was set high in a valley of the Rocky Mountains under a series of snowcapped peaks. The winters were cold with snow and the summers were hot, dry, and windy.

"Welcome to the major leagues," a tall skinny black correctional officer said to a room full of tattooed convicts.

"You're now in the state correctional system and the rules of survival are a lot different in here than what you are used to," he continued with a sense of the military within him.

His dark shades worn indoors made him more of a character within his own presence. His overwhelming sternness shadowed his pace as he stepped from side to side in front of the thickly glassed windows of an orientation room. It was then I felt the power of the state correctional system; a power of self-fear and loneliness; a power unknown to any other man other than those who've sat in the seats surrounding me. It was this power that changed my life forever.

I spent three years in an old concrete building which was originally built as a juvenile reform school now conformed into an adult prison. It was surrounded by large security towers and chain linked fences mounted with razor wire. There were four wings holding three tiers: North, East, South and West. The tall exterior walls were painted white standing under a dated copper roof of a light green patina. Each tier was lined with thick metal security doors fortifying sixteen cells in a row on each level. With cells on both sides of the wing, each unit held close to two-hundred inmates. The walls were painted tan and you could feel the tension of conviction in the air.

My cell was 6 'ft. by 9 'ft. holding a stainless steel toilet on one end and a painted steel desk directly across, but on the same wall. Opposite the toilet rested a set of bunks which were welded to steel plates fastened to a concrete cinder block wall. At the edge of our bunk we had a large glass window secured by steel diamond shaped screening. It was large enough to see out of, but not large enough to escape from. The worst part, the place smelled of disinfectant resembling that of a sterile hospital.

Everyone had a job. I worked in the kitchen at nights serving meals off the line. The line I worked on only served the South and West wings. The North and East wing meals were served in a connecting chow hall to our right keeping order within the penitentiary during feeding times.

I hated that kitchen. There was just something about it.

When I wasn't working, I was allowed out of my cell for yard time two hours per day. My days were spent lifting weights with my cellmate James, A.K.A Peckerwood. He was a red haired kid around my age with a sturdy build. He talked a lot of shit, was funny as shit and while we lived together he discovered his only child who he adored since birth for five years was actually his best friends. I had to laugh when he told me the story in our cell one night after he found out from his mother while talking to her on the telephone.

"Fuck you Boo," he said smiling behind watered eyes knowing it was actually funny shit.

He ranted and raved for hours before I told him to sit down and shut the fuck up. He stopped in mid-sentence, started to laugh then tackled me while I was sitting on the edge of his bunk. We wrestled friendly for a while before he calmed down. Before I got off him, I wisely said, "What do you care, it's your best friends kid anyway."

He laughed once again before saying, "I loved that little fucker."

He spent the rest of the night telling me stories about his kid and his lady. I listened attentively thinking it was good for him to get it off his chest.

Chris was my first cellmate in the joint. He was a tall medium sized guy with a Go-tee and tattooed arms from his elbows to his shoulders. He had a tough way of talking, but underneath he was a kind heart.

At night, Chris and I liked to watch Jeopardy from our thirteen inch television screen seeing who could answer the most questions first correctly. I have to say he was pretty quick at the game beating me most of the time even though I was always there for the challenge. I had some good times with Chris and I always wonder how he's doing.

Showers and phone time were an hour at night usually around eight o'clock. There were six man showers which you always had to stand in line for. When time became scarce, inmates would share a shower head. While one washed off the other lathered up.

During the countless hours I spent in my cell thinking about life, I was able to seek out the true me. What I discovered was a proud kid who lost himself in a world of drugs and alcohol. Angered by my decisions in life, I chose to overcome my barriers framing myself into a more complete person. My first step was to humble myself.

By doing so, I spent most of my time reading books. When I wasn't reading, I was taking advantage of the many programs prison had to offer. I even worked in the graphics department painting huge advertisement billboards for the local softball and little leagues. It was here that I had begun to feel a sense of self admiration. A sense I still carry with me today.

Prison was full of hate for most of the inmates. It wasn't abnormal to see a weekly fight or two over money or drugs. Other times, it simply came down to a couple of cellmates just not getting along. Confinement in small areas sometimes challenged ones mental stability. This instability tends to make an inmate act out; usually in violence.

To stay away from the violence, I minded my own business only hanging out with a small group of guys which I chose wisely. These guys were usually the more mellow types who didn't get caught up in the prison political system; meaning involvement in racism or gang association. Involvement in politics usually ended up in disaster.

I managed to stay out of trouble most of my incarceration. I got into a couple of scuffles but nothing major. I stayed away from the drugs and the pressures inmates brought upon one another while incarcerated. It wasn't an easy three years, but it was the right three years. I had time to find myself and a chance to discover a place I never wanted to be involved with ever again. It was a place of hell.

A year into my term, I was witness to an outrageous act of violence. Peckerwood was staring through the window of our cell door when he heard a large black man named, Shasta, yelling from a cell across the way.

We had been back from morning chow for almost a half an hour so most of the inmates were already in their beds sleeping. The place was silent except for Shasta's yelling.

"You keep banging that broom against those stairs I'm going to fuck you up white boy," he would say.

He was shouting through his cell door toward a porter who swept the tier. Each morning while the porter swept, he would bang the wooden broom end against the side of the steel stairs as he descended to the next level. Shasta's cell was next to those stairs, so every morning he was disturbed by the disruption.

"Go ahead mother fucker bang that broom again," Shasta continued with rage in his voice.

Beginning to laugh, Peckerwood looked towards me from the cell door and said, "Hey Boo, check this out. Shasta is over here freaking the fuck out. James the porter is pissing him off with the broom. You know that annoying banging we hear every morning. Well, Shasta's not having it anymore."

My curiosity had me jumping from my bunk to observe the situation. As I scuttled toward the cell door, Peckerwood stepped out of the way allowing me to see for myself. As I peered across, I could see Shasta yelling through the window of his cell.

James, the porter, had his back toward Shasta. The more Shasta yelled the less James paid attention. I could even see a slight smirk at the corner of James' lips. He was antagonizing Shasta.

James was a white kid about medium build and height. His skinny neck and small head supported a set of coke bottle glasses. He was known for having a temper and I believe the boy was crazy.

As James continued to sweep the stairs, he also continued to bang the broom. It even seemed he was putting a little more into the noise since Shasta was so ticked off. This action outraged Shasta even more. The more James banged the broom, the more Shasta yelled.

"You stupid mother fucker I'm going to get you," Shasta exclaimed!

James having enough of Shasta's shit turned around going from calm to spastic. He shouted toward Shasta's cell, "Shut the fuck up you dumb mother fucker."

At this point, Peckerwood and I had our heads squeezed together so we could both see out of our window at the same time. We were laughing hysterically.

As soon as the words left James' mouth, we noticed Shasta's reaction. His mouth stopped moving and his face scrunched in anger. If he wasn't black, I would bet he was red as an apple. He couldn't believe the words coming from James.

Peckerwood and I couldn't believe it either since Shasta was doing life in prison without the possibility of parole. This meant he was a killer and wouldn't fear killing again.

"Oh shit it's on now," Peckerwood said excitedly.

I continued to stare out the window anxious to see how Shasta was going to handle the situation. He was no small man by any means and definitely not a guy you would want to fuck with since he was doing life.

"Fuck you white boy," Shasta said in an almost tranquil state.

But, he was anything but tranquil. He had the look of a man who was about to kill. James, showing no fear towards Shasta, continued by starring Shasta down. When James had enough of the starring contest, he gave Shasta a cocky look before saying wisely, "What?"

Shasta raised his chin high in the air. With lighting speed he jabbed his index finger against the glass window towards James. With vengeance, Shasta said, "I'm going to get your punk ass."

James, holding no fear returned, "Whatever bitch."

Two words you don't say in prison to another man unless you're prepared to fight; the word punk and the word bitch. These are fighting words. There is nothing worse than these two words.

James was ready to get his ass kicked.

In those moments, Shasta disappeared from the window. Peckerwood and I waited in anticipation. James went back to sweeping the stairs still banging the broom as if the confrontation had meant nothing. Peckerwood and I knew it wasn't over. We stood there watching waiting to see the outcome.

Minutes later, James made his way to the bottom of the stairs as the unit Sergeant's voice echoed through the building from the intercom, "Morning work lines. Doors will be opening."

At the same time every morning, cell doors opened for inmate work crews. It was at this time Shasta decided to make his move.

Still starring through the window, Peckerwood and I watched as Shasta's cell door slid on its track opening. Before it was all the way open, Shasta squeezed through the door running at full speed towards James. In his hand, he had a wooden spike formed into a shank about ten inches long.

Wooden shanks were preferred by inmates and obtained from the wood shop. They were preferred because they were able to make it through metal detectors without detection.

Knowing the doors had opened, James turned from the stairs towards Shasta's cell surprised by Shasta's violent approach. Not knowing how to react or what to do, James stood there in astonishment. Before he knew what was happening, Shasta was on him. With Shasta's right arm out wide and dagger in hand, he swung the pointed end towards James' lower rib cage in an attempt to reach his heart.

Shasta was out to kill James and everything on his face said he wasn't going to stop until James was dead.

The first blow bounced off James' rib cage stilling the dagger. With quickness and furry, Shasta pulled the dagger back swinging for a second time. But, James had moved his hand to his side where the first blow had struck. While his hand was covering the first wound Shasta stuck the dagger with enough force to penetrate through James' hand continuing into his body pinning his hand to the side of his chest.

Leaving the dagger in place, Shasta walked away. At least six inches of the shank's point was inside of James. James was horrified.

Blood immediately poured from James' side as he lie on the ground with a glazed look over his eyes from behind his thick glass lenses. Shasta continued towards his cell leaving James to bleed out and die. Peckerwood and I couldn't believe it.

And what I saw next astonished me even more. As inmates approached the stairs, they walked by James as if nothing had happened. As if he was meant to die. I couldn't help but feel bad for the kid as I watched blood pour from his body pooling by his side. He was going to die and nobody made an attempt to do anything about it.

Standing there watching, my thoughts were interrupted by the Sergeants voice over the intercom.

"Lock down. Lock down everyone," the Sergeant shouted.

Immediately, inmate workers returned to their cells as groups of correctional officers raced down the stairs towards James.

James was coughing and rolling around in his own blood. Behind a parade of officers, the Sergeant followed with a body board to put James on so they could carry him to the infirmary. Within seconds James was strapped to the board. As they lifted him to the air and as they raced up the stairs blood flowed down his side leaving a trail in his path all the way to the infirmary.

I didn't know James well, but I hoped he had survived.

We stayed locked in our cells for the next couple of weeks as the correctional officers investigated the situation. We were stripped naked cell by cell and lead to the gym where we were questioned by the correctional officers. When I was asked if I saw anything, I kept my mouth shut and moved on with the rest of the crowd. As we were being questioned, our cells were shook down making sure there were no other weapons in the facility. Later on, we were informed that twenty-eight shanks were found throughout the unit. I was shocked to say the least.

For the rest of my incarceration, I thought a great deal about James. The officers did tell us he had survived, but the occurrence left its mark on me. It made me realize how serious things were in the penitentiary and how fucked up it could get real quick.

In the end, I was glad to hear James was okay.

Throughout my remaining time in Eastern Colorado, I decided to lay low. Peckerwood was a tattoo artist so I let him tattoo the shit out of me while we made the best out of the time we had. He had a way of making life inside the walls not so bad and I loved him for it.

Thank you Peckerwood...

CHAPTER 2

After prison, I was released into my parent's custody for a parole term of two years. I was free, fresh, and in search of a better way of life. I felt I had the ability to tackle the world. But, I was wrong. Within months, I was back to my old destructive behaviors with drugs and alcohol. I found myself locked in a room with a bottle in one hand and a pipe in the other doing nothing but hurting myself once again.

After a couple months of partying, I had dropped my second dirty urine screen for the parole department. With my parole officer upset with me, I was told to enter a drug treatment program for a period of six months. Feeling I let myself down, I was eager to enter the program.

The drug program which I had entered was located in a renovated community from the early 1940's. It was a gray home of Victorian Design with large windows on the side and an enclosed porch out front. The paint was peeling from the siding and the white window trim was in shambles. There were grass yards in both the front and back of the home with patches of dirt thrown about from many long dry summers.

The interior of the home wasn't much better than the exterior. There was old cheap short haired wall-to-wall carpet worn thin from the many years of foot traffic from recovering addicts who passed in and out of the program's doors. The walls were scuffed from the backs of chairs which lined the dining area and meeting rooms meant for group discussions. The whole place had the smell of old furniture from a dusty attic. A smell I did not like.

Behind the dining area was a kitchen with a large stainless steel basin and a four burner stove top just as you walked in. Next to the burners was a flat grill cleaned by the clients every night after dinner. A small room just beyond the kitchen housed a double steel door refrigerator.

The main floor was primarily for group discussions such as AA and NA meetings. It had a dual purpose as a dining area. Both the upstairs and downstairs were fit with sleeping quarters. The upstairs had three separated rooms with two beds in each room. Standing at the end of the hallway stood a rundown bathroom with a leaky sink faucet and a moldy tiled tub. Each room including the hallway was lined with tread-bear brown carpeting.

The basement also had three rooms except these rooms were larger than those on the second floor and each room had three beds with one large closet. In-between each bed stood old wooden night stands with a small drawer for storing personal items. The carpet was much the same as the upstairs, worn thin in many areas. Outside of the bedrooms was a large room with a couch, a reading chair and an old color television which could only be watched at night during certain hours.

The whole house was rundown and outdated. To me, it was a very depressing place to be. But, I decided to make the most of it.

My first day in the program was a bit awkward. A majority of the clients were much older than me and the house reminded me of that of a third world country. I didn't like it here and I didn't want to be here.

With fifteen members on the male side, we spent our days working in a donation center which supported the rehabilitation program. I spent my days assembling old computers and stereo systems while the others sorted through donated clothing. I figured I had a good job.

At night, we spent our time in AA meetings around town. I didn't mind since the stories people told always seemed to amaze me. Some stories were funny while others were depressing. But, each story was unique in its ability to describe the character of the tale; the person telling the story which usually ended up with him passing out in somebody's front yard or caught by the police pissing in some random area around town. You can imagine the amount of time I spent laughing.

After a couple of weeks in the program, I became very board. I tried reading books, but my mind wasn't right at the time. I had to find something more exciting. There was this one guy, Jim. He was a retired history and gym teacher with one hell of an alcohol problem. While at work one day, I began answering the man's questions before he had asked them. I figured since he was a teacher, he would be smarter than the rest.

After days of answering Jim's thoughts, Jim became very suspicious. I overheard a conversation he was having with another member of our program. He said, "I think Boo is a fucking psychic."

"No way," the other man exclaimed while keeping his head low looking cautiously in my direction.

"I think he is," the teacher went on.

"He knows what you're going to ask him before you even ask," he continued.

I smiled as the conversation went on. Each time one spoke, the other curiously gazed in my direction.

Three days had gone by as I telepathically toyed with the teacher. Finally, I decided to let him in on my little secret.

We sat down for dinner the same as any other night. Proceeding dinner, I went down to my room where I wrote on a yellow sticky note, "I'm not a psychic. I'm a telepath."

I then took the note upstairs to the teacher's room where he was standing in front of a mirror combing his hair.

"Here," I said handing him the sticky.

He gave me a crooked look before grabbing the note from my hand. I gave him a short smile then turned towards the door heading for the stairs. Descending, I took hold of the railing thinking, *"He's going to trip out after reading that one."*

Once I was on the main floor, I waved to our cook who was a man with twenty years in the military as a Marine. He gave me the same curious smile he always had by tilting his head to one side smirking. With a sly smile, I turned the corner and headed down another set of stairs towards my bedroom in the basement. I then laid down waiting for the game to begin.

No more than 10 minutes later, I heard the teacher on the main floor speaking to some of the members of the program including the cook who had been working for the rehabilitation center for many years. He said, "He's not a psychic. He's a real telepath."

The men in the room couldn't believe their ears.

"No way, how do you know," many responded?

"He gave me this," Jim continued as I imagined him handing over the yellow sticky.

The chatter upstairs was expected as curious minds assembled with talk of a real telepath. I rolled over on my bed clenching my pillow within my arms. As I lie there listening, a colossal of voices filled the kitchen as more and more members gathered.

Many of the members were in shock as I heard them ask, "A real telepath?"

Jim was into telling his story. He said to the group, "Yah, he always knows what I'm looking for at work before I ask him."

"That's cool," a member answered.

After a few minutes, the crowd seemed to disperse. But before they left the kitchen, a man named Bob decided to put my telepathic abilities through a test. He said to the other members, "Let's ask him questions telepathically and see if he answers."

"That's a good idea," the group answered.

Moments later, a tall skinny elderly man with fourteen years' experience in the Navy stood in my doorway. His arms were held high with his hands hanging from the door trim above his head. I gazed down the length of my bed over my toes towards him observing the expression on his face. His eyes squinted and a thought left his brain entering mine. He thought, *"Are you a real telepath?"*

Peering back at him, I answered his question, "Yes, I am."

His eyes immediately opened widely as he began to smile. Shaking his head in amazement he said, "Alright kido."

He then turned away and walked out the door trudging up the stairs. Moments later, I heard him talking to the others.

"He really is telepathic," I heard him say.

"No way, how do you know," they responded.

He then said, "I asked him if he was telepathic, telepathically and he answered me."

The others began to laugh shouting, "A real telepath. Who would of thought?"

The next day, I woke early in the morning. A few programmers passed my direction with strange glares on their faces as others asked me questions telepathically. I answered each of them individually watching as their faces

The American Terrorists

formed in wonder. For the first time in my life, I was able to feel the effects from people knowing I was a real telepathic. I had put myself out there. And I must say, as weird as it was, it felt good.

For the next week, I answered everyone's thoughts as they were projected towards me. Their responses were the same every time, complete and utter astonishment. I even began answering some of the employees at the donation center since word had gotten out. The reactions were all the same. Some opened their mouths in awe as others furrowed their eyes in disbelief. Some turned red in the face with shock and others laughed. I even had a couple of girls say, "That's fucking cool."

It wasn't long before word of a real telepath had gotten out. Between the rehabilitation center and the clothing donation warehouse, close to 50 people had become aware of my abilities. It was at this moment, I decided to write a book about my life.

Part of our responsibilities at the rehabilitation center required we attend AA meetings around town four nights out of the week. Every time we went to an AA meeting, the members of my program would speak of me. Before and after meetings, I heard chatter about my abilities amongst small groups of people.

As I continued showing up for AA meetings, I started to notice more and more people from town filling the seats of Alcoholics Anonymous. It seemed I had become a hit with the locals; famous in a way.

It wasn't long before the entire town of Grand Junction knew of a real telepath. Everywhere I turned, the story was being told. I even think someone took my picture and put it on the internet because I ran into people whom I've never seen before who recognized me as the telepath.

"There he is," they would say passing by.

I couldn't believe how fast my fame was spreading.

After a while, I wondered if I had done right by letting people know my secret. I even began having thoughts of the government coming after me.

"They may think I know too much. Maybe they would even try killing me," I thought.

I shook off the thoughts with a dull smile telling myself it would be alright. I shrugged my shoulders thinking, *"It's already too late. Everyone already knows who I am and I might even be on the internet. If they come for me, I'll just act stupid like I don't know what they're talking about. Yah, that's what I'll do."*

As time passed, people in the program had become overwhelmed with my ability. It even began making some of them jealous. A majority of them also became insecure with their thoughts. They didn't want a real telepath around. They didn't want me in their thoughts and I was becoming an outcast by the members of the program.

Eventually, people stopped talking to me altogether; something that has never happened in my entire life. I was always a very popular kid, but telepathy was suddenly making me very unpopular. It had gotten to the point where they began making fun of me in order to feel better about themselves. They started calling me a homo sexual. Some even made statements like, "I bet he's a transvestite, or he was probably a girl."

I was saddened by the accusations. Being a tough kid, I lashed out and called them on their bullshit. This made things even worse. It wasn't long before I had many enemies within the program. Only time would cure the situation. They were just going to have to accept a real telepath around.

And it did cool down. As the days went by, members of the house adjusted to my presence. They even began talking to me once again even though I didn't have much to say because of the way I was treated. Being a strong minded person, I was able to forgive them after a while.

The members of the program were made mostly of ex-military from the Vietnam era. All branches were accounted for including the Army, Navy, Marines, and Air Force. Because of the manner in which I stood my ground, they began thinking that I may have been in the military.

But, I wasn't…

*

One Sunday afternoon, the director took us miles away over the desert landscapes to a cave leading out onto a rocky face. Inside the cave, a crack nine feet below us rose from the ground to a mantle where we stood. The only way to continue was to descend down the rock faces of the crack where the trail picked up once again.

Watching members of the group descending before me, I noticed their struggle as their feet quickly slid down the sides of the crack causing them to scrape knees and elbows. I was quiet with my humor as I watched their uncoordinated movements.

When it came my turn, I decided to descend upside down. Since I grew up rock climbing and hiking, the task would be no problem. I placed my hands out from my body pushing against the sides of rock faces and began walking my fingers downward on both sides with my palms sliding with the movement. Soon, I was descending like a spider with my feet curving over the edge of the mantle holding my legs in place. Once I was completely upside down, I firmly pushed against the rocks with my hands holding my body in place then lowered my legs to the floor. With my feet planted firmly on the ground, I let out a deep breath before looking over my shoulder towards the director who was standing at the top of the mantle. He cleverly smiled shaking his head from side to side. Knowing I had his approval, I turned around exiting to the other side.

At the end of the tunnel, I heard the director's voice echo off the cavern's walls. He said to the others, "I'm telling you guys, this kid's not only a real telepath he's in the military as well and he's one of their best."

On the way back to the van, I stayed close to the group. Behind us, I overheard the counselors speaking of me. From what I could here they couldn't believe I was a real telepathic. And after a few minutes of them talking, the director whom had twenty-two years in the Navy said, "I'd even bet this kid's a Navy SEAL.

"Really," the others spoke astonished.

The Director continued, "I bet he is. The way he climbed those rocks and the way he acts he's definitely military and probably a Navy SEAL."

Back at the van, I stood on a rock away from the others listening for what the counselors would say to the group. Just as I expected, he whispered, "I think he's a Navy SEAL."

The group was in awe.

*

The air was cold with overcast skies supporting white cirrus clouds. A light January wind crossed our path as we scuttled from the van's sliding side door one by one lining up in front of the rehabilitation center's front door.

While I waited with the others for the front door to open, the oddest thing happened. I was standing just opposite the American flag which hung from a pole attached to the side of the house. It blew briskly in the wind. Noticing the colors of our flag, I took a moment to gaze at its presence feeling the power of our country; the power of the United States of America. As I stood there lost in thought, the wind seized to exist. Immediately, the flag dropped down by my side missing my shoulders by mere inches. It was at this moment, I felt proud to be an American.

The site must have been even more amazing to those who stood around me. Gasps filled the sudden silence. Next, the telepathic readings I received were most intriguing.

"That was amazing," I heard from many.

But, the words catching my attention the most were, *"This kid has powers. He just stopped the flag with his head."*

It made me wonder if I had other abilities besides telepathy.

Inside, I laughed as their thoughts entered my brain thinking to myself, *"I truly am a miracle."*

With everyone thinking I was a Navy SEAL, I began to imagine I was one of them. I liked the idea and it sat well with me. I decided I wanted to be a real United States Navy SEAL.

A couple of days after the flag dropped by my side, some of those at the rehabilitation center began going back to their old ways. Seeing the possibilities of powers made them more jealous than ever. Once again, they started talking under their breath to one another. They began to bash me as a SEAL when I never actually told them I was a real SEAL. In reality, they were only bashing their own imaginations.

I heard comments like, "He's not a SEAL he's not tough enough." And, "That boy's no killer. Navy SEALS are straight killers."

With the house made mostly of ex-military, I had a tough time arguing with their judgment. They were wrong. I was definitely tough enough and I knew I had the ability to become a killer. War against America meant war against me. If you were against our country, than you were against the people I love like my mother, father, brothers, and friends. This meant I could kill the enemy. I could do it. With this in mind, I set out to prove everyone wrong by turning myself into the perfect Navy soldier.

It started at dinner one night as I sat in my chair eating spaghetti and meatballs. Directly across from me sat a man in his late fifties who had many years in the Marine Corp. Obviously he had since retired, but he still had his military pride.

Knowing SEALS were smart, I figured they would also have excellent table manners. Because of this, I made sure I had perfect manners the way my father had taught me since I was a child.

With manners in mind, I had one arm by my side resting on my lap. My back was right against the chair as I held my fork with that of a proper mannered man. I began eating my spaghetti by raising my food to my mouth without bending my head over my plate. Waiting for the Marines approval, I took a moment to gaze in his direction.

To my surprise, he had a look of disgust. With his look, I wondered what I had done wrong. Then, a thought from his head entered mine.

He thought, "*You're no SEAL.*"

Instantly, I blushed at whatever mistake I had made. Not knowing, I took another bite from my plate in the same fashion as the first. Once again, I was rewarded with the same reaction except this time he grunted while banging his fork against his plate giving me the most unwelcome expression I had ever seen.

His thought, "*You're no SEAL. You're a boy born with a silver spoon in his mouth.*"

I couldn't believe his thoughts. I even became devastated by the situation. I had pulled the wrong move. Not wanting to change my manners, I continued with my meal hoping his attitude would change. It had not. He gave me the same unappealing look time after time through the course of our meal.

After dinner, I went down stairs embarrassed with myself. I began thinking, "*Where was I mistaken. Surely a real Navy SEAL would have proper manners being a disciplined soldier.*"

Then it hit me, SEALS were killers. They were trained to kill and untrained in manners. A SEAL wouldn't care about proper manners because he is a true warrior. True warriors eat, sleep, shit, and fight. They were good at killing not eating. That's where I had gone wrong. I needed to act more like a killer; more like a warrior.

The next morning, I woke for breakfast heading to the dining area with the others. With the thought of a true Navy SEAL in mind and the art of owning my food, I went through the breakfast line choosing a seat across from the Marine once again. Looking directly into his eyes, I set my plate hard on the table making sure I made my presence known. With my eyes drilled into him, I pulled my chair from its position and took my place at the table. Next, I rested both my elbows in front of me while wrapping my arms around my food grabbing my fork with my right thumb and palm as if I had no manners at all. I then bent over my meal and began shoveling food into my mouth like a Neanderthal.

"*I'm a soldier,*" I had in mind.

Within seconds, the Marine had a smile from ear to ear. Inside, I was smiling too. His thought, "*Maybe, he is a real SEAL!*"

I was overwhelmed with joy. I had pulled it off. I wanted the respect. I wanted the respect of a true Navy SEAL.

Over the next week, I continued to learn telepathically from the men of ex-military. The more I paid attention to their thoughts, the more I learned from them. I learned how to eat, sleep, act, and attack like a SEAL. I never broke eye contact, I slept straight like a board and I only bent over when eyes weren't on me. When I finished learning all I could from them, I had become the structure of the perfect Navy SEAL.

It wasn't long before the entire town of Grand Junction knew there was a real SEAL in their presence. Word had gotten out through the AA meetings and soon the meeting rooms were packed with new members anxiously waiting to see a real telepathic Navy SEAL. Amazing didn't procure the expressions on their faces and their thoughts were much the same, "*Oh my God, a real telepathic Navy SEAL.*"

The funny thing was I never actually told anyone I was a real SEAL. I just let their imaginations get the best of them. And the more I learned from the ex-military, the better my presentation had become.

*

What happened next, took me by surprise. My presence as a SEAL began to intimidate members of the program. They even became a little scared of me. My character had become so tough they began accusing me of terrorism.

"Be careful around that guy," they would say.

"He might me a terrorist."

I was saddened by the remarks. My plan had backfired. Instead of being portrayed as a SEAL, I was now being gazed upon as an evil being; a devil; a terrorist. The situation wasn't good.

Back at the rehabilitation center I had to act fast. With murmurs of terrorism on their lips, I needed a new plan. Leaving a group of skeptical programmers upstairs, I walked confidently down to my room where I began to think. Instantly, I had an ingenious idea as I looked across the room toward the closet where an array of colored plastic coat hangers dangled from the rack. My eyes sifted through them seeking out the proper colors. Yanking the colors of our national flag, I arranged them in their proper order; red, white and blue.

Walking out of the room, I made my way up the stairs toward the dining area where skeptics sat around chow tables in small groups whispering to one another about the situation. They had scared eyes and weary looks. They thought I was a terrorist.

Walking past them, I jingled the hangers in my hand making sure everyone could see the colors I was holding; the colors of our country; red, white and blue.

I continued into the kitchen where the cook stood with a knife in his hand slicing onions. Lifting his head from his work, I noticed he wasn't wearing his usual friendly smile. When he looked down upon my hand holding the three hangers, he took a step back.

His thought, *"He's an American!"*

For a brief moment, we stood there laughing at one another. He even nodded his head in approval. He knew I was an American and he also knew it was a clever act. He was once a Marine himself and I could tell by the expression on his face he now understood me. He also understood my purpose as a United States Soldier.

Next, I moved around the house making sure everyone saw what I stood for. I made sure they knew I was an American and I made sure they knew I was proud to be an American.

In the end, it was as I had expected. I was granted a sigh of relief and a newly refreshed warm welcoming. I was no longer a terrorist in the eyes of the beholder. I had done it. I had changed the tide in my favor.

Knowing I had succeeded, I walked down to my bedroom where I awaited the responding gossip toward my patriotic act. Within minutes the whole house was talking. I heard, "He's not a terrorist. He's one of ours."

Laughter filled the rooms above. I even heard a couple of the military guys shout, "We're going to war."

Their response made me smile as I imagined the expressions on their faces. I remember thinking, "*They believed in me. They finally believed in me.*"

*

My situation in the program improved as time went on. The members began respecting me as both a person and a real telepath. With the previous hype, I have to say I was glad it was over.

But, it wasn't. What happened next was completely out of line. One of my roommates, Josh, who remained jealous of my abilities decided to steel money from a dresser drawer in my room. With the money, he bought a large bag of rolling tobacco. Each time he rolled a cigarette, he would rub the theft in by laughing in my face. He would look at me and laugh making sure I knew he was the one who had stolen from me.

Totally pissed by the situation, I grabbed the bag of tobacco and flushed it down the toilet. In the process of my actions, I was busted by the cook.

"What are you doing? Was that good tobacco you just flushed," he asked.

"Yup," I responded a little wary.

The cook unaware of the situation asked, "Why did you do that?"

Blushed in the face, half because I was pissed and half because I had been busted, I said, "Because it was mine."

Confused, the cook stared at me before saying, "You're crazy!"

I knew he didn't understand my actions and I wasn't going to tell my reasoning. To the best of my ability, I made an attempt to smile before sadly answering, "Only if you knew."

Stealing from another member in the program was an automatic dismissal. Knowing this, I was at risk of being kicked out of the program even though I was stolen from first.

Shortly afterward, Josh heard of what had happened. With the news, he came barging into our room finding his tobacco missing. Steam spouted from his ears as he gave me the most hateful look in the world. A look I enjoyed most dearly. I laughed in his face. I laughed as he stomped out of the room.

That night, I was approached by the director. Josh had squealed on me. The director asked if I had stolen Josh's tobacco. Not saying a word,

I just smiled. I wasn't one to tell on someone and I figured the director knew my character well enough to figure there must have been a reasonable explanation for my actions. Assuming he would discover the truth in due time, I decided not to continue on with the conversation. Instead, I shrugged my shoulders before going about my business.

The next day, I had a sad awakening. My parole officer drove down to the donation center while we were working. As he approached, I noticed his hand reaching behind his back pulling out a set of handcuffs. Knowing what was coming next, I thought, *"Fuck, this can't be happening."*

He then said the words. The words no convict wants to hear. The words a kid like me didn't want to hear since I never belonged in prison in the first place. Sure I made my mistakes, but I never believed I was a bad enough to deserve prison.

He said, "Boo, can you turn around and spread your legs for me?"

I boiled over. I was ashamed of myself. I knew where I was heading. I knew I was on my way back to the penitentiary. Obeying his command, I turned around spreading my legs.

"Do you know why I'm here," he asked?

"Yah," I answered.

When I turned around to face him, he presented an unwilling expression before saying, "You're going back to prison on a parole violation."

Then, the sound of cuffs...

There was nothing I could do. I was broken and wouldn't show it. Once again, I had let myself as well as my family down. I was on my way back to the pen.

My parole officer and I had gotten along fairly well, so I understood his concern. The only problem was, it was mandatory that I complete the program since I screwed up on parole once before. There was nothing else he could do. It was over. I was on my way back to prison for some really stupid shit.

With my hands cuffed behind my back and my parole officer leading towards his vehicle, I decided leaving the program wasn't such a bad idea. I had been going through really emotionally weird shit and I thought it best I was being removed from the situation.

Weeks later, I heard Josh had been kicked out of the program. After I had gone, members from the rehabilitation center had concern for me.

They told the director Josh had stolen to buy the bag of tobacco. I was then informed by the director I was welcome back to the program if I chose to do so. Deciding prison was a better place for me, I declined the offer. In reality, I was tired of the criticism. I simply wanted to be left alone.

CHAPTER 3

On our way to the County jail, my parole officer asked why I had stolen from Josh. I laughed saying, "I didn't steal from him; he stole from me."

I then explained the story in further detail. Glancing over his shoulder, my parole officer said, "If I didn't know any better, I would say you're excited to be out of there."

I was truly glad to be out of there. Not wanting to answer too quickly, I took a moment to think before saying, "I am."

Leaning further back in my seat, I sighed with certain calmness and a feeling of relief. My officer chuckled and said, "You'd rather be in prison than in rehab?"

Taking another pause, I answered, "Yes, yes I would."

John, my parole officer, chuckled once again before saying with concern, "Alright, it's your life. You would just think it would have been easier to stay in the rehab for six months. All you had to do was keep your shit together for six months and you were home free. Now you have to go back to prison."

I knew he would never understand, so I just laid back and sighed. All the horrible memories from rehab struck my brain. When I thought about it, I was honestly happy to be out of there.

*

When we pulled into the county jail, we entered through a back gate leading us into a sally port where two sheriffs wearing green uniforms with gold badges hanging from their breast pockets stood awaiting our arrival.

When our vehicle stopped, the officer closest to me opened my door saying, "Alright kido, let's go."

With the door open, he reached inside grabbing my arm with his hand. He directed me from the vehicle advising that I watch my head on the way out. We then proceeded to a large green steel door where we stood while the other officer spoke into a radio strapped from his shoulder. He said, "This is 431. We have one in from sally port."

Moments later, the steel door clanked while popping open. Inside was a large room surrounded by cinder block walls with thick glass windows. Two female officers stood behind each section shuffling through paperwork.

I was told to face the far wall away from the paper shufflers while the officer holding my arm released the handcuffs from my wrists. I was then stripped of my clothes while standing there naked as the other officer instructed me through a series of body checks. One of these checks included bending over and coughing. Not one of my favorites in the series.

Once I finished with the strip check, I was handed a set of green scrubs; the standard Mesa County jail uniform. Most jails use orange but Mesa County used colors separating each housing unit.

I put on the outfit and was directed toward one of the heavy glass windows where one of the Mexican ladies asked a series of questions which consisted of my name, social security number and charges. I informed her I had no charges; rather I was here on a parole violation. She smiled sliding a small stack of papers through a two inch rectangular section under the glass.

She said, "Read and sign here."

I had been through the routine many times, so I reached under the glass snatching a pen with my two fingers and began signing on the dotted lines.

When finished, I was directed to another room where I was placed in a cell for eight hours until the booking process was complete. The only way to do this time was to sleep. So, I slept for eight hours.

After eight or so hours, I was pulled from my cell then led to a room where I was given two sheets, a towel, two pairs of socks, a hygiene pack, two wool blankets and lastly a green bed mat consisting of two inches of foam encased in plastic. With my newly acquired possessions tucked under my arm, I was escorted through another steel door down a long corridor to a pod filled with 30 cells.

After a brief orientation process with the shift sergeant, I was given a cell number and informed of feeding times.

"Don't be late because you won't get fed," the sergeant said sternly during his speech.

Turning from him, I searched for the cell number written on an index card which was handed to me during orientation. Once in my cell, I rolled out my bed mat then stretched one of the two sheets around its corners tying knots on end so it wouldn't move from its place; a trick I learned from many years in the penitentiary. Stuffing one of the wool blankets in a spare shirt, I made a pillow before laying down to rest.

Intake was a seven day process, so I would be sleeping a lot awaiting my placement in general population. Having the ability to hibernate made this an easy task. Not only could I sleep for a week straight, I could sleep for months on end.

This had nothing to do with depression. This is how I am. This is how I do time. I just keep sleeping.

After twelve days in the intake pod, I was moved to general population. I wasn't there for more than five minutes when the pod officer recognized me as the telepathic Navy SEAL.

"*There he is*," he thought.

He must have seen me on the internet or been around one of the Alcoholics Anonymous rooms. He was standing behind a large round control center which was used to open cell doors for recreation times. Knowing I shouldn't have answered him, but unable to resist I turned to him and said, "Here I am."

His mouth hit the floor with my words. He said, "You heard that?"

"Yes sir," I answered.

He then said in surprise, "Holy shit a real telepath."

I laughed from the expression on his face. I also laughed knowing I had just screwed up by blowing my cover.

"*Well, so much for remaining under the radar,*" I thought. "*Now the sheriffs know who I am and I'm going to have to go through the same bullshit I just went through at the rehab. This is just great.*"

After some thought, I decided, "*I'll just have to give them the same show I gave the people from the rehabilitation center. I'll give them a real Navy SEAL.*"

Later that night, I was in my room gazing through the thick rectangular glass window on the cell door towards the control booth where the sheriff who recognized me stood with two other deputies chatting. He was facing the two deputies telling of a story I could not hear. I knew by his body movements that he was talking about me. While he was in the middle of his story, the two deputies pulled their heads away making it possible for me to read their lips.

They said with an expression, "No way."

"Yah," the unit officer answered before turning in my direction to point towards my cell.

To their surprise, I was peering upon them no more than forty feet away. Instead of looking away guiltily, the two deputies waved. Happy to see them so excited, I returned the gesture by waving back as they nodded their heads in disbelief.

I have to say it was a relief to see they were on my side.

During recreation hours, I hung around the control booth answering the sheriffs telepathically. They were in utter astonishment. Soon, deputies were coming two and three at a time to see who I was and if I was indeed a real telepath. I proved I was.

Because I am a real telepath, the sheriffs also believed I was a real Navy SEAL. As you know I wasn't. But to make sure they believed I was a SEAL, I kept up with the show. I ate, slept, and walked like a warrior. I never put my head down and I never bent over. Between my actions and telepathy, the officers were convinced I was the real deal; a real SEAL.

After weeks of putting on my show, the sheriffs were so overtaken by the thought of a telepathic Navy SEAL they decided to call the Navy to find out if I was in fact a real Seal. They soon learned the Navy had never heard of me, but were willing to check me out.

Two days later I was in the jail yard which was a fifty by fifty concrete enclosure with a chain link fence for a ceiling. I was in the middle of the yard doing pushups when I began to hear two male voices speaking through thin air. With the military instilled in their voices, one of the gentlemen said, "If he does a hundred of those he's going."

Since I had already started my workout, I was only able to do 86 pushups. Not bad considering I had already completed eight-hundred push-ups in a series of sets. Curious to where the voices were coming from, I looked around the yard. Nobody was around except for me. I even peered through the glass windows leading into the control booth. There was nobody. I then brought my focus back to the yard where I noticed a video camera in the corner high above me.

The voices said, "He's looking for us."

Taking a second to think, I guessed the camera had some kind of microphone attached to it making it possible for me to hear the deputies speaking from the security room. Satisfied I was correct, I went back to working out.

Working out my triceps, I had my hands on the edge of a wooden bench with my legs stretched outward doing dips. In the middle of my first set, the voices came back and said in the same military tone, "If he does a hundred of those he's going."

"*Going where,*" I thought curiously?

Still confused to where the voices were coming from, I began to wonder, "*Maybe it's the guys from the Navy.*"

Whoever it was, I was able to show them I could do a hundred dips without stopping.

The voices then said, "You're going."

I wasn't sure what it meant, but I was fairly certain it meant that I was going into the Navy and the voices were coming from Navy boys. The only question was, how was I hearing them?

At the time, it didn't matter who they were or how I was hearing them. I just wanted to finish my workout. So after I finished with my exercises, I ran around the yard for an hour to burn off some steam.

I never heard the voices after that night and I wondered for months who they were and what they were talking about. But I'll tell you my gut feeling, they were definitely military and probably Navy SEALS. The problem was most of the sheriffs were ex-military so it was hard to distinguish between the two. Considering the circumstances, I would say they were probably Navy SEALS.

A couple weeks into my incarceration, I was informed by the sheriff behind the control booth my parole officer was on his way over to serve my papers for the parole revocation hearing. He also informed my hearing would be later on in the afternoon so I should be prepared. Thanking him, I turned around and headed back to my cell.

When my parole officer arrived, he had me sign some paperwork. Later in the afternoon I was called to the visitation area where a member from the parole board met with us. She was an attractive lady in her early fifties wearing a black dress with white stockings. She had nice gold jewelry hanging from her neck and a wedding ring that said her husband was very well off.

After being escorted into the visitation room, I was informed to pull up a chair across from the lady who introduced herself as Mrs. Jenkins. Since shaking hands was not formal with parole board members, I quietly took my place across from her.

"Mr. Marx," she said with a short temper and a look as if she had been doing her job for a very long time.

"Looks like you were unable to complete drug rehab. What was the problem," she continued?

I didn't want to tell her it was because of a guy who had stolen from me and of a town who had discovered I was a real telepathic making rehab very difficult and annoying. Instead, I solemnly nodded my head and shrugged my shoulders as if I had failed and there was nothing I could do. With these gestures, she quickly gazed at me understandingly like she had seen the scenario many times before from the thousands of inmates passing through her doors.

She continued by saying, "Well, that' too bad. Now you'll have to go back to prison for a period of six months. We'll give you credit for the days you were in the county jail which will leave you four and half months to do in the penitentiary at which time you will be released back into society. Do you have any questions?"

Eager to get the hearing over with, I looked her softly in the eyes and said, "No Mam."

"Okay," she said pressing a large stamp against an ink pad stamping my papers one by one. "Stay out of trouble while you're in there. You don't want to get any new charges."

I acknowledged her advice and thanked her before leaving.

Outside the hearing room door, an officer stood waiting as my escort back to the pod. "Good news or bad news," he asked jokingly as we walked down the long corridor.

"Good news," I answered. "I'm going back to the penitentiary."

"How could that be good news," the sheriff chuckled.

I looked deeply into his eyes and said, "You don't know what I just went through. It was a nightmare."

Chuckling once again the deputy looked at me and said, "Your right I don't."

We left the conversation as we continued down the corridor. At the entrance of the pod, I thanked him for the escort before walking into my cell thinking how four and a half months back in penitentiary wouldn't be so bad.

CHAPTER 4

A couple of weeks later, at three o-clock AM, the jail house was completely silent except for the clanking of cell doors as sheriffs let out those inmates who were to be transported to prison. "Boo, get up and pack your belongings you're ride to prison is here," a male voice spoke from the intercom into our cell.

At three o'clock in the morning, I wasn't so pleased to hear the words. "Okay," I shouted back.

Taking a quick second to wake, I then began stripping the sheets from my bed.

"*This sucks*," I thought as I untied knot after knot from each corner.

I had gone through this routine many times and I knew the transportation van wouldn't be leaving for another five hours. We would be placed in a cell down in booking and fed breakfast while deputies prepared our transportation papers. This meant, at least fifteen people would be crammed uncomfortably into a small cell for hours; hours which seemed to be an eternity. The worst part of going to prison was getting there. They are the longest hours of your life.

In the booking area, a sergeant I never saw before looked at me before saying telepathically, "*When you get out of prison, go to the Navy recruiting office. They're waiting for you.*"

Without expression, I acknowledged his thought by saying, "Okay."

In return, he smiled knowing I had heard him. Then as I walked away, he turned to me one more time and said, "Good luck. You're an amazing kid."

I thanked him as I continued with the other inmates as we walked toward a holding cell.

When the paper work was finally finished and the transportation officer was ready to go, we packed in a passenger van holding nine inmates. The others were placed in a smaller van which only held six inmates. I was lucky to ride in the larger van because the other was built like a dog cage out of steel with horizontal benches. The steel seats made it very uncomfortable and it was either extremely cold or extremely hot depending on what time of year it was.

The trip to Denver took over six hours when it normally only took three and a half. Not all the passengers were going to prison. Some had warrants in different counties along the way, so we had to stop and drop them off accordingly; a pain in the ass when you're trying to get away from bad breath and body odor from the inmates who didn't practice proper hygiene.

When we arrived in Denver at the Diagnostic Center, we were unloaded from our van an escorted into a large room filled with electronic equipment for taking finger prints and logging inmates in as they walked through the door. Once we were tagged, a correctional officer directed us with his hands toward a wall where three other correctional officers stood waiting to take off our shackles and cuffs. A moment longed for since riding with medal tightly wrapped around your ankles and wrists is quite unpleasant.

While the correctional officers moved their way down the line of inmates and as I heard each crank of a hand cuff or shackle, I overheard one of the correctional officers speaking with the driver of the transportation van.

I heard the sheriff say, "That one right there is a telepathic Navy SEAL; a real bad ass."

"No way," the correctional officer shouted loudly.

The sheriff continued by saying, "We called the Navy and they said they're taking him when he gets out. So if he isn't one already, they're going to make him one."

The correctional officer returned in astonishment, "Is he really telepathic?"

The sheriff answered, "Yup, but they say if you're funny with him he won't talk to you. He has to like you."

"Unreal," the correctional officer continued.

They both began to chuckle as I turned in their direction. Staring down the correctional officer without blinking, I wanted him to realize I didn't want anyone knowing my business. By the expression on his face, he understood very clearly. He threw his head back in surprise and looked away. I was satisfied with the gesture.

I meant him no harm; I just didn't want to undergo the same shit I've been going through from one institution to the next. It was a real pain in the ass keeping up with the whole telepathic Navy SEAL thing. There was too much judgment involved.

I spent thirty days in Denver getting my blood checked and seeing doctors for this and that making sure I was mentally sane and healthy; which I was. I showed a few of the inmates as well as a few of the correctional officers I was telepathic. I gave them just enough to let them know I was the real deal. I couldn't help myself. I didn't talk about it or go any further with it and it worked out just fine. I really wanted the whole situation to be over with, but no matter where I went some officer always told the next about my abilities as well as the possibility of being a real SEAL. It brought on way to much attention. Attention I didn't need or want.

After thirty days, I was transported to a State Correctional Facility in the desert of Canyon Colorado. The prison consisted of six t-shaped buildings structured from medal, concrete and aluminum siding. They were two stories high and modernly built; housing over five hundred minimum security inmates. The yard had a weight pile, basketball court, and walls for playing handball. On the north end of the yard stood a gymnasium and on the south end a library. The west side held the t-buildings while the east held the chow hall and kitchen. The place was dry, hot and sometimes smelled like shit from the cattle yard across the way which produced milk for most of the prisons in Colorado.

When I arrived, I stood in a single file line with clanging shackles around my ankles as the remainder of the inmates unloaded from the bus.

"Against the fence," officers shouted as our group scuttled towards it's heavily razor wired top.

Once we were in place, the officers directed us through a staging area made of concrete, thick glass and a medal roof with an overhang. Two officers stood behind the glass as one by one we yelled our names and DOC numbers.

"Boo Marx, 116079," I said as I passed an elderly man in a light blue uniform.

He had a clipboard in his hand scrolling down with a yellow highlighter. When he found my name on the list, he smiled before looking into my eyes. He said, "Go soldier."

I smiled back because it felt good, but at the same time I couldn't fucking believe it. The damn officers at the Penitentiary already knew who I was. I was back in the joint and I was going to have to deal with the situation. It was inevitable. No matter where I went, my reputation as a telepathic Navy SEAL was going to precede me. "*So fuck it. Bring it on,*" I thought.

After we passed through the security gate, we were lead to a chow hall where dinner awaited. We had missed normal chow hours due to a late drop off, but the kitchen had warm meals for us. I was grateful because I was starving and it wasn't a bologna sandwich.

The chow hall was a rectangle cinder-block room painted white with square tables seating around one-hundred inmates. In front of us, as we walked into the building on the right, stood the serving line which was behind a four foot concrete enclosure with a steel sliding door hovering above for security purposes. Small square windows surrounded the room more towards the ceiling on three sides letting in minimal light compared to the bright florescent lights above.

As I sat with a bunch of fellow convicts eating meatloaf and mashed potatoes, I heard the kitchen officer speaking to a couple of his inmate workers who were assigned to the kitchen.

"There he is," the correctional officer said to the inmate workers as they peaked over a short concrete barrier.

All three of them had curious smiles on their faces. One looked over to the officer and said, "He's a Navy SEAL!"

"That's what they say," the officer responded.

With a brief pause, he continued. He said, "They also say he's telepathic."

The mouths of both inmates dropped in shock. They couldn't believe it. "A real telepathic," they said almost in unison.

The officer said proudly, "Yup, a real telepath and a real fucking bad ass."

A couple minutes later, the two inmates circled the nearby tables from where we were eating. They had wash rags and spray bottles in their hands wiping down tables. Every couple of seconds they would glance in my direction. I could tell by the way they were acting they were sizing me up. As I paid attention to what they were observing, I caught one of their thoughts. It was the guy closest to me wiping down a table which was messy from chow time. He was looking in my direction from under his armpit as his thought entered my head.

He thought, *"He isn't a Navy SEAL. He's too soft."*

Quick to react, I thought, *"What could have brought this on."*

Immediately I scanned my body structure to see if there were any imperfections. From my experience, body structure was the first thing people observed before passing judgment. Instantly, it hit me. I had my arm by my side and my fist standing straight up on my thigh. The only problem was, my wrist was slightly bent and curled under my forearm. A sign stating I wasn't very masculine. So, I changed it up as soon as he looked away by placing my fist directly on my thigh without bending my wrist; like I was ready to attack anyone who got in my way.

When the inmate had finished wiping down the table, he took another glance in my direction. When he noticed the adjustment, his head shot back and I could tell by his expression I had changed his point of view. He even had wonder in his eyes.

His thought, *"Maybe he is a SEAL."*

Before long, the inmate was back in the kitchen. I could hear him having a conversation with the officer.

Speaking quietly he asked, "He's a real SEAL?"

The officer answered, "That's what they say."

The inmate was amazed. He was no small man by any means, so I understood his challenge. The best part, I had the ability to hear his thoughts. I was ahead of his game.

After we left the chow hall, a correctional officer was standing outside the double door with a clipboard in his hand. He called out our names one by one giving us a unit number to where our cells were located. I was informed I would be staying in Unit-B.

Once inside B-Unit, I was greeted by a short pudgy Mexican officer with sunglasses tucked in her dark hair. She assigned me to a cell handing me a bed roll consisting of blankets, sheets, and a pillow; the standard prison issue. Before I turned around to leave, she pointed me in the direction of my cell. I thanked her before heading down the corridor.

Yard was in session so my cellmate wasn't around when I had arrived. Taking a quick look around, I set my bedroll on the available bunk before sitting down beside it. Running my hands through my hair, I took a deep breath and sighed. With the inmates knowing who and what I was, I already knew what was coming next. The same shit I had been going through for the past five months; judgment.

As I was making my bed and putting my belongings away, my roommate came in and introduced himself as Joe. He was of medium height with a large masculine build. But what was most awkward, he had these skinny little legs which usually came from lifting too much with your upper body and not enough with your lower. I had to laugh with the observation. It made him look goofy.

Joe came off as a tough guy, but I could tell it was all an act. He was just putting on the attitude to fit the prison mentality. But there was one thing for sure, after five minutes of talking with him I could tell he wasn't very bright. In fact, he was dumber than a box of rocks. And the way he presented himself, I could tell we weren't going to get along very well.

The next day, I woke early for breakfast and it seemed all eyes were on me as I walked through the chow line. Inmates would stare in my direction then turn to their buddy sitting beside and say, "There he is."

When I made it to the end of the line, I grabbed my tray and thought to myself, "*The fucking nightmare is starting all over again.*"

With this crew, it was going to get ugly. I was definitely in for a long four months.

I sat at the first table available and as I sat curious eyes observed my every movement. Pulling my fork from my chest pocket I began eating without saying a word to any of those around me. But, I could tell they were eager to say something since I was the talk of the yard.

Within a few moments a tall slender kid with a shaved head broke the ice. He looked over his tray and said, "I'm Mike. Did you just get here last night?"

I nodded, "yes."

I then began eating my meal once again without continuing the conversation. I could tell he was unsatisfied by the way I had left the conversation, but I didn't care much since I tended to stay to myself.

I found from previous incarcerations it better to stay to oneself because you're more likely to find less trouble this way.

Mike gave me a look of disgust. His face turned a different shade of red and I could see in his eyes he had something to get out. Instead of using words, he stretched his hand across the table and said, "Well, welcome to Four Mile. The food sucks but the place isn't too bad."

I had to laugh at his overzealous reaction in our greeting. I also figured he wasn't such a bad person, so I reached across the center of the table and shook his hand. For the brief seconds we shook, a satisfied smile crossed his face; a sense of satisfaction like I made his day in some odd sort of way.

As soon as our hands separated, the rest of the guys at the table began introducing themselves. They were a young crowd, but I could tell by the way they presented themselves and the way they wore their hair they were alright guys. I gladly approved their gestures of introduction and the four of us continued with a simple conversation on the lifestyle of the yard. I laughed at most of their stories and I even began to loosen up a bit thinking it wasn't going to be such a bad place after all.

After chow, I went back to my room so I could take a nap since chow started at five-thirty in the morning. Joe was back in the room huffing and puffing as he put on boots, jacket and a pair of gloves.

"You want to hit the weight pile," he asked hyped on too much coffee and an egotistical head.

"I'm good," I returned as I unlaced my boots and crawled under the covers.

He let out a "Psss," as if he was disappointed.

He then started mumbling, "Okay, okay. I got it, okay."

Whatever the fuck that meant, I don't know...

Joe was too much to deal with as a person and I could only imagine what he was like on the weight pile. As I lay there, he continued to sip on his coffee making loud slurping noises. I couldn't help to think how much of a looser the guy was and the thoughts made me laugh as I couldn't wait for him to leave. All I wanted to do was sleep.

After lunch, I decided to hit the weight pile for some exercise. It was a nice sunny day in the warm desert climate of the Canyon. There were about fifteen other people exercising when I arrived. I walked over to one of the bench presses and began setting forty-five pound circular weights on each end of the bar. Again all eyes were on me as I set each weight in place. Since I had a crowd, I decided to warm up and work out with two hundred and twenty-five pounds. Not a whole lot of weight, but good enough to work out with. Good enough for a Navy SEAL.

As I lay on the bench pressing out reps of ten, I could hear the inmates around me whispering to one another. They said, "Maybe he is a SEAL."

A smile crossed my face as I continued pushing the weight.

After I finished with the bar routine, I grabbed a couple of ninety pound dumb bells before lying back down on the bench to continue my chest exercises. When I couldn't handle those anymore, I went for a set of seventies and worked my way down to the fifties finishing off with some butterflies. It was my first day back in the weight pile and I knew I was going to be sore the next day, so I decided after my butterflies it was time to go in.

I put my weights away where I found them before grabbing my t-shirt from the bench. I headed inside. As I was leaving the weight pile, I could hear a couple of Mexican inmates speaking to one another.

"That kid's a real bad ass," they were saying.

Another chimed in with, "And a real telepath."

I just continued walking without turning my head. Inside, I was laughing.

Within two weeks I was the conversation of the yard; being in a prison atmosphere brought out the shit talkers as well as the jealousy. I heard things like, "He's no Navy SEAL. He's a fucking cop." Or, "He ain't no killer. He looks more like a girl."

They even went as far as putting a green light on me. A green light in prison meant that anyone could stab you at any time.

I kept hearing people say, "He's got a green light on him."

Since I knew the prison yards well and I knew how to handle myself, I wasn't too worried. But at the same time, I had to put a stop to the situation. If I didn't handle myself now, people would think I was scared. I wasn't scared of shit.

Over the next couple of days, I went to the weight pile to lift weights. I also had another motive. I wanted to see who was running the yard for the whites. By the second day, I had my man. He was a tall white guy of medium build who thought he was a biker with prison tattoos running up both sides of his arms. His hair was dark brown and he wore a go-tee with side burns. His name was Dave. I could tell by the way Dave looked and the way he presented himself he was no match for me.

Later on that night in the chow hall, I had a chance to meet Dave face to face. He was carrying his tray towards the trash bins when I hopped up from the table I was eating at and walked in his direction. When our paths met, I stopped dead in front of him two feet away and starred him straight in the eyes without saying a word. He stutter stepped, not used to someone in his path, before looking up to see who it was. Instantly, his head shot back as our eyes met. I noticed he could see the pure hate behind them; a hate that wasn't going away. I wasn't moving. I wasn't backing down.

Within a split second, his eyes hit the floor not wanting to match mine. Broken, he stepped to the side of me as I looked straight ahead. Once he was a couple feet behind me, I heard him say to the guy he was walking with. He said, "I guess that kids not moving for anyone."

His friend returned, "Yah, you dumb ass. You put a hit on a real Navy SEAL."

Dave answered, "Well, he definitely isn't scared of me."

"I don't think that kid is scared of anyone," Dave's friend returned as the two of them laughed walking away.

For me, the war had just begun. I turned around from where I was standing and followed them out of the chow hall dumping the contents of my tray in the trash. I stayed a good ten feet behind them listening for their talk as we headed back to our building. Dave looked over his shoulder noticing I was there, but dared not say a word to his friend. He just kept his head down and continued walking quietly.

I snickered at his ego. He was once a proud man; now, a pride taken man. And it still wasn't over. These kinds of things never went away. These guys always came back.

That night, I let Dave's imagination get the best of him. I wanted him to know I knew he was the one who sent the green light and I wanted him to know I was after him for it. Only the imagination had the ability to get the best of a man. I was willing to bet his would get the best of him.

The next day after breakfast, I went to Dave's room. Knocking on his door loudly, I was quickly answered.

"Come in," a voice shouted from behind the thick glass pained steel door.

The room was dark except for a glimmer of light shining through the blinds from a far window. Standing in front of the window was Dave taking his shirt off. His body was riddled with prison ink. His cellmate was lying on the bed. Both of them had skeptical expressions.

"What's up dude," Dave said as if nothing was wrong between the two of us.

We hadn't actually spoken to one another, so this made for an awkward moment. Starring him in the eyes, I said with a look of anger, "Did you put a green light on me?"

My eyebrows were furrowed as he immediately glanced to his cellmate acting surprised. Looking back at me he said, "No, I didn't do that. You're alright man. We're cool."

As I saw him backing off, I decided not to take the situation any further. I just wanted him to know I was aware of his shenanigans. I also wanted him to be fearful.

Keeping the same gaze, I said, "Alright then."

Without saying another word, I walked out of his cell making my presence known. I wasn't playing with the mother fucker.

Hyped up from the situation, I strutted down the hallway towards my room which was down the adjacent corridor. Once inside my cell, I climbed in bed staying out of the covers leaving my boots on in case Dave came for a fight. I laid there awake for an hour before I decided he wasn't coming. Part of me wanted to believe it was over, but knowing prison I knew it was never over.

*

Later on that afternoon, I was out in the yard playing cards with a bunch of poker addicts when I overheard a conversation between two white guys. The one on the left said to the one on the right, "Dave pulled the green light off the kid."

The man began to laugh. He then said, "Great, we got a Cop running our yard."

A smile crossed my face as I raised the pot to three dollars. Stakes in prison were low since we used Ramen noodles and hygiene to buy chips. To me, money was money.

Talk of a SEAL was high on the yard. People were jealous I was a real telepath and even more jealous I might have been a Navy SEAL. After

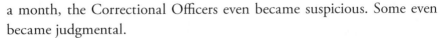

a month, the Correctional Officers even became suspicious. Some even became judgmental.

One of the officers who had spent ten years in the Navy was most judgmental. On certain occasions he worked the day shift in our dorm. One day, he and a couple of inmates were standing in front of our unit leaning over a metal rail with their feet propped on the bottom post as I walked the track.

As I walked by them, I heard one of the inmates ask the officer, "You were in the Navy. Do you think he's a real Navy SEAL?"

The officer answered, "Na, he's not smart enough."

I chuckled at the comment knowing I was a really smart kid.

As I continued to walk around the yard, I kept thinking what the officer had said. And the more I thought about it, the more it pissed me off. When I arrived at the far corner of the track, I glanced over in the direction of the officer which was a little over a football field away. To my surprise, he was no longer standing with the two inmates. Wondering where he had gone, I began to feel the need to prove myself. Somebody calling me dumb just wasn't happening.

By the time I walked the length of the track, the officer had reappeared from the unit. He took his place next to the two inmates and even though I made it look like I wasn't interested in them, I still glanced in their direction. As I passed them on my right making for another lap, I could see the officer had something on his mind. He had this weird look on his face. Almost as if he was completely baffled. Walking further ahead of them, I heard the officer say with a slight country accent, "Well, maybe he is a SEAL."

The two inmates, acting like a bunch of kids, returned, "How do you know?"

The officer then said, "He's smart enough alright. He's real fucking smart."

"How do you know," one of the inmates questioned?

The officer continued, "I just went in to check his file with his counselor and do you know what his file says? It says he has the IQ of a fucking Genius."

"No way," one of the inmates exclaimed.

The other in awe asked, "Do you think he's a SEAL?"

The officer answered, "I do now. I've seen them in the Navy."

The inmate spoke again, "What do they look like?"

The officer laughed saying, "Just like that."

With the three of them laughing, the officer spit out, "A Real God Damn Navy SEAL. I can't believe it."

The news had shocked me. I've been taking those IQ tests for a long time but nobody had ever gone over the results with me. I knew I was smart, but I had no clue I had the IQ of a genius.

Word had gotten out fast. Having the IQ of genius made the scenario of a real SEAL even more likely. People would start backing off.

With the whites off my back, the Mexicans started becoming suspicious. They were going around telling everyone I was probably a cop. They said I was using the Navy SEAL act to cover for something.

"He's scared of something," they would say suspiciously.

Soon I had the look of every Mexican on the yard. They were man hungry and I could tell they wanted a piece of me. With this in mind, I decided to stir up some shit.

Since everyone was skeptical I may have been a Cop, they didn't like me walking the yard so freely. So, the Mexicans decided to challenge to see if I was scared of something.

I was sitting on the edge of my bed one day getting ready to lie down to read a book when I noticed from the corner of my eye one of the biggest Mexican in the yard pass by my door. I knew something was up because this guy had no reason for being on this end of the corridor. Also, my cell was the last on the block and he had gone right by toward an emergency exit door where he stood gazing out the window for a few moments before turning around heading back in the direction he came from.

It all became clear as he passed by the second time. As I sat on the edge of the bed with my book in hand, he stared through the cell window directly at me. If I looked away, it would mean I was scared. But I wasn't, so I just stared him down as he passed. Immediately a thought left his head entering mine.

"*Shit*," he exclaimed.

Hearing this, I definitely knew Sammy was there for a reason and I would even bet he was there to fight to see how tough I was.

Listening to Sammy's boots clunking on the floor as he walked further down the hallway, I rested my book by my side on the corner of the bed before heading to the window on my cell door. Leaning the side of my head flat against the pane of glass, I peeked down the hallway in Sammy's direction. I could see the back of him as he walked to the end of the corridor.

Sammy was a big guy and if I had to fight him I knew I would have my hands full. So instead of fighting him, I decided to psych him out. Knowing Sammy, it would only be a matter of time before he gained the nerve to fight. So thinking fast, I opened my door all the way grabbing a small shampoo bottle from a shelf in the room propping the door open. I wanted to give Sammy the idea I was inviting him in for a fight. I wasn't scared, but if I had to fight we were fighting.

Sure enough, moments later I could hear the same thumping as before as Sammy's boots came trucking down the corridor. Anxious for his arrival, I stood at the far end of the cell with my boots on ready to fight. Suddenly, the sound of Sammy's boots stopped for a brief second in the middle of the corridor. I could tell he was thinking of backing out because he didn't stop to talk to anyone or knock on another cell door. Instead, he turned around quietly and walked back in the direction he came from. Knowing my psych maneuver had worked, I began to laugh quietly.

At the end of the corridor, I heard Sammy talking to a group of his Mexican buddies. Even though he was trying to be quiet while speaking, the sound of his voice traveled down the length of the corridor to my cell. He said, "That kids not scared of me either."

One of his buddies asked, "How do you know?"

Sammy returned, "He propped open his door inviting me in for a fight. He knew why I was down there."

His friends began to laugh as one of them spurted out, "Fuck!"

Another one of the Mexicans shouted, "We should all jump him."

Sammy disagreed. He said to his crew, "If we fuck with that kid, he's just going to keep coming."

"You think so," another exclaimed?

Sammy spoke for the last time. He said, "If that kid isn't scared of me, he isn't scared of nothin. And if we keep fucking with him, he's going to come after every single one of us."

After he spoke, the others had taken his advice. They left the corridor without another word. By Sammy backing down from the fight, it meant I had just taken over the Mexicans. I was on my way to taking over the yard.

With the Mexicans and whites out of the way, I figured the war was over. And it seemed to be. Talk of the yard said I wasn't scared of anything. And as I passed groups from different races they would size me up before saying, "A real fucking Navy SEAL. Who would have thought?"

One guy even went as far as saying I was a recruiter. The comment made me laugh even though I thought it a good analogy. The fact of the matter, I was just doing time like the rest of them.

My life at Four Mile changed after Sammy backed down from the challenge. It seemed he had a lot of pull in the yard and people respected his opinion. We even began saying, "What's up," to one another other as our paths crossed; kind of a mutual respect. When I thought about it, I didn't find Sammy a bad person. He had some character and I thought he would be able to do well in life if he was able to keep his shit together. But prison is one of those places where it's tough to get out of the system once you're in it. You don't realize you're institutionalized until it's too late and mentally you have to overcome the barrier in order to move on with your life. A problem I have today.

The Asians were cool with me and since there weren't many of them in the penitentiary they usually kept to themselves. But, I did have a run-in with the blacks.

*

I like to play poker so I spend most of my day on the card table when I wasn't lifting weights. After about a four hour run on the table, I had a black man named Sweet Water down thirty-five dollars. He had sweat dripping down his forehead which he cleaned with a blue bandana which soaked through his chest pocket in-between hands. I could tell he was pissed, but I just kept coming at him hand after hand. His anger soon got the best of him and he began betting erratically trying to catch up. When this happens a person starts to lose dramatically. Within another half an hour, I had him down fifty-five dollars; big money in terms of prison poker. The problem was, I knew he didn't have the money. I could tell by the look on his face.

After the game, Sweet Water pulled me to the side and asked if I could wait a few days for payment. He said he was waiting for his girl to put some money on his books which was like an inmate bank account. This allowed you to pay for commissary and other miscellaneous items in the penitentiary. Agreeing, I said I would discuss it with him later.

A few days later, I was passing by the dayroom on my way to my cell from the yard. At one of the card tables, Sweet Water's cell mate was sitting down ironing cloths. He was a large black gentleman with a really big head and pony tails like Snoop Dog. He walked slowly with a skip in his hip from being overweight for so many years. His age had taken the gangster out of him and he was now considered an OG; an old gangster. To me, he was an alright guy by the short conversations we had in the past.

While he was sitting at the table, I walked up to him and asked, "Do you think your roommate is going to be able to pay me my money?"

He smiled saying with a little slang in his accent, "He told me you got him pretty good on the card table the other day. How much does he owe you?

"Fifty-five," I said as if it was no big deal.

"Woo wee," he exclaimed.

"He'll get you. His girls pretty good about taking care of his books," he continued.

We laughed for a brief moment before I walked away.

Forty-five minutes later I was lying in bed in my boxers when Sweet Water knocked on my door. I crawled from under the covers answering. As soon as I opened the door, Sweet Water came barging in. He was disturbed and very irate. Within seconds he was yelling with spit flying from his lips. I had to take a step back to insure I wouldn't be hit by the projectiles.

"Why you asking my celly if I'm good for the money," he exclaimed in a very harsh tone.

"I told you I was good for the money so I'm good for the money," he continued.

I knew from past experiences these kind of actions usually meant the man was trying to start a confrontation in order to get out of paying his debt. Seeing through his epiphany, I walked to the door and asked politely for him to leave. Opening the door, I said in a calm cool manner, "Get the fuck out of my room."

With rage still in his voice he tried keeping the confrontation going.

"Get out," I said one more time.

Seeing I wasn't trying to fight, he put his face inches from mine and began yelling something about paying the money. He balled a fist and raised it above his shoulder as if he was getting ready to strike. Reacting quickly, I took a swing at him repeatedly hitting him in the side of his head until he was up against the wall. He let out a scream as I continuously beat him. At one point my fist slid across his face hitting the wall leaving a hole where it had struck. This didn't stop me. I just kept going until he was on the ground curled up in a ball. When I decided he had enough, I grabbed him by the shirt collar and slid him across the linoleum floor into the hallway.

Calmly I said, "I told you to get the fuck out of my cell."

Sweet Water laid there for a moment before he climbed to his knees spitting blood from his mouth. He stayed there on all fours for a few seconds before shaking his head from side to side. Sighing he said, "I haven't seen somebody that fast in a long time. You whooped my ass white boy."

I had to laugh at his remark. Sweet Water then climbed to his feet without looking back in my direction. He held the right side of his face and walked to the end of the hallway as I heard him saying to himself, "I just got my ass kicked by a real Navy SEAL. Woo-we."

I smiled knowing the war was finally over. I had just taken over the blacks.

(I felt bad for having to fight Sweet Water. It's not something I wanted to do and I wondered if I had caged anger from what I had been going through for the last six months.)

In the end, they decided I was scared of nothing. I had taken over the entire penitentiary in under ninety days. The correctional officers were even impressed. I heard one of them say, "That boy just took over our prison in ninety days. I haven't seen that happen in over ten years."

He chuckled...

Astonished, the correctional officers decided to call the Navy to see if I was a real SEAL. They couldn't believe I had taken over their yard in such a short amount of time, so they decided to find out for themselves. They wanted to know if I was a SEAL.

As I walked the yard one day by myself, I passed the kitchen crew on my left; a group consisting of five inmates and two correctional officers. They were leaning against a cinder block wall chatting as I walked by. One of the CO's blurted out, "That boy's a real SEAL."

A couple of inmates immediately returned, "How do you know?" The officer pulling on his pant buckle shimming his hips said, "We called the Navy. They said he's going when he gets out of prison. So, if he ain't one already they're making him one."

The inmates were surprised to hear the news. "No way," one exclaimed.

Another said, "Well, I guess we fucked with the wrong kid."

I smiled at their remarks keeping with my pace. I knew I wasn't a SEAL, but I now knew I was going in when I got out. I was going into the Navy. I was going to be a Navy SEAL.

CHAPTER 5

My time in the yard had gone by fairly quickly even though I suffered through the daily challenges of criticisms and judgments. I said good-bye to the few people I made friends with before the gate officer drove me to the local airstrip where my brother picked me up in my father's new Cessna. I could see the air tower from the back gate which made the thought of going home send chills down my spine. I was excited to say the least.

The officers loaded five inmates including myself into a transportation van. The six of us were to be released on the same day. We were all ecstatic to say the least. After a ten minute ride, the five inmates were dropped off at the local bus station before the officer driving the van headed to the airstrip.

When we arrived, the officer pulled in front of an old tan shack which acted as the airports control center. When the van came to a stop, the officer put his hand out. Taking a moment to notice the gesture, I thought it odd. The reason being, correctional officers never shake the hands of inmates. As I reached across my lap to grab the man's hand, he faced me with a molded expression.

He said, "Serve our country proud kid." Surprised by his comment, I looked him in the eyes and said, "I will Sir." We then shook hands.

As I walked away from the van, I had a feeling of pride. The officer made me realize what an honor it was to serve for my country. It was a feeling I had not felt until I heard his words. It made me realize I was going to be a Navy SEAL.

Inside the control center, I sat on a couch observing the room's character thinking it had no resemblance of an airport whatsoever. If it wasn't for the radio gear strung about and the continuous echoes of pilots reading their coordinates over the air waves, I would say it resembled that of a hunting cabin. It even had an Elk head with beady black eyes hanging from the wall opposite from where I was sitting.

The man running the shack was an old country guy around the age of sixty who didn't say much. He wore old blue jeans, cowboy boots, and a plaid shirt with pockets on either side of his chest. Standing over six feet tall with a weathered face from too much sun, he had a sense of toughness to his presence. But, I could tell he had a big heart and was a very nice man.

As I sat on the old worn tweed couch with a cup of freshly brewed coffee in my hand, I gazed down upon a map of the Colorado Rockies which was sealed under an old glass table. My mind was running wild as I imagined all the places I had not yet explored. With the thought of hiking through the mountains with a backpack on, I was interrupted by my brother's voice over the radio. He said through his microphone, "This is RG19940 approaching tower 419."

The sound of his voice brought back so many great memories.

With his approach, the cowboy said to me as I sat quietly overcome with joy, "I think that's your brother coming in now."

"It is. I can tell from his voice," I returned.

He smiled pointing through a large glass window over my shoulder saying, "he will be coming in right over there if you want to meet him outside once the plane stops."

I stood from the couch finishing off the last of my coffee before throwing the Styrofoam cup into the trash. I thanked the man for his hospitality then preceded through the doorway where I watched my brother land my father's plane. To my surprise he made a perfect landing.

At the end of the runway, Jay circled around taxiing in my direction. As he approached, I could see a bright smile on his face as he gave me the classic side to side sway of his head. He did this every time we saw each other. The reason being, he knew I was in trouble a lot so it was his way of calling me a dumb shit without actually having to say it.

He parked his aircraft next to a couple of old tarp strewn planes which appeared to have not been in great use. As the sound of the engine dissipated and the propeller slowly came to a stop, I was already halfway in his direction. Rounding the front of the aircraft, I observed Jay taking off his headgear while pushing some buttons on the console. I couldn't wait to see him.

"What's up shit head," he said opening the cockpit door stepping down from the plane.

I put out my hand for him to shake but Jay blew it off giving me a hug instead. I have to say it was nice having family around once again.

The cowboy from the control center walked in our direction as Jason and I stood chatting. With the cowboy catching Jay's attention, Jay asked where he could fuel up. The man waved with his hand saying he would grab the fuel truck, but first he wanted to check out our plane.

"That's a nice bird," he said smoothing his hand over the prop. Jay acknowledged his comment before opening the door of the cockpit for the man to peer inside. I could tell he was impressed by the state of the art navigational equipment by the way he turned into a little kid as he looked around. I was a little envious since I didn't know how to fly, but decided it was something I would educate myself on in the future.

After the two of them went over the plane from head to toe the man said he would bring the fuel truck around. I was excited to get home, so I hoped the refueling process wouldn't take very long. And it didn't. Within twenty minutes, Jay and I were in the air.

As we ascended to fifteen thousand feet, I looked back at the prison yard thankful I was no longer behind its razor wired fences. Thinking how much the place sucked, I was awed by how big the prison seemed from high in the sky. My brother noticing the expression on my face asked, "Are you glad to be out of there?"

Blowing out a breath of air, I said, "If you only knew how good it feels."

We both had a quick laugh before Jay exclaimed, "That's got to suck."

Because of the high mountain peaks, Jay kept the plane between fifteen and sixteen thousand feet. Since we were at such a high altitude he said it might be easier to breathe if I used the oxygen mask which plugged into a console between our seats. Agreeing, I strapped the mask to my face as Jay turned on the gas. To my surprise, it worked very well. We could even talk to each other through a microphone system which was built into the mask.

Ten minutes into our flight we passed between two large snowcapped peaks of the Rocky Mountains. Once we made it through to the other side,

Jay asked if I wanted to fly the rest of the way home. I eagerly agreed, so he began explaining the navigational equipment in a few short sentences.

"This is us here," he said pointing to an arrow on the navigation screen.

"All you have to do is keep that arrow on the dotted line," he continued.

"This is our destination, so when you get close let me know and I'll land the plane."

I nodded my head excitedly before taking over the controls.

Flying was fun and easier than I had expected. I figured the hard part was in the takeoff and landing. Something I was sure I could do with a little practice since I have the ability to learn very fast.

An hour and fifteen minutes into our flight, we were through the dessert approaching a flat topped Mesa. It was here Jay gave me the look. The look saying we were about to do something completely fucked up.

"Do you want to have a little fun with the plane before we land," he said mischievously.

I could only imagine what he was intending to put me through. Growing up with my brothers meant you weren't allowed to back down from anything. Knowing this, I had no choice but to go along with his adventure.

"Let's do it," I replied sheepishly.

As Jay took over the controls, I removed my hands from the steering wheel. He had this childish look on his face and I immediately knew I was in for it.

Without warning, Jay pushed the steering wheel all the way toward the dash board dropping the nose of the plane so we were heading straight for the ground. As he did this, he turned the plane spinning in circles as we descended thousands of feet in a matter of seconds. My hands were glued tight to the ceiling as we twirled through the air. My stomach was in my throat as the weightlessness tickled my belly. Jay had control of the plane, but for me I was dizzy as hell.

As the ground came nearer, Jay pulled back on the controls sending us straight up in the air. With the plane climbing in altitude, the weight from my body pushed against the seat giving me a moment to gain my composure. But it wasn't enough time. Jay turned the wheel once again thrusting my body towards the center console. When I looked through the passenger window, the ground was straight below us. Once again, he spun the plan descending for earth one more time. And once again, my stomach was in my throat as my belly tickled. Within seconds I was dizzy and disoriented, but every time I looked over at Jay he was in complete control with a shit eating grin on his face.

"*What an asshole,*" I thought.

"*What an asshole.*"

Soon Jay had had enough fun. He steadied our flight looking over at me only to see the most disgusted expression on my face. With my mouth watering, I felt sick to my stomach. I knew it wasn't long before I threw up. All I could do was swallow the saliva in hopes of fighting it off. But, it was useless. I was going to blow chunks all over the place.

Searching for something to vomit in, I sought out the plastic bag I brought from prison with the remainder of my belongings which wasn't more than a tooth brush, some tooth paste and miscellaneous discharge paperwork. Quickly, I poured its contents onto the floor then stuck my head over the opening and began projectile vomiting. Jay laughed his ass off as streams of bile protruded from my nostrils into the bag. I coughed, I spit and I vomited hating the feeling and the moment all at the same time.

Before long, we approached the landing strip of the Monuments Airport. I was overcome by a great sensation as I gazed down upon the city. It felt good to be home.

Landing, Jay taxied through a series of hangers before reaching ours. After a series of procedures, the plane was then shut down. As the prop stopped spinning, I grabbed my bag of vomit exiting the plane feeling woozy. Jay pointed me in the direction of a dumpster, so I could dispose of the vomit. Glancing at the bag in my hand, Jay began to gag himself.

"There's something about somebody's throw up that gets me every time," he said making us both laugh.

Once the plane was safely secured in the hanger, Jay locked the door then led me around the corner to where his truck was parked. As I opened the door, the fresh scent of leather hit my nose making me realize how long it's been since I had ridden in a vehicle other than a prison transport. Even though the smell gave me a headache, I was glad for its scent since it signified freedom.

*

My parents were waiting for the two of us at their favorite Italian restaurant in downtown, so Jay and I drove over to meet them for lunch. With the windows down, the hot desert air felt amazing as it swept across my face. I thought of how good the trees smelled compared to that of the cattle fields of the dairy farm at Four Mile Penitentiary.

When we arrived downtown, Jay and I drove down Main Street in search of parking. With the hot summer weather, the girls on the street had my attention with their short shorts and tanned legs. It had been a long time since I had bedded a female and I could only imagine what it would be like once again. The things you miss while incarcerated: women, good food and cold beer.

Once we had the car parked, my brother and I walked the few blocks to where we were meeting my parents. As we walked toward the restaurant, I could see the two of them sitting outside on the patio area under a green awning umbrella. My mother, spotting me first, had a huge smile across her face. My father, noticing her reaction, turned in my direction and I could tell by the way the two of them expressed themselves they were more than anxious to see me. Prison was never an easy situation for them to go through, so I knew it must have been a relief for them to see me safe and well.

Jay and I walked through the doors of the restaurant to the outside dining area where my parents were seated. My mother, anxious to see me, rose from her chair and gave the biggest most comforting hug. My father, being my father, put out his hand for a shake. He wasn't much for hugging but my brothers and I knew he loved us very much. Once we were seated, my father asked, "So, you glad to be out of there?"

I smiled nodding my head thinking, *If he only knew what I had gone through.*

"Yah," I returned nonchalantly.

"That had to suck," he said with a smile on his face.

I laughed because Jay had said the same thing in the air plane.

"It did," I answered back.

During Lunch, I broke the news to my parents about going into the Navy SEALS. I had a feeling they weren't going to believe me, but I wanted them to know anyway. Preparing to let loose big news, I leaned back in my chair rubbing my palms together and said to my parents, "I have something to tell you."

My father, with a mouth full of food, looked over his plate towards me as my mother leaned back in her chair awaiting the news. I then said confidently making sure they knew I was serious, "I'm going into the Navy SEAL program. They want me."

My father opened his mouth taking in air then coughed as he choked on his food. I knew he wasn't going to believe me. My mother burst out laughing and said, "They're not taking you into the Navy. You're a felon Boo."

My father had his napkin pressed to his face shaking his head as he continued to cough. When he finally finished coughing, he set his napkin at his side and said, "Boo, let's be real here. You're a felon who just got out of prison and the Navy is never going to take you."

My brother was almost in tears with laughter.

As the three of them had a good laugh, exactly what I had expected, I decided I would prove them wrong.

"Okay, wise asses. You just wait and see," I exclaimed.

Knowing they didn't know my situation, I decided to let the conversation end. I finished by saying, "I'm supposed to go down to the recruiting office and check in. I'll let you know what they say."

My father, still coughing a little said, "Well, it doesn't hurt to try. Maybe they will take you."

My mother, not very optimistic about the situation said, "They won't take him Pat. He has a record."

I decided to call the Navy Recruiting Agency in Grand Junction to prove to my parents I was in fact going into the Navy. I looked over at my father and said, "After lunch, I'll prove it to you."

My father laughed once again then said, "I'll bet you fifty bucks they won't take you in."

Knowing I didn't have fifty dollars since I had just been discharged from prison, I gladly accepted his proposal.

When we finished with our lunch, I asked my father for his cell phone so I could call information for the number to the recruiter. He smiled passing his phone over saying, "This is going to be the easiest fifty dollars I ever made in my entire life."

Quickly snatching the phone from his hand, I gave him a wise smile as if to say I was going to show him up. He acknowledged the wise attitude.

I dialed the number for information asking the operator if I could have the desired number for the recruiting agency. Once I had it, I hung up with the operator and dialed the number. Within a few short rings, a young gentleman answered the phone saying, "Navy Recruiting, how may I help you?"

Stumbling for words, I said in a calm voice, "I'm the telepathic kid. I was told by the Sheriff's Department to call you as soon as I was out of prison."

The kid took a deep sigh before saying, "No, we never heard of you. Sorry buddy."

Disappointed with his answer, I asked one more time, "Are you sure you never heard of me before?"

He answered, "Yes we're sure."

But before I hung up the phone, he said in a wise tone, "You can try the Army. They have different rules than we do. We don't accept felons but they might."

Angered by his remark, I was eager to get off the phone. I thanked him for his time before ending the conversation.

As soon as I pressed the end button, my father had his hand out looking for his fifty bucks.

"I told you they weren't going to take you in," he said.

"They're taking me," I returned.

My mother laughing at the conversation then gave a speech. She said, "Why do you want to go into the Navy? Besides, a lot of those guys are gay."

I looked at her quizzically and said, "What do you mean they're gay?"

She continued completely serious and said, "They spend too much time out at sea together so they get lonely and start sucking each other's dicks."

My father, brother and I busted out laughing hysterically. With my mother coming from an Army family, this was the obvious answer for her not wanting me in the Navy.

"Whatever," I answered fairly blushed. But, I still had a good laugh at the comment.

CHAPTER 6

T he next day I decide to head over to the Navy recruiter to talk to the guys in person. I knew they heard of me, so I wanted some answers. I had come too far to quit now.

Pulling into the parking lot, I had to wipe the sweat off my palms because I was so nervous. I kept thinking to myself, *"Please want me. I'm ready to go into the Navy. I had come a long way and there was no way I'm taking no for an answer."*

I opened the front door of the building then followed the signs for the recruiting agency which lead up a set of stairs to a row of offices. There were three suites in order from right to left: Navy, Army, and Marines. The front of each suite was structured of thick tinted glass with posters strung about advertising the armed forces. I have to admit, the posters alone made me want to join. The only problem was, the place was empty of personnel. Taped to the front door was a white letter with blue writing. It said, "Gone for Country Jam. We won't be back until Monday."

"Great," I thought. The boys are partying at one of the biggest concerts in Colorado and I'm here ready to join the Navy.

Disappointed, I turned around and headed for my truck thinking, *"It wasn't over, I was definitely coming back."*

The only problem was I had to wait out the weekend for the recruiting boys...

I stopped by my brother's house after leaving the recruiting office. I told him I went down to sign up, but they were at Country Jam. He laughed and said, "There is no way they are taking you into the Navy.

Embarrassed, I answered, "You just wait and see."

I spent a couple of hours with Jay before deciding to leave for my parent's house. When I got to the bottom of the stairs outside his front door, I overheard his wife say, "Do you think the Navy will take him?"

He answered, "Once they see him they will."

I smirked at the comment. I was proud my brother believed in me.

Monday arrived quicker than I had expected. Once again, I found myself in the parking lot outside the recruiting office with sweaty palms. And once again, I headed up the stairs to the suites with the large armed forces signs. As soon as I rounded the corner, to my joy the office was open.

Walking in, I was greeted by a sailor around the age of twenty-five. He was tall, skinny and barely filling in his Navy Uniform. He had huge round eyes which were magnified behind his thick coke bottle glasses and I could tell by the way he smiled he had one hell of a sense of humor.

"What can we do for you," he asked genuinely.

"I need to talk to somebody about joining the Navy," I answered without expression.

Seeing I meant business, he directed me to another sailor who sat behind a desk facing my direction while talking on the telephone. As I approached the second sailor, I overheard him say into the phone he had just been promoted to a second class petty officer. By the smile on his face, I would say he was quite proud.

Walking toward the sailor, he set down the phone motioning for me to take a seat in front of his desk.

"You're here to join the Navy," he immediately asked with a smile from ear to ear?

I knew these boys were always eager to have somebody sign up, so the smile was half that of a wise ass and half that of a sincere person.

"I am," I answered.

Before I would let him talk again, I said, "The sheriff's department said for me to report here. I'm the telepathic kid you're looking for."

He had red hair no eye glasses and was a little thicker than the sailor who greeted me by the door. His eyes squinted and I knew right then it was going to be bad news.

"No, we never heard of you I'm sorry," he said.

My face began to flush and I didn't know what to say, so I sat there for a moment before saying, "Are you sure you never heard of me before. The sheriffs called you guys and they said for sure you wanted me."

Without hesitation, he shook his head from side to side saying, "No," one more time.

"We've never heard of you," he continued.

I couldn't believe it. After all this time I was under the impression the Navy was taking me into the Navy SEAL program. Now this kid is sitting in front of me telling me otherwise. I was about to explode. My frustration was beyond comprehension.

"Are you sure," I asked one more time.

"I'm sure," he returned.

In one last effort I said, "I'm telepathic. Do you know what that means?"

He said, "I know what it is, but I still never heard of you."

"*Fuck,*" I thought.

Not knowing what to do, I stood from my chair and began to head for the exit. Just before I arrived at the door, the recruiter said with a wise tone, "You can try the Army. They have different rules than we do."

I shook my head in disgust without looking back. I left the office.

Outside the office door, I decided to leave my number for them to call in case they heard of anything. I grabbed a pen from a Navy mug which stood on the first recruiter's desk to write my number on a Navy pamphlet from a stack in the corner.

"Call me if you hear anything," I said lightening my tone a bit.

"Will do," the recruiter said.

In my mind it was over. There was nothing I could do since I was a felon and the recruiter was telling me I couldn't go in. I was saddened by the thought. I had the Navy in my head for so long. I even fought for the belief in prison. It sucked. It was all over just like that.

*

Just before my release from prison, my parents purchased a new twenty-four foot pull behind camper for me to live in until I decided what I was going to do with my life. I rented a space at an RV Park in Colorado about ten miles away from my parents. It was your typical RV Park with rows of campers. There were very few trees, but rent was cheap and I had all the hook ups including cable which was a plus.

Not having a job, my father put me to work painting his house so I could make some extra cash. He paid me more than enough and I think it was because he felt bad I had just gotten out of prison.

At night, I built fires in a small portable fire ring while cooking food over a small Coleman charcoal grill. As my food cooked, I sat in a nylon lawn chair with a cold Budweiser in one hand and a fire poker in the other. The stars were always bright over my head and I couldn't stop thinking how good it felt to be free.

As I sat in my chair at night drinking beers, I couldn't help thinking about the Navy. It just didn't make sense. The officers at the jail told me to go to the recruiting office when I got out and the officers at the prison had called the Navy and said the Navy was taking me into the Navy SEAL program. Something was wrong. Surely, I was going in and there had to be more to the story, but what? What was I supposed to do and what was I missing? I couldn't get it out of my head.

Five days had gone by and still no word from the recruiters. I was in my parent's garage with a paint brush in hand jamming out to the Steve Miller band when I heard a man's voice.

He said, "Look at this, a real telepath painting houses for a living."

I stopped dead and began looking out the garage door in hopes of seeing some guys from the Navy. I was so excited my hands began to tremble. But as I looked, there was nobody there. I was so crazy over this whole Navy thing I was beginning to hear voices. I laughed at the thought since I'd been hearing voices for a majority of my life.

After work, I drove to the grocery store to pick a few things up for dinner. I decide to make shish-kabob, so I needed skewers, chicken and some vegetables. While in the checkout line paying for my items, I heard the gentleman's voice again. He said, "Who do you think you are, Martha Stewart?"

I laughed at the comment before turning around to see who was behind me. To my surprise, the only person was an elderly woman stacking her groceries on top of the conveyer belt. When I looked at her, she smiled.

I said, "Hi, how are you?"

She answered with a little country in her accent, "I'm doing just fine."

As she spoke, I began thinking I was going insane.

"*Where was the voice coming from,*" I thought. "*Maybe it's the SEALS.*" But how in the world am I hearing them.

I left the grocery store in complete wonder. When I returned to the campground, I immediately put my groceries away before starting the grill. This was always fun because I liked putting on a lot of lighter fluid making sure I had the coals fired up nicely. Something a man liked to do to his grill.

Once the coals were lit, I crunched up some newspaper and began building a fire so I could drink some beers under the night sky. The atmosphere was clear, so I was hoping to catch a few shooting stars. They always fascinated me.

To get the fire started, I decided to add lighter fluid to the mix. With the strike of a match, flames exploded from the wood. Life was good: fire, a cold beer and shish-kabobs. It didn't get much better than this.

Six beers into my adventure, I burnt the Shish-kabobs and spilled a full beer on my lap. I was cursing myself while laughing at the same time. The skewers even caught on fire. "Nope, not Martha Stewart," I chuckled as I pulled the kabobs from the grill.

After some close observation and a few obscenities, I decided only one side of the kabobs were burnt leaving the other side edible. I had a good buzz going and I was hungrier than shit so I didn't really mind.

After dinner, I sat under the stars dreaming of how cool it would be to travel in space. Something about what goes on up there completely blew my mind. I visualized earth from a space shuttle. The same scene we've all grown up with from the many space movies in our day. Green lands and blue water shadowed by white clouds, what a wonder.

It was about ten o'clock at night before I decided to get some sleep. I had to be at my parent's house early for work, so I couldn't afford a hangover in the morning. Inside the camper, I turned the air conditioner off and opened the windows. Even though the summer was hot, nights in the desert cooled down to a more than comfortable temperature. Due to the many beers I had consumed throughout the night, I was very tired. Once I had my pajamas on, I was in bed and fast asleep.

At one o'clock in the morning, I awoke from a dead sleep having to take a vicious piss. On the way to the bathroom, I stubbed my toe on the corner of the barrier wall separating the kitchen from the dining area.

"Fuck," I yelled hopping on one leg still on my way to the bathroom.

In the bathroom, I turned the light glancing down toward my big toe. I noticed there was blood coming out from under my nail. Paying more attention to my toe and throbbing pain, I didn't realize I had begun to pee on the floor. The only thing catching my attention was the different sounds the pee made spraying off the back wall.

"Shit," I shouted redirecting my aim.

In that same moment, I swore I heard somebody laugh. It was a high giggle. Still a little buzzed, I decided to answer whoever it was.

I said, "That shit isn't funny. My toe's fucking killing me."

There was no reply, so I continued peeing. When finished, I was too lazy to wipe the pee from the back wall. Instead, I headed back to bed figuring I'd clean up in the morning.

Then it happened. Lying in bed starring at the ceiling, I was startled by three or four different long drawn out voices.

They were saying, "Boo...Boo...Get up Boo."

The voices kept repeating themselves. It sounded as if the voices had surrounded my camper. They were outside coming from every direction. Thinking it was some kind of joke, I rolled out of bed opening the camper door turning my head from side to side.

To my disbelief, there was nobody there. The only problem was I could still hear voices speaking my name. Curious, I took a step down to see if anyone was hiding around the corner, still nothing. The only noticeable difference was a large blue RV camper with a long gray pinstripe directly across from me.

"*It must have come during the night,*" I thought.

With the voices so close, it was hard to tell if they were coming from the direction of the RV. They appeared to be, but as I gazed through the windows of the RV, I noticed it was pitch dark. Also, there didn't seem to be anybody moving around. It was completely quiet except for the call of my name.

"*Weird,*" I thought.

Standing there, I began to laugh at the insanity of the situation. As I laughed, the voices immediately stopped. What happened next was the most amazing thing I had ever experienced in my entire life. It started with six distinct cricket chirps sounding from the bottom of the blue RV. Once the sounds had my attention, the chirping moved to the bottom of my feet. It was as if I was being attacked by crickets. Quickly, I reached inside my camper to turn on the outside light. Once the light was on, I glanced down at my feet. To my surprise, there was not one single cricket in my presence

"What the fuck. What is this," I thought!

Noticing my demise, one of the voices began to laugh.

Then it hit me. I looked across the way towards the big blue RV and began to laugh saying out loud, "Well, the Navy SEALS are here."

One of the voices then said, "We're not the Navy, but we're here for you. We're here to train you."

Another voice, quite a bit younger than the first, fell in behind saying, "No fair. Nobody ever figures those things out." I assumed he was talking of the crickets.

These people called themselves the trainers, but I didn't know if they were affiliated with any branch of the military.

"If it wasn't the Navy then who was here," I thought.

Too tired to play games, I decided to head back inside my camper for the night. I had to be up early in the morning knowing my father would be upset if I was late.

As I turned around to go inside, one of the voices said, "That kid's going to be one cold mother fucker when we're done training him."

Another guy said, "Yes he is."

I was happy to hear the trainers thought so highly of me.

Back in bed, I began to feel my throbbing toe. With all the excitement, I had forgotten how bad it hurt. Then with the start of just a few crickets, my entire camper soon filled with their sound. It was as if a hundred crickets had taken over the premises. In complete awe, I laid there thinking, *"Wow, these guys have some pretty cool technology."*

The crickets lasted for close to five minutes before going silent. The trainers hadn't spoken afterward and I started to think maybe I should have hung around outside a little longer to show how excited I was for their arrival. Deciding they would understand I had to work in the morning, I brushed it off falling fast asleep anxious to see what the next day would bring.

At six-thirty AM I rose to the sound of my alarm. Groggily, I reached over hitting the snooze button in hopes of gaining a few extra minutes of sleep. But as soon as I rolled over, the trainers began with their chatter.

"He's up," one had said.

Another said, "Rise and shine, it's time for work."

The excitement in their voices immediately roused me from bed. Rubbing the sleep from my eyes, I grabbed a towel from the cabinet above my head and walked over to the bathroom to take a shower. When I shut the bathroom door, I noticed their voices had remained in the kitchen area just outside the bathroom door.

With this observation, I thought, *"I must be hearing through their bugs and it seems they only bugged my kitchen and sleeping quarters."*

I knew I could hear on the same frequency as radio waves, but I never dreamed I would be able to hear through a bug system. Who would have thought?

After showering and not knowing if the trainers had cameras installed as well, I decided to wear my towel out to the kitchen until I was able to dress myself. Once dressed, I began my search. I was determined to find where they had hidden their bugs, so I began going over every inch of my camper.

In the beginning of my search, one of the trainers said, "Look he's trying to find our radios and cameras."

In surprise, I thought, *"They can see me."*

After I was sure I had searched every square inch of the place, I concluded these guys were good; actually the best. I couldn't find one single bug or camera. They must have been using some kind of Na-no Technology. Something the human eye could not see.

I cooked a quick breakfast of eggs and toast before heading out the door to my parents. So far, I had only listened to the trainers through their bugs. Overwhelmed by the situation, it did not occur to me I could talk and they would be able to hear. Not saying good-bye, I locked my camper door walking toward my truck for the ten minute drive to my parent's house.

Opening the truck door, I slid inside punching my key through the ignition. Once the vehicle was started, I put my seat belt on before pulling away from my designated parking area saddened I had to leave the trainers behind.

I turned left onto the main road just outside the RV Park. It was a long winding road that followed the Monument which was a series of curved sandstone cliffs all the way to my parents place. My parents lived at the base of the Monument, so it was always nice to make the drive.

The scenery is amazing!

Two miles up the road, I decided to listen to the radio. Pushing the on button, country music began to pour from the speakers. I didn't listen to country often, but sometimes it was the only station that played good music.

"That boy's going," a voice said in a thick southern accent.

My reaction, "*Holy shit, they bugged my truck too.*"

I couldn't believe these guys. They were all over me. Deciding I was glad they were still with me, I began to laugh. Another trainer, with almost the same accent, but much different yelled, "You're going in boy!"

Excited by the thought, I returned with much enthusiasm. I said, "Yes I am, Sir."

Pulling into my parent's driveway, I shut my truck off thinking how much my parents would trip out if they knew what was happening. Thinking I should probably keep it a secret since these guys were very secretive, I concluded I should probably keep the whole situation to myself. Besides, I didn't really know who they were. My parents would just have to wait until I was being trained for whatever it was I was being trained for.

"Alright, you guys be good. I'll come back and check on you throughout the day," I said to the trainers before exiting my truck.

One of the country boys then said, "We ain't leaving ya. We'll be here."

I smiled before shutting the door.

"*This was some pretty cool shit,*" I thought.

My parents were sitting at the breakfast table having a cup of coffee while reading the newspaper when I walked in.

"There he is," my mother said with a big smile on her face.

My father, glancing up from the paper with his reading glasses over his nose said humorously, "it's about time you showed up."

"What do you mean," I answered. It's only 7:30."

My father chuckled before saying, "I'm just fooling with you."

After I poured myself a cup of Joe, I sat down next to my father asking if there was anything good in the newspaper.

"Same old stuff," he replied.

I thought to myself, "*I have a story for you.*"

Not wanting to disclose the good news, I kept my mouth shut. They probably wouldn't have believed me anyway.

"Well, I'm going to get started on the painting in the garage," I said getting up from the table heading for the door.

"Okay," my mother replied.

My father answered with another wise ass remark, "Don't fuck it up."

I laughed at his humor.

In the garage, I grabbed my paint supplies from a metal cabinet along the far wall. I had a tarp set up next to the back door where I kept a few gallons of paint for the project. As I began prying one of the paint lids off, I had a bit of a struggle. Noticing a sign of weakness, one of the trainers remarked, "You girl, you can't even get a paint lid off."

My head shot back in shock before I said out loud, "holy shit. You guys bugged my parent's house too."

"Your parent's house too," a man replied.

I couldn't believe these fucking guys. They bugged my whole existence in one night.

"You guys were busy last night," I continued.

Another guy then spoke, "We're the best kid."

Not doubting him and amused by the situation I said, "I guess you are."

My mother, opening the laundry room door leading into the garage, poked her head in and said, "Who are you talking too?"

Coming with a quick response, I said, "I'm having a struggle with this paint lid and it's pissing me off."

"Use a screw driver," she said. Thinking my mother was the genius of all geniuses I replied, "What do you think I'm using?"

She then said, "Well, bang it on its side maybe that will help."

"That only works on food jars," I answered wisely.

"Well, I don't know what to tell you then," she continued.

"I'll get it. Don't worry about it," I exclaimed.

Shutting the door behind her, my mother walked back inside. Waiting a few moments, I said to the trainers a bit more quietly, "Bang it on its side. What is she thinking with that shit?"

We all had a good laugh.

Not wanting my mother to hear my conversation with the trainers, I decided to turn on the radio. I knew some of the boys liked country music, so I tuned the radio to the proper station. I wasn't a big fan of country, but it would do.

I spent the rest of the day painting my parent's garage while talking to the trainers. We had some good laughs at random stories I was telling and it seemed we were getting along quite well. By the way they were joking I knew they had taken a liking towards me. But when I asked them when we were leaving, they said, "We're not ready for you yet."

Satisfied with the answer, I left it at that.

CHAPTER 7

For the next couple of weeks, I spent my time working and hanging out around the camper conversing with the trainers. I didn't have much privacy, but I was okay with it. In fact, it was nice to have the company since I had just gotten out of prison and all my friends had since moved on.

One day, I decided to have a little fun with the guys. I said jokingly, "I'm tired of you guys always following me around. Now it's my turn to have some fun."

"Oh yah," one of the trainers replied.

"What are you going to do," he continued before I could answer?

Confidently answering, I said, "When it gets dark I'm going to find out which RV you're in and sneak up on you."

I already knew some of the older trainers were staying in the blue RV directly across from me because once in a while I would see them tooling around towards the back of their bus. They wouldn't pay me much attention when I walked out to say hi, but I knew they were in charge by the way their feet pointed forward and by the way they wore their baseball caps high on their heads. I figured there was another RV close by housing the younger trainers. I counted fifteen voices over the last couple of weeks and there was no way all of them were crammed into the same bus. They had to be located somewhere in the RV park close by. I intended on finding them.

"Good luck," one of the boys said.

I returned, "I don't need luck I'm telepathic remember."

"That's why we're here kido," a trainer answered.

"You're going to be one of our best," he continued.

Hopping in my truck, I drove around the RV Park looking for possible buses. Since many of the RVs looked the same, I decided to check license plate numbers. With the blue RV across from me having California tags, I assumed the other bus would have the same.

As I drove around, I was unable to locate another vehicle registering the same tags. However, I was able to locate an RV with Texas plates. Knowing many of the trainers had southern accents, I determined this was the RV in which they were staying.

An hour after dark, I packed a duffel bag with a black t-shirt, dark pants, and black boots. Since the trainers had my truck bugged, I was also going to need a clean vehicle; one without bugs. My brother lived in town, so I drove over to his place in hopes of exchanging rides.

When I arrived, I parked down the street from his home so the trainers wouldn't know where I was going. Since they had cameras in my ride, I didn't want them seeing which house I was going to. I hadn't been to my brothers since they started watching, so I figured they wouldn't have his place bugged or know what I was up too.

Jay wasn't home, but after a quick look around back I noticed his truck was parked in the driveway. Walking through the back door, I was greeted by Simba; our dog which I grew up with since high school. He was a boxer chow mix and the coolest dog you have ever seen.

Once inside, I threw the duffel bag on the floor unzipping the top compartment to begin changing into my all black outfit. I was determined to sneak up on these guys and I was very excited by the idea.

When I had finished changing, I walked into the living room looking for the keys to my brother's truck. The first place I checked was the coffee table. My eyes brightened as I saw the glimmering keys just beside the remote control.

"Thanks Jay," I said snatching the keys from the table.

"*I owe you one,*" I thought.

Before I left his home, I dropped down to give Simba a hug and a kiss. I missed the little shit after so many years in prison and it was good to see him. Outside, I unlocked Jay's truck before hopping behind the wheel.

"*This is going to be fun,*" I thought as I turned over the ignition. "*These guys are never going to expect the change in rides.*"

Pulling out of the driveway, I turned off the radio to concentrate on a plan. Down the road a ways, I had it. On two sides of the RV Park were open fields. If I parked Jay's truck on one of the side streets, I would be able to sneak through somebody's back yard before hitting the field. Once I made it to this point, it would be at least a two-hundred yard hike to the side of the RV Park. The only problem, there was a six foot high wooden slat fence separating the RV Park from the field. Not a huge task, but maybe a little noisy to climb over.

Ten minutes later, I checked my rear view mirror making sure I wasn't being followed. Turning right on the side street just before the RV Park, I slowly drove through the neighborhood looking for the best point of entry. To my luck, there was an open lot in-between two houses leading straight toward the field. It couldn't have been set up much better.

Parking the truck a few spaces down from the entry point, I turned off the engine waiting in dark silence for a few moments making sure I was not being followed. I even trained my ears on every sound making sure the trainers didn't have my brothers truck tapped as well. The only sound heard, was the clinking of the engine as it cooled down. Satisfied nobody was watching, listening or following; I opened the truck door before quietly walking in the direction of the open lot.

There was a three foot high chain link fence surrounding the property to keep intruders out. After some quick observation, I noticed a gate in its center with a sliding metal latch.

"*Perfect*," I thought lifting the mechanism so the gate would open.

I didn't want to look out of place, so I did this as quickly as possible.

Once inside the lot, I quietly shut the gate without latching it. I then sprinted towards the back of the yard before being stopped by another three foot high chain link fence. Not wanting to waste time, I put my hand on the top rail leaping over to the other side. As soon as my feet hit the ground, I ran about twenty yards into the field dropping flat on my stomach near a patch of low desert brush facing the direction I had just come from. Once again, I wanted to make sure I wasn't being followed.

Within thirty seconds, two trainers appeared at the back of the lot on the other side of the fence. They were quiet, but I could see their silhouette as they moved about. One was tall wearing a black beanie cap while the other was much shorter with the same apparel.

"Where did he go," the taller of the two asked?

I recognized his voice from the bugs.

"I don't know he just disappeared," the other answered.

"This fucking Kid," the taller trainer exclaimed.

They both began to laugh before the taller trainer said, "I can't wait to take this kid in. He's going to be one of our best."

They both hopped the fence.

Once they were on the other side of the fence, the shorter of the two trainers asked, "Can you see him?

The taller trainer answered quietly, "No, where in the fuck did he go?

Making sure I had not followed the fence line, the two of them followed the line in both directions. When they were satisfied I had not gone in either direction, they turned their attention back to the field.

The shorter trainer whispered, "Well he's out there somewhere. We can't let him beat us."

Before the trainer was finished with his sentence, the taller trainer shouted, "I think I got him."

I could see from the position of his body he was gazing in the opposite direction of my location. He then raised his arm straight out in front of him. Twenty feet to my left, I heard a high pitched beeping noise coming from the grass. He had the distance right, but he was off in direction.

"*Holy shit*," I thought. "*These guys are using some kind of remote control device that uses a laser which you can't see to leave noises where they target.*"

I couldn't believe the technology these guys were using. I was absolutely fascinated.

Next, the shorter trainer had his hand out in front. He was using his laser to make cricket chirps. Where ever he pointed, a cricket would sound from the grass close by. They were still twenty yards away, but their lasers were reaching me no problem.

"*What in the fuck would they use those for*," I thought to myself. "*This shits crazy.*"

Laying still and quiet, I began laughing in my head. The shorter trainer kept asking, "Do you see him yet?"

"No," the other trainer replied.

The shorter trainer then asked, "Wouldn't you be scared if you had us on you?"

The taller trainer exclaimed, "I would be!"

The taller trainer then switched his laser over to crickets matching his partner. In the tall grass, he left cricket after cricket in search of me. Fifteen minutes had gone by and they still hadn't located my position. A few times they had gotten close, but not close enough.

The taller was a foot above my head with his laser making crickets. He would move it over a couple of inches and sound again. He must have left close to ten crickets in the vicinity of my head, but he was yet to hit me directly as I lay there quiet as a mouse.

Frustrated, the two of them gave in.

"I don't see him," the taller trainer exclaimed with the sound of defeat.

The shorter trainer answered dumbfounded, "He just disappeared."

The two of them giggled with wonder. After a moment, the taller trainer said, "That kids going to be one bad mother fucker."

"Yah he is," returned the shorter.

Before giving in, the taller trainer yelled out into the field, "We'll give you that one. Next time you're ours."

Turning around, the two of them scaled the fence. Before I knew it, they had disappeared.

Not making a sound, I waited a few minutes making sure they had gone. Satisfied they had, I rose from my position making for the fence. On the way over to the fence, I noticed my arms were sore from the way I was laying on them. I smiled thinking I was thankful they had given in.

When I hopped over the fence, I took a moment to search the lot. I wasn't able to see the trainers, but I had this funny feeling they were near.

"These guys *don't give in that easy,*" I thought. "*I know they're here somewhere.*"

Still gazing about, I spotted part of a head sticking out between a garage and a tool shed. It was hard to see, but it was there. Not knowing what to do, I yelled, "I can see your head between the tool shed."

Instantly, the taller trainer snorted through his nose trying to hold back laughter. I chuckled as well thinking it funny because these guys were supposed to be the best but I got the better of them.

With this, I headed in their direction keeping my distance by staying in the center of the yard. I was a little nervous to meet them, so I decided not to make my introduction. To be honest it felt a bit awkward.

When I arrived at the gate, I stepped through before turning around. Yelling softly in a loud whisper, I said, "You guys aren't that good. I had you two."

Keeping quiet, the trainers had nothing to say in return. Feeling the victory, I decided I no longer had to sneak up on their camper. Instead, I had beaten them at their own game.

After that night, I noticed a change in the trainers. It was as if I had earned their respect in some odd sort of way. They kept indicating that I was going into some kind of program. They wouldn't tell me which one, but they did say it was going to be tough. I was nervous, but I was ready.

They say I'm the best...

CHAPTER 8

My parent's house backed the Monument. It's a maze of high sandstone cliffs with hollows and arches made from thousands of years of wind erosion. The valleys are filled with Pinyon Pines, Juniper and Aspen trees. Low to the ground, prickly pear cactus as well as many other native plants thrived in the dry desert climate. And as the saying goes in Colorado, if you don't like the weather just wait five minutes.

On the weekends, my father and I enjoyed hiking through the many trails the Monument offered. One of our favorites was a trail called the Ute. The Ute wrapped around a windy road below in a canyon along the Monument Pass. Making sure we didn't have to walk in the same direction we came from, we would park a vehicle at the top of the trail and another at its base. This made the walk a lot easier since the trail was mostly downhill.

My father was outside washing his car when I arrived at my parent's house one Saturday morning. I could tell by the early temperature it was going to be a hot sunny day. Before getting out of my truck, I had a few words with the trainers. We were laughing about how my father babied his new Porsche. He was like a kid in a candy store. His eyes were bright with glee. He had this smile across his face as he slowly washed the beads of water from the car hood.

"He loves that thing," I said to the trainers as I opened my door stepping from my truck.

"Yah he does," one of the guys answered.

Walking towards my father, I had my hand in the air saying good morning. Looking up from his car, my father replied, "Your mother is in the kitchen with breakfast if you're hungry."

I was hungry, but it could wait. I wanted to check out the new ride. Opening the driver's door, I peaked in. It had the smell of fresh leather which always gave me a headache.

"Nice," I exclaimed while looking over the interior."

"Not bad," he answered.

Through the windshield, I watched my father pick up a large cigar from an ashtray sitting upon a plastic crate. The cherry had gone out, so he reached inside his pocket relighting with a wooden match. Blue plumes of smoke emanated as he puffed away. The sight made me laugh at his character. The character I loved him so much for. What made him even more entertaining, he was five-seven in height, kind of stocky and funnier than shit. He was always dressed casual and ready for anything.

"Where are we hiking," I asked shutting the car door.

"The Ute," my father responded.

"We taking this," I asked pointing towards the Porsche?

"You are," my father exclaimed!

I had not yet driven his Porsche, so I was mildly excited.

"I'm going to take the 4-Runner. You can follow me in this," he continued.

"We'll park one at the top and the other at the bottom," he said as ashes fell from the tip of his cigar.

Already knowing the routine, I nodded my head asking, "Do you need any help?"

Getting back to his work, he declined the offer. I smiled knowing he liked to wash his cars himself making sure there were no scratches.

"Alright," I said heading inside to see how my mother was doing.

In the kitchen, my mother stood in front of the sink washing dishes. She was fifty-six at the time, the same age as my father. She had blond highlighted hair and a soft kind heart. If she wasn't cooking a gourmet meal, she was painting with water colors or out in the garden messing with a variety of flowers and vegetables. Like Martha Stewart, she was a woman of all traits.

After breakfast, my father threw the keys to the Porsche towards me.

"Don't fuck it up," he said with his usual wise ass remarks.

"How fast is it," I asked?

His eyes lit up before saying, "Faster than you'll ever go."

"We'll see about that," I answered walking quickly toward the garage.

Chasing after, my father shouted, "Don't beat on it. I just bought the damn thing."

Looking over my shoulder, I could see him pointing with his finger as if to scold. Still running, we were both laughing while entering the garage.

Starting the Porsche, I listened to its engine. It was perfectly tuned. Pulling out of the driveway, I waited at the stop sign towards the end of the street. Once my father followed behind in the 4-Runner, we made the five minute drive through the backstreets toward the front entrance of the Colorado National Monument. Inside a brown wooden booth stood a Park Ranger where I paid a seven dollar entrance fee to enter the park.

After paying the ranger, I accelerated through the gate. Halfway up the hill, I grabbed a water bottle from my backpack lying next to me on the passenger's seat. As I sprayed water into my mouth, a trainer's voice appeared. He said, "Let's see how fast that car can go."

Shocked, I spit a burst of water from my mouth all over the windshield choking on the rest.

"You guys bugged my dad's Porsche too," I exclaimed while wiping water from the steering wheel?

"Come on kid. Were the best," the man responded as I thought how amazing these guys were.

With peer pressure on, I shouted, "Okay, here we go."

Slamming my foot against the gas pedal, the Porsche jumped in speed leaving my father in the dust. Looking in the rear view mirror, I could see my father shaking his head in disgust. The trainers and I laughed.

Taking the first sharp turn at fifty-five miles per hour, the Porsche maneuvered nicely.

"*What a great car,*" I thought as I whipped into the next turn.

Noticing my driving skills, a trainer with a New York accent yelled, "That's how we do it."

His voice gave me a sense of exhilaration making me go even faster. "*Now we are having some fun,*" I thought.

With my father nowhere in sight, I sped through the switchbacks. It seemed we were having a good time and we were until one of the guys with a country accent said, "You've got your dad nervous back there, you might want to slow down a bit."

I was having so much fun, I had forgotten about my father. Ahead, I noticed a sign for a photo opportunity. There was room to pull over, so I did. I waited for my father.

Five minutes later, my father pulled in next to me shaking his head

"I told you to take it easy," he said trying to hold back a smile.

"I was taking it easy," I replied.

"The car handles good around those turns," I continued with a smile from ear to ear.

"It's nice isn't it," he returned.

I agreed before taking another sip from my water bottle knowing it was hard to upset my father. He had a lot of kid in him.

Wanting to get moving, my father said, "The bottom of the trail head is up here a ways. Follow me the rest of the way so you don't pass it."

He put his vehicle in gear and pulled in front of me.

We parked the 4-Runner at the base of the Ute before driving another eight miles in the Porsche to the top of the trail. The guys were quiet since my father was in the car making me laugh at how sneaky they were. I wanted them to talk so my father could hear. Then I realized he wouldn't be able too since he didn't have the ability to hear through radio waves. The thought bummed me out. My father would have shit his pants if he knew these trainers were around. He was a war buff and everything he read had to do with war.

With the car parked, I took an extra minute for my father to exit the vehicle. Wanting to say good-bye to the fellas before leaving for the hike, I waited for my father's door to shut before quietly whispering, "Alright, you shit heads. I'll see you in a couple of hours."

A trainer whom I have grown to admire very much said with his country accent, "We'll be here. We're not going anywhere."

I figured he was in his early forties. The way he talked, I could tell he was a nice guy with a genuinely good heart always speaking with a good sense of humor.

"Okay," I returned before stepping out from the vehicle.

Strapping my pack to my back, I followed my father along the Ute trail. The first two hundred yards were nothing but steep switchbacks and rugged rocky terrain. Five minutes into the hike, the oddest thing happened. I heard one of the guys talking. Glancing over my shoulder

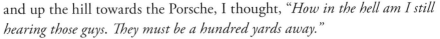

and up the hill towards the Porsche, I thought, *"How in the hell am I still hearing those guys. They must be a hundred yards away."*

Laughing, I continued to think, *"I must have good range."*

When I was three hundred yards away, I could still hear them. They weren't talking to me; instead they were talking to one another other. I couldn't believe my ears.

Four hundred yards later I stood dumbfounded at the base of the Ute as my father stopped in the middle of the trail taking a water break. When he turned around he asked, "What are you laughing at?"

Feeling weird telling him the guys had his Porsche bugged and how I had one hell of a range in hearing them I said, "Oh, I was just thinking of how well your car handled around those turns back there."

Having a good laugh, my father gave me a friendly shot in the shoulder before saying, "You do that again and I'm going to kick your ass."

Then something even stranger happened. One of the trainers began laughing after my father popped me in the shoulder for driving his car too fast.

"Can these guys still see me," I thought turning back towards the hill where the car was parked?

Thinking there was no way they could since I couldn't even see the car from where we were standing, I shrugged it off.

"Maybe they were laughing at something else," I continued thinking. *"If I couldn't see them they definitely couldn't see me."*

After our short water break, my father and I began hiking the trail once again. No more than a hundred paces along, I heard one of the trainers say, "When are we taking this kid?"

An older gentleman, one whom I've never heard before, returned, "We're waiting for his spot at camp to open."

Another trainer then said, "Let's get him now. This kid's amazing."

"We're waiting," the older gentleman responded.

He had authority in his voice making me assume he was the man in charge. It seemed the trainers listened to what he had to say and they didn't argue with his decision to wait.

As I listened to their chatter, I was aware of how far I was getting from the car. We were at least a mile away.

"How could it be humanly possible to hear someone at that range," I thought?

This whole situation was becoming unreal to me.

Two miles into the hike, I listened to the trainer's converse with each other. I also had this odd feeling they could see me. They didn't show any signs they could, but for some reason it felt as if they were watching over me.

My father stopped a ways down the trail to take another water break. It was hot and by this time we were both poring sweat from our foreheads. Our shirts were soaked with sweat as well as we stood there drinking water like it was the last sip on earth.

Standing there, I heard one of the guys say, "You drink too much of that you're going to cramp up."

I almost dropped the water bottle on the ground as my head rose towards the sky in surprise with the sound of his voice.

"*How in the fuck can these guys still see me,*" I thought.

I was completely amazed by the way these guys operated.

I thought, "*I wonder if they can hear me as well.*"

Turning my shoulder away from my father, I whispered, "Can you guys still hear me?"

Since I whispered, I didn't think they were able to hear. But, I was wrong. My favorite country guy yelled out, "Yes sir. I told you we weren't going anywhere."

"*Holy shit,*" I thought smiling over my water bottle making sure my father couldn't see the expression on my face.

"*How were these guys seeing me?*"

No more than two seconds after the thought left my head, the older gentleman with authority spoke. What he had to say completely and utterly shocked me. He said, "This is commander Knapp. Those aren't bugs you've been hearing through. We've discovered you're the only kid in the world who can hear and communicate on the same frequency we use for our spy satellite system. We found your capabilities in the jail yard one night while you were doing your exercises. You heard our voices. That was us who said, "If he does a hundred of those he's going." After one of my boys spoke, we noticed you looking around for the source of his voice. That's when we discovered you could hear us. Congratulations kid! We're here to train you for an agency. You're a walking radio."

I was dumbfounded to say the least.

"*A fucking agency,*" I thought.

I had to take a moment to let the thought settle in. I wanted to tell my father, but he would never believe me. I was a felon just out of prison. Who would have ever thought I was going into an agency. Shit, who would have thought these guys even existed. And even more so, who would have thought somebody could actually hear through a satellite. Hearing voices through a satellite is like the ultimate paranoid schizophrenic diagnosis.

I turned my head once again so my father wouldn't hear and said, "Thank you sir. I appreciate you taking the time to check me out."

The commander answered, "You're welcome. You're one amazing kid. We're glad to have you."

For the rest of our hike, I stayed a good fifteen yards behind my father so I could chat with the fellas. I didn't want him to think me crazy for talking to myself. And as I walked, I couldn't get over the idea I was communicating through a spy satellite system.

The whole concept was a lot to handle, but I think I dealt with the situation maturely. I didn't get overwhelmed; I just accepted it for what it was.

CHAPTER 9

For most of my life, new technology had always seemed to amaze me. Since high school, I was always inventing new gadgets in my head. I wanted to put flat touch screens on kid's strollers so they could learn the alphabet and watch movies. I wanted to build a double sided TV for bars and airport terminals. I even came up with a few different ways to save energy that I hope to get out to the right green energy company someday. Technology has become a way of life for me. So the more I knew, the more intrigued I had become.

After the trainers informed me that I was able to communicate through a satellite system, I decided to put the satellites capabilities through a test. I wanted to know exactly what this satellite could do.

Knowing these guys were very secretive about their satellite system, I had to be very sneaky in how I went about this. Since I could hear their voices inside the house, I already knew they were able to hear through walls because we were able to talk to one another. The question was, how well could they see. If they were able to track me when I moved through buildings, then they were definitely able to see me in some way.

I was at my parent's house one afternoon finishing up with some of the painting chores when I decided to make my move. In the hallway next to the kitchen was a watercolor painting my mother had painted after taking a class from an artist in Aspen Colorado. It was definitely one of her coolest paintings ever, so I decided to show the guys. In reality, I was testing their technology.

Stepping off the ladder which I was working from, I laid my brush across the top of the paint can. I didn't want the guys to know what I was up to, so I said, "Man, I really have to take a leak."

I then walked through the kitchen making a right down the hallway. I was hoping they didn't notice I was going totally out of my way to use the restroom. Just before I was about to pass the painting on the wall, I stopped and said, "My mom painted this. Pretty cool, huh?"

Instantly one of the guys replied, "Yah that is cool."

Immediately, my heart jumped from my chest while thinking, "*Holy shit, these guys can see in full color.*"

Not missing a beat, making sure I didn't give myself away, I quickly continued down the hallway towards the bathroom. Along the way, I kept thinking to myself, "*This shit keeps getting better. This satellite is amazing. I wonder what else it can do.*"

While I was in the bathroom peeing in the toilet, I started to doubt what had just happened.

"*How could a satellite see through walls,*" I asked myself?

Then it hit me. Maybe they were able to see through one of the windows along the front of the house. We had plenty of large windows leading from the study into the hallway, so maybe they had a view to the painting.

"*That had to be it.*" I had to put them through another test.

On my way back to the kitchen, I passed the living room on my left. In the cabinet next to the television, my mother kept a plastic container filled with baby pictures.

"Do you guys want to see some of my pictures from when I was a kid," I asked turning towards the cabinet?

"Sure," one of the guys answered.

Opening the cabinet door, I reached for the top shelf pulling the bin from its place. Choosing a spot on the couch away from all window views, I sat down making sure there was no possible way the trainers would be able to see other than from their satellite. Taking a stack of pictures in my hand, I began shuffling through them one by one. Every time I found a good shot, I would describe to the fellas where we lived and how much fun my brothers and I had growing up.

As I passed through the pictures, I was yet to spark the trainer's interest. Then the picture proving they could see passed through my palms. My brothers and I were sitting on a rock along a river in Lewisburg

Pennsylvania. We had these bowl haircuts straight out of the seventies. One of the guys started laughing before saying, "Nice bowl cuts."

I had to laugh as well with his remark. All three of us had the same hair do. Making a joke, I said, "Hey, we were some cool kids in those days."

He returned, "You're a pretty cool kid now too."

Words couldn't explain my feelings. This was the most remarkable technology I had ever come across. The best part, the test was successful. I had proven they could see in full color through walls. My imagination started running wild from the satellites capabilities. I was in complete awe.

I wanted the guys to know I had put them through a test. Sitting on the couch I said, "So, you guys can see in full color?"

Putting the pictures away and closing the bin, I then said, "I showed you the pictures to test your satellites capabilities."

Immediately, a guy grunted through his nose. A couple of the other guys began laughing as well.

One of them said, "Yah we can, so don't tell anyone because it's one of our secrets?"

He tried to act serious but since they were my trainers, I could tell they didn't care too much. Besides, their cricket and bird system was much more amazing then seeing through walls.

I answered, "Don't worry about it. I got your back."

The trainers laughed thanking me.

CHAPTER 10

A few days had passed since I had become aware of my ability to hear through a satellite frequency. Everywhere I went, indoors and out, I conversed with the trainers. I talked of how I grew up and all the stories along my time line. I was having fun with the satellite, but it seemed as if I was having a one way conversation since the guys didn't want to reveal much about them. They were funny that way.

I had also discovered in the days passing, I didn't have to talk very loud for the trainers to hear my voice. I could faintly whisper barely making a sound and they were still able to hear. It was very surprising because I was so quiet with my speaking I could hardly hear the words myself.

I had become so comfortable with my communications at times; I didn't realize I was in public talking to myself. If it wasn't for the guys, I would have never caught on.

I was at Home Remodeling Center with my father buying supplies for the house when the trainers made me aware. I was in the paint aisle grabbing caulking from a shelf. As I read the label, I was also in a conversation with the guys speaking of how well I could swim. I didn't realize as I spoke I was moving my head around while gesturing with my hands. One of the guys said, "Careful kid. That lady next to you is picking up on your conversation and movements. She thinks you're crazy."

I immediately stopped what I was doing turning in her direction.

She was a tall country girl like the many the Monument had to offer. Her hair was cut like she was still in the seventies with feathering along the sides and bangs frozen stiff to the front of her head. She had tight jeans and a pair of brown work boots on.

Turning to face her, she had this look on her face I couldn't really describe. Not knowing what to do or how to explain myself, I just smiled. She immediately busted out in laughter. I too had to laugh at my demise.

"You alright over there," she exclaimed!

"Looks like you're having a real good conversation with yourself," she continued.

Quickly coming up with an excuse, I said, "You know, have you ever laid some caulk down and it shrinks when it dries? I hate when that shit happens. It makes your work look like crap. I'm just trying to find one that won't shrink on me."

She started laughing once again before saying, "I wouldn't know anything about that honey. My husband does all the painting around the house."

"Oh," I responded.

Shrugging my shoulders wanting to end the conversation since I had completely embarrassed myself, I threw the caulk into the shopping cart saying, "This one should work. It's perfect. Have a good day mam."

She looked at me raising her eyebrows and said, "Bye honey. Don't talk to yourself too much."

I laughed at her sense of humor.

Turning the shopping cart around, I headed down the aisle to find my father. Along the way, I realized how blushed I was from what had just happened.

"*I must be more careful,*" I thought. "*I don't want anyone to know I'm talking through a satellite.*"

The following day, I was at the gas station buying a drink when I noticed a clear container filled with tea tree oil tooth picks.

"*Perfect,*" I thought. "*I'll chew on tooth picks so nobody notices my mouth moving while I talk to the guys.*"

I bought the picks thinking it was a brilliant idea.

What do you know, they worked. Everywhere I went, I had a tooth pick dangling from my lips silently talking away. The best part, not a single person noticed I was having a conversation with someone else. Not even my father.

*

My situation with the trainers took a dramatic turn for the worse.

I was walking out of my camper early one morning when I was struck by the site of an immensely large woman. She had short red dyed curly hair rising close to five inches outward from the top of her forehead. She had back arms like a professional heavy weight fighter and the body of a Sumo wrestler. When she moved, the fat from her body swung loosely in every direction. She looked like Bart Simpson with tits.

The site of her made me stop dead in my tracks as she walked in my direction. Since I had no clue who she was, I figured she worked for the RV park. Joking around with the fellas, I turned my head to the side and whispered, "Hey guys, look at this hotty. I'd hit that with one of your dicks."

Instantly, I heard the commander's voice as he yelled through the satellite. "That's my wife you little prick," he shouted.

"Are you making fun of my wife," he continued.

Confused, I answered, "Oh no sir, she's a real cutie. She's not fat or anything. I was just having a little fun with the guys. She's beautiful, I swear."

"You wise ass kid. That's my wife you're talking about," the commander shouted.

I didn't know what to do, so I started laughing. I thought for sure he was screwing with me. Some of the Special Forces guys were even laughing. Thinking it was a joke, I said, "I was just telling the fellas here how hot your wife is and how I would hit it."

The commander wasn't joking. He yelled at the top of his lungs, "That's it. You're not going into the program. You're off."

Shocked by the sudden turn of events, I returned, "Relax, I didn't know it was your wife. It could have happened to anyone."

Then I added, "She's not bad looking. She's cute."

With my words, I heard what sounded like a fist slamming down on a table. The commander said to his team, "That boy's not going into our program. We're leaving him here."

The guys answered, "He didn't know. He was just having some fun with us."

"I don't care, I don't want him," the commander continued.

My heart sunk. I had completely screwed up and I didn't have time to apologize because his wife was now three feet in front of me. When she noticed the expression on my face, she asked, "What's wrong honey, you look like you've seen a ghost?"

Standing face to face with her, I thought, *"Don't worry you'll find out when you get back to the bus."*

Instead of speaking my thought, I said, "Oh nothing mam. I thought you were campground staff here to tell me I had done something wrong."

She looked at me surprised and said, "Nope, I'm here to give you this."

She pulled a note from her pocket.

It said: Boo, so nice to meet you. Come say hello in Santa Barbara; best of luck. It was signed by her with her email address.

Standing there humiliated, I felt the redness of my cheeks as the guys laughed hysterically. She had no idea what had just happened. All I could do was pray the commander would forgive me.

When she turned to walk away, I said, "My bad fellas. I didn't see that one coming."

One of the country boys answered, "You've done it now you pissed off the commander."

Wanting to apologize, I said, "Sorry commander. I had no idea she was your wife. Do me a favor. Don't tell her when she gets back in, alright."

The boys started laughing once again as the country boy answered for his commander. He said, "He doesn't want to talk to you. He doesn't like you anymore."

I was ashamed of myself. I couldn't believe what just happened. Dropping my head to the ground, I walked back to the camper.

That night, the guys and I didn't have much to say to one another. I tried making things right with the commander and I even apologized to his wife a few times. Neither of them had anything to say in return. The whole situation had me bummed out.

The next day, I tried diverting the commander's decision back on the right track by showing him how good of a swimmer I was. Across the street, there was a state park with a lake. I decided to take a swim.

*

Standing in my camper, I put on a bathing suit. It was hot outside and I was ready for a swim.

"I'm going to the lake," I told the fellas.

One of them answered, "Who cares. We don't want you anymore."

Not liking the words, I returned, "Why don't you pussies go home then?"

Not liking what I had said, one of the guys answered, "Are you calling us a bunch of pussies?"

I returned, "Yah, I am."

My intentions were to get under their skin, so they wouldn't quit and go home. I knew their commander was upset I had called his wife fat, but I still wanted the job. Knowing these guys had a reputation for not quitting; I wanted to work the angle.

I yelled out, "Quit then pussies."

To my relief, one of the guys shouted back, "We ain't quittin."

Happy for his words, I returned, "Good, because I'm going for a swim."

Jumping into my truck, I drove over to lake paying a five dollar admission fee to enter the park. Once I had my vehicle parked, I walked towards the sand beach where families were scattered about having a good time. Some sunbathed on top of beach blankets while others sat in lawn chairs under umbrellas seeking shelter from the sun.

Finding an open area among the ruckus, I threw my towel in the direction of the wind spreading it nicely along the sand. Taking my shirt off, I threw it atop my towel walking down to the water's edge where I quickly wadded through the water. Knowing cold didn't bother these guys, I showed no concern for the waters temperature.

When the water reached my waist, I dove under swimming towards a set of buoys marking how far a swimmer could swim. Since the lake was small and there wasn't much room to swim, I decided to tread water.

A half hour had gone by and I could tell the guys were still upset. They were having conversations with themselves, but they wouldn't talk to me. I began to wonder if calling them a bunch of pussies was such a good idea. After some thought, I decided they were a bunch of pussies if they couldn't handle some light humor.

An hour had gone by and I had plenty of energy to go on. I was in excellent condition from prison, so it seemed I could swim for hours. To my relief, one of the guys yelled to his commander, "You want to leave this kid behind."

The commander answered, "We can't. He already knows too much about us and our technology."

I figured he was talking about their key communication system. Happy with the commander's response, I began treading even faster.

After an hour and a half, I had become bored with the exercise. I knew I could go further, but there was no telling how long I could go on for. It seemed I could tread water forever. Turning my back to the crowd of swimmers, I said to the trainers, "I can keep going, but I'm bored. I'm heading in for the day."

One of the guys shouted back, "You pussy. You can't do more."

I laughed at his payback, but I didn't care. I just wanted to go home and start the grill for a cookout.

On my way back to where I had placed my towel, I noticed a couple of girls playing with a beach ball. The site of them having so much fun brought a smile to my face. I could remember when my brothers and I were around the age. The thought brought about many childhood memories from the Jersey Shore.

As I passed the two girls, one of the guys said in a wise ass tone, "Maybe this kids a pervert and he's into those girls?"

Not wanting to believe what I just heard, I immediately responded, "That's fucked up that you would say something like that."

He answered, "You are. You're a raper. I saw that smile on your face."

Angered with his disposition, I said, "I was smiling from the fun they were having. They're just a couple of girls. Don't you think they're cute?"

"No, I don't," the trainer responded.

He was pissing me off. Rage filled my brain. I didn't know what else to say, so I said, "Well, your fucked in the head then."

Infuriated, I snatched my t-shirt and towel from the sand heading towards my truck. The entire way, I cursed thinking, "*This dirty mother fucker wants to say I'm a rapist.*"

I wasn't sure if he was joking, but none-the-less I was furious with the comment.

In my truck, I kept thinking, "*If these guys think I'm a rapist, there is no way they will take me into the program.*"

I had to prove them wrong. There had to be some way to show them I wasn't the way they were insinuating.

Noticing my frustration, the guys continued working me over.

"You're a raper, you're a raper," they chanted.

Enraged, I yelled, "Fuck you mother fuckers."

Angered with my words, one of the trainers shouted back, "Fuck us? Fuck you bitch."

I knew they were mad because I called them a bunch of pussies, but this was no way to have fun with somebody. It was beginning to feel as if they were turning their backs on me. I would even bet it had something to do with calling the commander's wife fat.

Slamming the palms of my hands against the steering wheel, I started the engine peeling out from the parking lot.

Speeding to the front entrance of the park, I remembered another component of the trainer's technology. They had some sort of MRI or CAT scan built into their satellite system. I discovered this while lying in bed one night watching and intense scene from the movie Heat. With my heart rate greatly accelerated, one of the guys made a comment about its rapidness. I didn't think much about it at the time, but now I figured I could use it to prove I wasn't into kids. If they could see my heart rate, then they could surely see if I was aroused over raping women. With my lips tight across my face, I said, "I'll show you fuckers I'm not into raping people."

Instead of crossing the street into the RV Park, I turned left heading for the freeway towards the mall. My plan was to drive around the mall parking lot seeking out women to put my genitals through a test. I wanted to prove I was not aroused by them in the way they were thinking. I wanted to show them the difference in arousal between a hot girl and the imagination of rape.

Once I pulled into the mall, I drove towards the front entrance of a department store. To my luck, a family of six stood on the sidewalk waiting for my pass. The mother was a bit older than me and one of the daughters was around the age of twenty. When I stared at them, I had no arousal. No sexual desires whatsoever.

With no feelings of arousal towards them, I yelled to the trainers, "See, no arousal fuckers."

One of them shouted back, "You're into rape and you know it."

Not wanting to listen to his words, I shouted back, "Fuck you."

The situation with the guys was heading in a very bad direction. They were becoming very rude and very obnoxious. I was hooked up to a satellite and there was nothing I could do to turn it off. I was stuck listening to their comments as they fed my brain ridiculous shit.

I kept thinking, *"there is no way they're acting like this because I called their commander's wife fat. There had to be another explanation."*

I wasn't giving up. Even though I knew they were feeding my brain these thoughts to get under my skin, I was determined to show them differently. I continued driving around the parking lot looking for women to prove them wrong. And each time I ran into one, I was with no arousal.

The guys didn't care. They would yell, "We don't care. You're into them. Admit it."

I couldn't admit to anything. They were totally off the wall with their acquisitions. All I could do was sit there and listen as they battered me. It didn't matter how many women I came across, the situation was the same. They continuously pounded my head with awful thoughts.

At one point, one of the guys shouted, "Bingo, you had arousal."

Knowing I had not, I yelled back, "Bullshit."

"It was there, I saw it," he continued.

Not wanting to listen once again, I yelled at the top of my lungs, "Fuck you. You don't know me and you don't know what you're talking about."

Instantly, the guys began laughing in a very creepy way. The way they were acting made me question their motives. I began to wonder what was really going on.

I was so irate, I couldn't control my temper. I was steaming with anger. Seeing they were getting the best of me, I decide to not let it get to my head. I said calmly, even though I wanted to shout at the top of my lungs, "I've had enough of this shit. You have me out here looking at people the wrong way and it's not right. I'm not doing this for you anymore. I'm going home."

With a moment of silence, one of the guys said, "Kill yourself just fucking kill yourself."

By the way he spoke those words, I knew he meant it. Something was definitely wrong.

For the next couple of days, I couldn't help but defend myself. As I drove from place to place, I kept my eyes out for attractive women. Each time one had passed, I would concentrate on my genitals.

"Look guys, no arousal," I would say.

There was no way to convince them. The reason being, they didn't want to be convinced. They wanted to believe I was a bad person so they could kill me. They wanted an excuse.

After weeks of this, I had become brain bashed. It was a constant battle between the fellas and me. Their commander even joined in on the fun. I hated him for it. I hated them for it.

Soon, some extremely horrifying events began to unfold. From concentrating on my genitals so often, I actually began to feel a tingly sensation at the base of my ball sack.

"*Oh no,*" I thought. "*This can't be happening.*"

The commander must have seen the expression on my face. Maybe he observed some awkward head movements which expressed my conflict of judgment because he said to his guys with a sense of glee, "I told you boys this kid's perverted. Something's going on with his nuts."

The guys began cheering all at once.

They shouted, "Woo, you're a molester, you're a molester."

"You have arousal in your nuts," they continued chanting.

With the sound of their voices and what was going on between my legs, I could feel myself beginning to break. At the same time, I wanted to scream while jumping out of my skin. The only problem was, if I expressed any signs of mental exhaustion they would attack even harder. I found the best way to maintain was to remain calm.

These guys were definitely a bunch of dirty mother fuckers.

As the days passed, I was tormented constantly. It wasn't long before the most devastating series of events began to occur. My imagination began to get the best of me. Ever hear of the expression "bad visual." Well, that's exactly what began happening. As I passed women in my vehicle, my brain began visualizing them naked. The more I tried to get the visualizations out, the worse it had become.

"No," I screamed.

"This isn't real. Leave me alone. You're changing my thoughts."

Observing my reaction, the guys menaced with the most evil tone in their voices.

They said, "What do you want to do to those girls? Do you want to fuck them? You do don't you?

"No," I screamed. "I don't want to do anything to them. They're just people out having some fun."

My heart was in my stomach. I felt as if I was going to vomit. My thoughts were filled with the most god awful visuals you could possibly imagine. The more I pleaded for them to stop, the more I was tormented.

"Fuck, fuck, fuck… You want to fuck those girls," they repeated.

When I had enough, I shouted at the top of my lungs, "Fuck you, you fucking dirty mother fuckers. You're all a bunch of bitches. I'll get back at you for this."

They wouldn't stop. Everywhere I went, I was confronted with the visuals of naked women. Every time one crossed my path, my head would shoot back hoping praying I wouldn't see them naked. It was the most horrible thing I've ever gone through. It was non-stop. The worst part, they laughed the entire time as thoughts continuously beat me down. I can honestly say I was undergoing severe brainwash.

At night, I would lay in bed with my fingers jammed into my ears hoping I wouldn't hear them anymore. It was useless. Their satellite had a volume control. They were able to supersede my defense. With nothing left and nowhere to go, I began crying my eyes out.

"Stop...Please stop," I pleaded.

"You're brain washing me," I continued.

With no regard for my wellbeing, they just kept on going, "You want to rape people. You want to fuck them. Picture them naked. You want to fuck. They're naked and you want to fuck them."

The images of all those around town continuously infiltrated my thoughts. Every time I tried to picture a good thought, it was crushed by their banter. All I could do was cry myself to sleep.

This went on for endless days and nights. Soon, the men and women I came across filled my brain with their nudity. Everyone was naked and my mind was having sex with them. The more I pleaded for the trainers to stop, the harder they came with their brainwash. My stomach was twisted in knots. My eyes had a constant flow of tears and all I could do was beg them to stop.

It was of no use. They were out to kill me.

*

When the guys discovered I was becoming brainwashed, they began using any angle in an attempt for my suicide. It turned out, the commander was so insulted by my comments towards his wife he no longer wanted me with them. Since I had discovered their key system which mimics bird and insect noises, they couldn't risk leaving me behind. They were scared I would write this book someday. Their only option was to use any means possible to make for my suicide since they couldn't kill me themselves. It would be murder, so suicide was their only option.

(This key system is unique because it is a form of communication for this elite crew. Instead of talking through a radio network when close to the enemy, they use bird and insect noises. They used crickets, humming of insect wings, water drops, stones bouncing, squeaks, beeps, whistles and much more. They can pretty much imitate any noise you can possibly imagine. So while they are using this system, the enemy thinks they are surrounded by wildlife. In reality they are surrounded by the Elite waiting to be killed.

Earlier in the story I spoke of the elite using their key system in the form of hand held remotes. Later on in the story you will discover they use it through a satellite system as well. Inside a control center, commanders use a laser sensitive computer monitor which has the capability to target any area on earth indoors or out. Once a spot is targeted, soldiers leave a key directing one another. A key can also be used straight through the monitor using their hand held remotes. As I said before, the monitor is laser and sound sensitive. This system is such a vital part of the Elite's communications they set out to kill me for knowing too much about it).

*

With the Elite having such success with brainwash, they decided to introduce other horrific thoughts into my head. Like brainwashing me on children wasn't bad enough.

I was sitting on my bed trying to figure out a way to control my thoughts, when one of the guys began yelling, "You're a killer. You want to kill people."

With the words, my eyes rolled into the back of my head as I thought, *"Great, now these fuckers are going to try and get me to kill someone."*

I didn't hear the commander often, but for some reason he decided to join his crew. He spoke through the satellite in a low tempered tone almost as if he was speaking to put me into a trance.

He said, "We want you to kill people kid. You're a killer. Everyone you see you will kill, Kill everyone. Kill...Kill...Kill..."

Instantly, my thoughts moved to kill. Everything and everyone in my brain was being killed. The worst part, the brainwashed mixed with what was already in my head; rape. I was now visualizing people being raped and killed.

I kicked and screamed. I had the palms of my hands pressed tightly against each side of my head thinking, "*This can't be happening.*"

For hours, I laid on my bed eyes bawling wondering when it was going to end. Once again, I had to cry myself to sleep.

When I went into public, everyone I saw was getting slaughtered or raped. I walked around like a zombie. I lost track of time. I didn't know which day of the week it was or even the date. Sometimes I found myself in a deep trance; I didn't even know where I was. I wouldn't know how far I had walked or what street I was on. I would drive endlessly. Things had become very unfamiliar very quickly. It didn't matter what I did, I couldn't get them to stop. All day, all I could hear was their voices as they chanted, "Kill..."

"Rape..."

"Kill..."

"Rape..."

At one point, I heard the commander's laughter as he was obviously enjoying himself. He said to his guys, "This kid's great boys. We can program him to do anything."

As he spoke, I thought how much of a horrible man he was for what he was doing. With nowhere to turn, I stayed optimistic hoping they would have some kind of remorse.

But, they had none...

Instead, they yelled things like, "Who's the bitch now, mother fucker? You want to call our commander's wife fat. Now you're going to pay."

In an attempt to plea in my defense, I tried to make them realize it was not my doing which created this. It was a simple mistake of having a joke when I called the commander's wife fat. I had meant no harm in my actions.

It didn't matter to them. There was nothing I could say to change their minds. They wanted me dead.

Abruptly, my life was in shambles. I couldn't think clearly. My mind was constantly filled with death and rape. I had loss of appetite. I went weeks with very little sleep. Sometimes, I even went two or three days with no sleep at all.

It was a fucking disaster...

It wasn't long before I picked up a bottle of Rum and started drinking. I couldn't handle the pressures of brainwash. The guys were determined to kill me and I had no means of stopping them.

Day after day I found myself feeling a touch of resolve from the bottom of a bottle. It didn't help with the brainwash, but it did help by putting many of my emotions into submission. The reality was, the situation sucked and alcohol was only a surface breaker.

Soon, I found myself drunk and angry in a constant battle with the guys. We were back and forth telling one another to fuck off. Seeing I had a will to survive only made them fight harder. I was determined to stay alive. I was determined to win.

When they became more aggressive, I became more aggressive. I told them I was going to fuck their wives. I told them I was going to track them down and cut their throats. I used any means possible to get into their heads. It had become a war of psychology and I wanted them to know I was going to overcome them. I wanted them to know they couldn't beat a kid like me.

When it came to the commander, I told him I was going to fuck his fat cunt wife. I told him I was going to act like Ted Bundy and cut his family into little pieces putting them in the freezer pulling them out to fuck them whenever I wanted too. They wanted a psychopath, so I gave them one.

I even Jerked off to the commander's wife one night while telling him of the positions I was putting her in. While doing so, one of the guys said, "Hey commander, he's beating off to your old lady."

The commander returned, "Don't worry about it. We're going to kill that kid."

By the tone of his voice, I knew I had finally gotten to him. The thought made me smile as I jerked away.

When the elite observed the alcohol was making me stronger, they retaliated with homosexuality in their defense.

"You're a fucking fag kid, you're queer and you know it. You like fucking men in the ass."

As they kept going it was inevitable for my mind to fill with the bad thoughts. They continued by telling me to stick a finger in my ass chanting, "You suck dick. You suck dick."

I have to admit, they were fucking with my man hood. Calling me a fag just wasn't happening. Once again they were getting to my head. It was frustrating and they seemed to be winning. I fought back the best I could, but I was verbally outnumbered as they broke my brain into little pieces. Infuriated, I picked up a bottle of rum drinking the entire bottle.

When I wasn't being brainwashed on killing, rape or homosexuality, I was brainwashed on terrorism.

"You want to kill the President of the United States," they would say.

"You have bombs and you're going to kill people," they added.

My thoughts had turned against society and the government. I even began thinking of how to build a bomb out of simple curiosity. Something I never dared to think about in my entire life.

Soon, I imagined myself blowing up buildings. I thought of killing people and raping them. I thought of shooting people execution style; right between their eyes; sometimes in the back of the head.

I would watch their brains splatter. I would watch limbs fly through the air as nameless people were massacred. I watched myself fucking their dead bodies as tears poured from my already soaked eyes.

All I could do was drink as thoughts continually pounded my head.

*

Three months had gone by. I was brainwashed the entire time. They had no concern for my wellbeing and they even became very violent towards me. What I couldn't explain is why they never left the RV Park. They stayed parked in their RVS in the same exact spaces from the day of their arrival; directly across from my camper and up the road a bit.

Because they never moved from the RV Park, I began to wonder if I was being put through some sort of test.

"Maybe they really did want me and maybe they're just seeing how much I can handle," I thought.

Since I was going into an agency, I thought this a very plausible explanation.

Wanting to get to the bottom of things, I decided to knock on their RV door. Since I never went anywhere without a beer in my hand due to severe brainwashing, I walked over drunk one night and began banging on the side of their bus.

"Come on out," I shouted.

I could hear them talking inside and I could also hear them through the satellite. I think I surprised them because they acted like they didn't know what to do.

When I noticed they weren't going to answer, I began banging once again. This time I knocked a little harder. I was angered because they wouldn't come out and talk. They were acting like a bunch of pussies.

"I'm out here. Come out and talk," I yelled while continuously banging.

Having enough of my obnoxiousness, one of the guys shouted, "Get away from our camper you fuck. Go home and kill yourself."

Angered by his response, I shouted back, "Fuck you bitches I'm right next door if one of you pussies wants to fight."

"Kill yourself," they would return.

I could hear them laughing and it pissed me off, but I couldn't do shit because they were hiding in their camper. They wouldn't come out. All they would do was yell obscenities while telling me to kill myself.

For many nights we had this back and forth behavior going on between us. Sometimes we even found ourselves yelling out our windows at one another. It had actually become fairly humorous.

One night I had gotten so drunk I walked over to their bus pulling out my penis and began peeing all over the side of their RV. I laughed hysterically as the piss of two horses soaked the side of their camper. I even tried writing my name as I walked the length of the bus pissing the entire way.

"He's pissing all over the side of our bus," one of the guys said in an almost serious manner.

All at once, the guys began yelling, "Stop pissing on our bus you fuck."

Their reaction didn't stop me. Instead, I stopped dead in my tracks, stood on my toes, pointed my penis straight up in the air, squeezed the tip of my head to get some pressure then pissed all over the back side window.

A few of the guys grunted through their noses trying to hold back laughter as others said, "I can't believe that kid's pissing on our bus."

I laughed at his remark.

When I finished, I zipped up my zipper and laughed uncontrollably. In the middle of my laughter, I looked straight up into the sky while staggering like an estranged lunatic. Putting my right arm high above my head, I gave the satellite the finger yelling, "Fuck you, you fucking bitches."

With this, one of the guys said in a wise tone, "He just gave us the finger."

After giving the satellite the finger, I heard the commander's voice in the background. He said completely baffled to his crew, "I can't believe that kid just peed on my bus."

I was exhilarated by the sound of his voice. Surely peeing on his bus was enough to piss him off.

Still laughing, I turned around and walked back to my camper. Once inside, I yelled, "That's what you fuckers get. Next time I'm going to burn that fucking bus to the ground."

Grabbing my bottle of rum from the freezer, I chugged away before passing out.

*

After I peed on the Elite's bus, the commander sent the guys out to follow me wherever I went. I figured he was trying to scare me in some odd sort of way. Like having the guys follow me would bring thoughts of them killing me.

I wasn't scared a bit. With my telepathic abilities, I have this sense when somebody is following me. Each time I sensed the elite following, I simply ditched them.

While driving in my truck sensing somebody on my tail, I would pear in my review mirror. Since the guys were military, I could easily pick them from a number of vehicles; mainly because they drove trucks instead of cars. Once I had my target in sight, I would get into the right lane making like I was going to make a right hand turn. When the light turned green, I would wait for the cars turning left to open a gap wide enough for me to pull through. Now I was turning left with the traffic making it impossible for the guys to follow. And if they did follow, I would be able to see them in the mirror making the correction.

Every time my move worked perfectly. I could even see them hitting their steering wheels in anger. The guys behind the satellite would even say, "This fucking kid. He just ditched them like it was nothing."

With these acts, one of the guys said to his commander, "If you leave this kid here, he's going to kill you."

I thought about it, but I wasn't a murderer so I quickly extinguished the thought from my head.

*

The Elite were on me like flies on shit; like white on rice. Because they had satellites trained on me, they knew my every move. Since they could see me indoors and out, it made it very difficult to ditch them. Knowing this, I still had to give them my best.

I was in the mall buying t-shirts when I was able to ditch them on foot. Sensing somebody behind me, I stopped by a dark glass window where I was able to see my reflection as well as anyone following. Just as I stopped, I noticed two guys about fifteen yards away. Wanting them to know I was onto them, I quickly turned around staring them straight in the eye. When my eyes met theirs, both abruptly dropped their heads in an attempt to cover their identity. With their actions, I knew I had my marks in sight.

Instead of continuing in the direction I was walking, I went back in the direction I came from. When I was able to head down another wing, I made the turn. On my right and just ahead was a department store. Taking a sudden glance over my shoulder, I checked for the Elite. Sure enough they were at a quickened pace towards the end of the wing making their way in my direction.

Once I was inside the department store. I cut through a set of clothing racks making my way for the main entrance. The only problem was, I wasn't going to have enough time to make for the doors before the guys caught up. Instead, I dropped low to the ground between the racks watching for their feet as they passed by.

Then I had another idea. When I was a child, my brothers and I used to climb inside the circular shirt hanging rods playing hide and seek. If you scrunched down in the center of the rack, there was enough room to fit a human body without making the shirts outside look out of place. I could even separate the shirts by sticking my arms out creating a gap wide enough to see through.

Climbing inside the shirt rack, I positioned my body so I was facing the linoleum walkway where the guys would be coming from. I opened a small gap to see through and waited. Within seconds, the Elite were in view. The funny thing, they happened to stop exactly in front of me three shirt racks away. I could see them perfectly. They must have come to the same conclusion I had about the front doors because the expression on their faces said it all. It said, "There is no way he made it to those doors."

Holding back laughter, I watched as they scanned the shopping area with their eyes. The soldier closest to me asked his buddy, "Do you see him?"

The other responded, "No, that kid's like a fucking ghost. If he ever finds out who the commander is, he's going to fucking kill him."

I laughed at their demise. I also laughed because I knew I wasn't going to kill their commander. But, I did decide I could use the tactic in my favor. I thought I might be able to scare them away.

Having no luck finding my hiding spot, the guys headed for the front entrance of the store. I guess they decided I made it to the doors in time. Once they were out of view, I waited a good five minutes before leaving my hiding place. When my head popped from the coat hangers, one of the guys behind the satellite yelled to his commander, "He just ditched Dave and Scott."

The commander grunted in defeat before his soldier spoke again. The soldier said, "You better take this kid. He's nothing nice."

*

Knowing I had beaten the Elite once again, I decided to use a scare tactic for their commander. I chose to fight him man to man.

Since I was hooked up to a satellite, I had to set the stage making my act seem more believable. I wanted the commander to believe I was coming home to kick his ass. Forming my face into the ugliest expression I could muster without breaking into a laughter I looked straight up towards the ceiling and said, "Now I'm coming home to kick your commander's fucking ass."

Immediately one of the boys said to their commander, "He's coming for you. And he's pissed off."

I walked out of the mall like I was a real bad ass. Once I was in my truck, I slammed the door starting the engine peeling away from my parking spot. On the way home, I made every turn with fury. And the more I thought about kicking his ass, the more I wanted to kick his ass.

I pulled into the RV Park as fast as I could. I took the turn a little short kicking dust from my tires creating a cloud making the scene even more plausible.

As soon as I made the turn, one of the guys said, "Well, he's back. You better go out there and talk to him."

The commander said nothing in return.

Speeding towards our campers, I made a sharp turn sliding across the gravel fishtailing to a stop. Opening my door, I jumped from the truck leaving the door open as I hurried towards the side door of their RV. When I was four feet from their door, I stopped with my feet set wide apart. I had my chest bolted outward and my arms crossed in front with my head held high. With the boldest tone of voice I could muster, I yelled to the commander, "Get your fucking ass out here and fight like a man."

The guys were laughing their asses off. Hearing them laugh made me want to laugh, but I had to maintain my composure. Then one of the guys said, "You better go out there and shake that boy's hand."

I could tell the commander was close to the satellite connection when he spoke. He said, "I'm not going out there. I'm telling you boys this kid's dangerous."

The fellas weren't having it. They were shamed. They said to their commander, "Get out there and shake that boy's hand. You started this mess and that boy right there is going to finish it. He's going to kill you if you don't make things right with him. It's in his eyes."

The commander spoke again saying in a sigh, "I ain't going out there."

I stood outside their door for a good ten minutes coaxing the commander to come outside. I banged on the side of their RV and I shouted for him to come out.

After a while, I heard nothing from the Elite. They were completely silent. There was tension in the air and they were speechless. They now knew they had trouble on their hands.

With no luck in having the commander out for a fight, I walked towards my camper. I had a smile on my face knowing I had won once again. But most of all, I knew the commander was scared of me.

The next morning I woke early to run some errands. When I was walking towards my truck, I heard the commander say to his guys, "I want that boy followed. I don't want him out of your sight."

The guys returned with a sense of defeat, "You can't follow him. He knows you're there and he just ditches you."

They were almost whining with their demeanor. The commander didn't care. He said with authority in his voice, "I don't care. I want that kid followed."

Then, for the first time in a long time, I heard the commander's wife. She said to her husband, "You leave that boy alone. He's going to come after you hun. You're too old for this kind of shit. Can't you see what you're doing to him? He's going to kill you!"

The commander didn't care. He said, "I want that boy dead."

His words made the skin on the back of my neck crawl. I thought, *"If this guy wants me dead then I'm going to make sure he pays. I'm going to make sure he spends the rest of his life in prison."*

*

A couple of weeks later, I began working construction for my parents business in Aspen Colorado. We were building a few large offices along with a couple employee housing units.

My first day on the job was horrible. Since I wasn't able to drink, I was butt ass sober which meant the brainwash was completely out of control. I couldn't concentrate. I couldn't remember what I was doing. I walked around in circles while talking to myself. And the worst part, I kept driving over everything in my path while operating heavy machinery. It was as if I was on a one way path of destruction and it wasn't good.

One of my father's superintendents, Carl, was the first to notice. Carl was a really nice guy from Texas. He had been working for my father for many years and they had become good friends. I saw a lot of Carl on the weekends. He would come over for cookouts or we would meet up in Lake Powell for boating trips. He always had a smile on his face and he never showed a care in the world.

While I was driving a large forklift, Carl walked over in my direction waving his arms high in the air signaling for me to stop. I had no idea what all the commotion was about, so I slowed the lift down. As Carl walked to my side, he looked up and asked concernedly, "Are you alright."

Even though I was not, I answered, "Yah, why?"

Carl continued a bit flustered, "Well you just drove over that man's surveying equipment. Didn't you see it?"

He was pointing behind me, so I turned around to access the damage.

Twenty-five yards away, I saw the man picking up his shattered equipment from the ground. He had a disgusted expression on his face as if I had destroyed his most prized possession. Too fucked in the head to care, I showed no remorse. All I could do was shrug my shoulders acting like it was no big deal.

I had been drunk for days and I hadn't been sleeping well from the constant harassment the Elite put me through. I must have looked a bit gray because Carl asked, "Are you okay. You don't look so well."

I knew I was a mess. I also knew I wasn't feeling well. I so badly wanted to tell him I was being brainwashed and there was nothing I could do. Since the story was so crazy, I didn't believe Carl would understand. The funny part, Carl had served in the Navy for many years.

"I'm fine," I said nonchalantly.

Carl thought otherwise. He gave me this odd look before saying, "Why don't you turn that thing off and get yourself some coffee. It looks like you had a late night last night."

I laughed thinking, "*If he only knew.*"

For weeks I walked around the job site in utter confusion. I even began overhearing some of the workers conversations. They would say, "I think Pat's son is losing his mind. All he does is walk around in circles all day yelling towards the sky. Sometimes it's like he's talking to somebody else, but there is nobody there."

They even began laughing as I passed their small groups. I have to admit, I was embarrassed to say the least. I knew when my father found out it was going to be an embarrassment for him as well.

Work was useless. I wasn't very productive and I was making an idiot of myself. I was ashamed and all I could do was drink the agony away. I consumed larger amounts of alcohol and my life was completely fucked up.

I was still living in the RV Park making the hour and forty-five minute drive to Aspen every day. Every morning I woke up next to a bottle of rum chugging away. Sometimes I made it to work on time and sometimes I had not. It just depended on how drunk I was from the night before or how long I laid awake screaming and crying for the elite to turn off the damn satellite.

With all the brainwash, I didn't realize I was isolating myself from society. When I wasn't at work, I found myself in the camper having bouts with the guys. I was no longer hanging out at my parent's house for dinner. I wouldn't meet up with them for hiking trips. I missed family cookouts with my brothers. I wouldn't call to let everyone know how I was doing. My friends thought I disappeared off the face of Earth. The worst part, it was like I was in some kind of time warp. Either time went by really fast or time went by really slow. I was missing everything going on around me. I wasn't myself. I wasn't Boo Marx. I was changing.

*

The elite finally moved to another RV Park. I figured they were scared I might try and burn down their camper in retaliation for their actions to my head, or maybe they thought I would call the police.

Who knows? All I know, I had one hell of a time pissing all over the side of their bus.

Even though the elite moved away, they still kept on with the satellite. They continually fed my head thoughts of murder, rape, suicide and homosexuality. My thoughts were a fucking mess.

With the guys no longer parked next to me, I began having barbeques outside my camper once again. I was standing in front of the grill double fisted with a beer in one hand and a bottle of rum in the other. I'd take a pull off the rum chasing it down with a beer. The entire time the Elite yelled.

They would say, "Kill yourself, just kill yourself and we'll be gone. It's your only option."

I was angered, but I kept thinking, *"Yah, let me kill myself so you can get away with what you're doing to me. That's not happening."*

To get under their skin, I returned, "You're not getting away with this. If you leave, I'm going to write a book about what happened here with all your classified technology in it. I'm going to publish the story and all of you are going to prison. You're going to get a taste of what you've put me through. Trust what I have to say, prison isn't the coolest place to be. It sucks and you're going."

Disgusted with my comments the guys answered, "Shut up and kill yourself."

I tried making stands for myself, but I was constantly outnumbered fifteen to one. These elite traveled in groups of fifteen plus a commander. If they saw I was verbally getting the upper hand, three members would immediately pounce on me. It was the most unfair scenario I had ever been in my entire life. They were a bunch of cheap bastards who only had the nerve to fight in a group. If you asked one of them to come over and fight like a man, they would say, "We're coming," using the word we. The pussies wouldn't even fight one on one. Some of them sounded like real tough guys, but eighty percent of them were a hundred and sixty pounds soaking wet light weights. You could tell by the tone in their voices how small they were.

When I noticed one of them acting weak, I would work on his ego in an attempt to belittle him. As soon as a guy a bit tougher picked up on my slander, he would jump in to protect his buddy. Total fucking pussies. And you know what, the entire time they hid behind the satellite. Not one time would they come over and fight like men.

*

I don't remember how much time had passed, but I do remember the situation had begun taking a turn in my favor. I guess I was in such horrible shape some of the guys started feeling bad for me. The problem was it got so bad I really couldn't tell. My mind wasn't able to look from the outside in. I wasn't able to comprehend what was going on.

The Elite soon turned on their commander. Instead of yelling at me, they began yelling at him. They would say, "You're not leaving this kid here. We're taking him with us."

They would even call me amazing at times.

But, I still hadn't won over the commander. He was continuously out to get me. He would respond, "I don't want him."

When asked by his crew, why? He would say, "I don't like the way he talks to me."

All day they would go back and forth with yelling at one another. Half the crew sat a ways from the receiver while the other half sat in front of the satellite feed telling me to kill myself. It was ridiculous.

Since the commander had his crew out to kill me, I retaliated by calling him and his family names. When the Elite would tell me to kill myself, I would respond by calling the commander a bitch and his wife a fat cunt. The commander hated me for it. Because he was the head of this Elite team, my name calling had hurt his ego in front of his boys. For a guy who was structured on self-control and discipline, you would think a simple thing like name calling was something he would be able to get over fairly quickly. But, he wasn't able to because he was and still is a pussy.

*

I had to figure out a way to get back on the commander's good side. I wanted him to know I was worthy of going with them. I wanted him to know I was strong.

Every day I passed over the Colorado River on my may home to the RV Park. While driving over the bridge, I would gaze upon the rumbling waters thinking how my mother always told my brothers and I not to swim in the river because kids were drowning from its fierce undertow currents.

When I passed over the bridge, I looked in my rear view mirror saying to the Elite, "I'm going to swim across that river today." I knew swimming was their thing, so I figured I would show them how well I could swim one more time.

I continued on my way to the camper pumping myself up for the swim. I never swam in the Colorado's waters before, so I was a bit nervous.

Opening the camper's door, I ran inside to throw on a swim suite. In the cabinet above my bed, I had an old Hawaiian style suit with white flowers against a dark blue background. They were my favorite, so I chose them for good luck. Next, I drank a couple large gulps of Gatorade from a quart I had in the fridge. I was a little hung over from the night before so the Gatorade quenched my thirst nicely.

"Alright, I'm ready fuckers," I shouted heading out the door for my truck. The river was a few hundred yards from the RV Park making the drive just a few short minutes.

Pulling off to the side of the main road onto a dirt drive, I parked my truck in front of a stand of trees which rose high above a thicket of thorn bushes. With my window partially down, I could hear the roaring waters from the seat of my truck. The sound exhilarated my body intensifying my focus. I was nervous, but I was ready.

Jumping from my vehicle, I walked a short distance through a clearing in the trees acting as a gravel boat ramp. The smell of clay was in the air due to the large amounts of sediment the Colorado carried within its agitated waters.

Standing on the river's edge, I watched as the rapid wakes swiveled and tumbled like a roller coaster. The river was moving fast; faster than it appeared from the bridge above.

Popping out of my sandals, I then pulled my shirt over my head laying it across a nearby tree branch. Walking back to the water's edge, I tested the temperature of the water finding it was bathwater warm.

Wading through the water, I was suddenly stopped as the water rose just above my knees. The pressure from the current nearly knocked me off balance making me contemplate the swim. Taking a few steps backward into shallower water where the current wasn't as strong, I stared across the river to the other side. It seemed a very long distance, but I was sure I could make it over.

"I can do it," I told myself.

"I can make this swim."

Turning my head, I gazed up river. To my surprise, I saw a man in his mid-twenties standing next to a dark gray Chevy Silverado parked in a small clearing between the trees just beyond the river's edge on the opposite side from where I stood. He was about a hundred-seventy yards away. The driver's door was ajar as he stood there with his feet planted wide. He was about six foot two tall with dark hair. He had his shirt off with his arms crossed in front of his chest. He was skinny and built like a swimmer. His face sought no expression at all.

"*One of the elite*," I thought.

We stood in our places starring at one another for a few moments before I turned my head down river once again to judge the swim. This time, the rivers bank seemed even further away.

I was in an awkward situation. I felt the Elite were putting me in a pressure situation to make the swim. I must have been standing there for a good five minutes deciding if this was actually a good idea as mother's voice filled my brain. She kept saying, *"Don't swim the Colorado boys, They say kids are dying from the undertow."*

I would take a glance at the member from the Elite then I would gaze downstream to the other side. I did this about three or four times trying to gain the nerve to swim. But, I could not. A few times I bent over swaying back and forth ready for the plunge. The more I thought about it, the more I wanted to back out. The worst part, my mother's voice continued to repeat herself in my head, *"Kids are dying in the Colorado, so don't swim in it boys."*

Standing up straight, I assessed the situation one more time. I was chickening out.

It wasn't long before the member of the Elite became tired of watching. As I stood there, I saw him from the corner of my eye. He threw his hands in the air giving up. Stepping into his truck, he slammed the door behind him reversing away from the lot. Dust kicked from his tires. Once he was gone, I had no choice. I had to make the swim. They would think me scared if I had not. I in return would be ashamed of myself.

Without thought, I dove under the water. When my head hit the surface, I went in an all-out freestyle swim as fast and as hard as I could. My arms pounded the water thrusting my body forward with each stroke. My legs kicked with those of a track star running the four-hundred meter.

Within minutes I was thirty yards away from where I stood and close to the center point of the river. Since I was putting everything I had into the swim, I was becoming tired. I could feel my shoulders losing strength as my heart pounded against my chest.

The concrete pillars holding the bridge were soon in front of me. I didn't want to get slammed against their hard sides, so I angled my body timing the passing perfectly. The shadow from the bridge above protected my body from the hot sun chilling my skin as I swam underneath. Its darkness brought about an eerie feeling.

I breathed heavily with every stroke. I was exhausted. My arms and legs had little strength. I knew if I stopped I was dead. I would not have the energy to go on. I kept telling myself, "Don't stop...don't stop. You can't quit now."

When I passed through to the other side of the bridge, the sun's intense heat beamed against my skin once again. I was twenty-five yards away from my destination. My arms began to flail. I could feel my body being pulled under. Not from the undertow, instead from the dead weight of my body. All I could do was keep pushing on.

"Don't give up," I kept repeating to myself.

"Just don't give up."

I felt like I was drowning. I wanted to give up, but I could not. The strength of the current would sweep me down stream with no energy to move on. I was a goner. Reaching deep inside my heart, I sought the strength and will to survive.

"I can make it," I told myself.

"I can make it."

Ten feet from the rivers bank I had nothing left. I was almost dead in the water. With my feet kicking and my arms scantly moving, one of the Elite yelled out, "Put your feet down. Your there."

Hearing his voice revived every limb on my body. I acted quickly. I folded my knees underneath my chest firmly planting my feet to the rocky basin. Completely drained, I slowly rose in a parallel face with the river's murky waters. Bent over with my hands held by my thighs breathing and coughing heavily, I was surprised to see I was standing in only two feet of water.

I laughed while shaking my head thinking, *"Two feet of water, fucking two feet of water!"*

The best part, I had made it and I was still alive.

Within seconds, I realized I couldn't see. Everything was as white and as bright as a welding ark. Wanting to get to dry land, I blindly walked through the water to the river's sandy edge. Soon, I could feel the dryness of land under my feet. Clumsily, I dropped to my knees rolling over onto my back. Lying there, I could feel my chest rising and falling with every exhausted breath.

It wasn't long before I was nauseous. With my head pounding from pressure, I rolled onto my side and began dry heaving. When I was unable to produce fluids from my stomach, I shoved a finger down my throat in an attempt to gag myself. The act was unsuccessful. Instead, my stomach violently contracted as my guts tightened with excruciating pain.

After a couple of minutes, I rolled back over. My vision was still at a loss and I began feeling a sense of heat exhaustion. Thinking quickly, I crawled on my stomach towards the water. My intention was to cool my core temperature.

In ten inches of water, the river poured over every inch of my body. Every now and then I would dunk my head under feeling the cold wetness of the waters energy reviving my body. It was working.

Soon I found myself thirsty, so I began drinking from the river. Opening my mouth, the water rushed over my lips as I drank away. It wasn't long before I discovered drinking the water was a bad idea. My stomach couldn't handle the liquids making me vomit. Along with the water, came yellow bile.

Ten minutes later, I found myself back on dry land. All I could do was lie there with my eyes closed hoping my body would restore itself to normal. And it had. I was still weak, but I was ready to make the move to my vehicle.

In my current condition, there was no way I was swimming back across the river. The only route was over the bridge by foot. Looking over my shoulder, I began searching for a passage through the dense underbrush leading to the road above.

Discovering a minor foot trail, I decided I was ready to move on. With my body asthenic from the swim, I was in a vexatious situation. I found it very difficult to motivate my limbs. My body quivered as my hands trembled.

Gaining the strength to proceed, I stood upright feeling the weakness of my limbs under me. Steadying myself, I turned in the direction of the highway. Instantly, I realized I was barely able to see. Everything was as bright as the sun. The bushes appeared white when they should have been green. Trees were blotches of brown. Rocks were simply shadows on earth. It was like a bad abstract oil painting; the worst canvas I had ever seen.

Since everything was so brilliant, I decided to create a cover for my eyes in hopes of blocking the sun's reflection. Forming my hands and fingers into make shift binoculars, I pinned them around my eyes enabling me to peer through, stunting the sun's reflection.

What do you know? It worked. Using my hands as binoculars drowned enough of the sun's rays making it possible for me to see clearly. I laughed at my ingenuity.

Pushing on, I stumbled through thick brush, tramped under trees and weaved my way around large boulders. When the brush dissipated to a more open area, I found myself trudging up a gradual embankment. With my sandals across the river, the sharp jagged rocks bit the bottoms of my feet with every bare step. I was in pain and the situation couldn't have gotten much worse.

At the top of the embankment, I was stopped by the sound of an oncoming car. Keeping my binoculars posted in front of my eyes, I turned in the direction of the vehicle. I must have looked funny because whoever was behind the wheel of the car honked their horn as they passed by. I laughed at the visual.

Taking a moment to catch my breath, I peered upon the road making sure there were no cars approaching in either direction. Finding it safe, I stepped onto the asphalt heading across the street where I would then pass over the bridge.

I was two steps away from the double yellow center line when I realized the bottoms of my feet were on fire. In fact, they were almost blistering from the desert heat radiating from the roads surface. I cursed myself for not having my sandals. It was a stupid mistake.

With a few more steps, I found I was unable to continue. Not being able to handle the sun's torturous heat against the black asphalt, I jumped in the air turning in the direction I came from. Too fatigued to run, I walked as fast as I could towards the road's shoulder.

When I was back to the safety of the shoulder, I sought out a small patch of desert grass to stand on. With my feet scorched, I found myself dancing from foot to foot in an attempt to cool down. My current predicament had me frustrated.

When my feet finally cooled off, I decided to take a moment to think. Walking on my tip-toes, I headed towards a large boulder which was high enough to sit on. Taking a seat, I rubbed the bottoms of my raw dogs. They were sore to say the least. But, I had bigger problems on my hands. I had to find a way across the bridge.

Sitting there utterly baffled, I needed a plan. Common sense told me I had to protect my feet.

"*Sandals,*" I thought cleverly.

"*I need to make a pair of sandals.*"

I quickly scanned the immediate area in search of sandal making materials. With the dense underbrush and river nearby, I was sure this would be an easy task. First, I thought of wood. When I was unable to locate the proper resources, I readily dismissed the idea. Next, I skimmed the dense under brush. As I picked through the odd variety of shrubs rejecting those which were incompatible for my task, I was immediately awed by an abundant green weed growing no more than ten feet away from where I was sitting. It was made of thick circular stems an eighth of an inch in Diameter.

"*Perfect,*" I thought raising my tattered body from its resting place.

Gently walking towards my prize, I thought of ways to make sandals out of the vegetation. With the weed being so thick, I decided I would be able to tie a bundle of stems together assembling a sandal. Once I had the sole secured, I would then have to find a material strong enough to connect the sandal to my toes and ankle. It was the best idea I could come up with.

Yanking handfuls of stems from their roots, I went to work with my creation. Placing stacks of eleven inch long strands next to one another, I laid out the sole of my sandal. Finding the stems were fibrous, I then took longer cuts threading the bundles together. The final result was a tightly woven sole five inches in width and approximately eleven inches long.

The elite were fanatic with my resourcefulness shouting cheers through the satellite feed.

They shouted, "That's the way to be Boo. That's how we do it, great job."

I was happy they were still with me.

Once I had my flats, I attached them to my feet by lacing strands around my toes then through the sole. For extra support, I wrapped stems around my ankles intertwining them with the heel of the flop. When finished, I had two primitive, but nicely woven sandals attached to the bottoms of my feet. It was a success, but the real challenge lie ahead. I had a two hundred and fifty yard hike across the scorching hot highway, over the bridge and down the dirt road to my truck and gear.

Two hundred feet into my walk, the sandals performed perfectly. They remained tight to my feet with no signs of falling apart anytime soon. I had a smile on my face from ear to ear. I even chuckled at my cleverness.

As I passed over the bridge, a sense of relief swept throughout my body. Just beyond the bridge, I could see my truck through a thicket of trees on the other side of the guard rail. I was almost there.

Past the guardrail, I turned right onto the gravel road. My stem sandals cushioned my feet from the jagged rocks. Just ahead, I could hear the flow of the river leaking between its rocky banks.

Shortly afterward, I arrived along the boat ramp at the water's edge. Tearing the makeshift sandals from my feet, I threw them in the river watching as they were swept downstream. Lifting my head, I gazed across the river to where I laid helplessly recovering from my almost but not near death. Shaking my head joyfully with adventure in my voice, I shouted to the Elite, "That sucked!"

We all had a good laugh.

*

After some time, I became tired of hanging out by myself. I needed to get out and see the real world for what it was. I needed something normal in my life. Most of all, I needed to get laid.

Out in front of my camper, I had a steak on the open grill with potatoes and onions rolled up in aluminum foil cooking to the side. To keep the brainwash at bay, I constantly drank from the bottle striving to stay alive. My nerves were shot and all I could do was drink.

I was wasted by the time my meal finished cooking. Sitting inside my camper at the kitchen table, I slowly lifted bites of steak to my mouth as I breathed heavily through my nose. Everything around me spun in circles as I tried to hold dignity by leveling my head high. It was of no use. My chin drooped to my shoulders as I mumbled words through my mouth defending myself from the Elite's attack.

Noticing my condition, the Elite pressed harder. They would say. "Kill yourself you drunk fuck. Do it; you're useless; you're depressed. Just fucking kill yourself. If you don't kill yourself, we will."

It was getting worse. They were now threatening my life.

"When you pass out, were going to come over and kill you," they shouted.

The words pierced right through me. It was like somebody had plunged a knife into my heart.

I wasn't going to let them beat me mentally. When they threatened to take my life, I was greatly angered. I wasn't scared, probably because I was intoxicated, but I definitely felt the pressure of death. Since I wasn't going to kill myself, they were going to have to do it themselves.

With some food in my stomach, I felt much better. I slowed down on the rum and my vision became much clearer. I even decided to go out and have some fun. The reason being, I didn't want the guys thinking I was depressed. If they knew I was becoming depressed, they may have worked the angle even harder.

"I'm going out to have some fun fuckers," I yelled while stripping my clothing to jump in the shower.

I laughed crazily, half because I was out of my mind on alcohol and half because I was playing the role of a psychotic. I wanted them to know I too had the ability to kill. I wanted them fearful of me. I wanted them unsure of my character.

After the shower, I pounded a beer outside of my truck. The sun was just over the horizon, so night was near. Above, the clouds the sky sprayed a purple and red. With my head tilted back finishing the last of my beer I gazed upon the beautiful colors thinking how amazing life really is. Then I thought, "*This sucks. My heads full of shit and these guys are trying to kill me.*"

I drove over to a local bar in downtown Grand Junction. It was off the main street in a seedy area. There were two reasons why people went here. One was to consume large amounts of alcohol and the other was to play pool. I liked both, so this was my bar of choice.

Inside, the bar was kind of dead except for a group of guys standing around a pool table shooting a game. By the expression on their faces, I could tell they were just as miserable as I was. A life of alcoholism had put them in a slumber they couldn't control. I knew the feeling because I had been their once before myself. Knowing this, I decided I had come to the right place. I too was here to drink my sorrow away. My brain hurt and there was only one way out; get drunk.

Beer advertisements filled the walls of this watering hole. The pool tables were worn out and the floor was soaked with spillage from drunks. I grabbed a stool from under the bar and sat down. With my elbows firmly planted to the bar, I took a deep breath while pushing my fingertips hard against my temples on either side of my head.

Soon, I was tired and unable to control my thoughts. I was under a spell. Suddenly, visuals of people being slaughtered and raped filled my brain. I was in a daze; in a trance. It wouldn't stop.

As I watched a guy get shot in the head and his brains splatter, I heard a woman's voice. "Sir... Sir... can I help you."

In my dream like state, a woman came beside me with the gentlest touch. She rubbed my shoulder as brains and blood painted her face. She did not flinch. She did not move. It was as if she was oblivious to the massacre unfolding around her.

Her voice,

Soft...

Sensitive...

"Sir... sir..." she continued.

A gun shot; a women screaming; a child crying for her mother. I was standing in a city made of brick walls. The buildings were streaked with blood. People were dead and dying in the streets. Some crawled while others lay still as a grave. All I could hear were shots of gun fire.

"Sir... sir... do you need help," as a warm hand touched my forearm.

I raised my head from my hands. Standing in front of me was a woman close to thirty years in age. My vision was a bit blurry, but I could see she was an attractive gale with blonde hair. She had on a black t-shirt with a bar rag tucked in the side of her apron. The only problem, she had a bullet hole in the center of her forehead with blood trickling down her nose.

Blinking my eyes, my vision came back to focus. The women kept saying, "Sir... Are you okay?"

Looking up at her, I had no idea where I was. It was as if I had just woken from an hour long nap. I turned my head over my shoulder gazing upon the crowd. Everyone had gunshot wounds to the head. They were still walking. They were still talking. Some were even laughing. To me, they were all dead.

Confused, I brought my attention back to the bartender while rubbing my eyes. I still hadn't said a word. I just sat there starring into her eyes.

"You alright honey," the bartender asked?

Suddenly my mind came too. The wound in her head disappeared. When I glanced over my shoulder, the pool players appeared normal. Shaking my head in disbelief, I said, "Yah, I'm fine mam."

Behind her, a man pored beer from a tap. I began to piece together where I was.

"I'm at the bar," I thought.

My voice was scratchy as I spoke saying to the female bartender, "I'll have a Budweiser and two shots of tequila."

She took a moment to assess my stability. Deciding I was fine, she nodded her head repeating my order, "Two shots of Tequila and a Budweiser."

With nothing else to say, she turned around and began pouring my drinks.

Six shots and two beers later, I was beginning to gain control of my head once again. With the alcohol pouring through my veins, I felt strong. I felt confident. Most of all, I felt the need for a girl. I needed somebody to talk to. I needed companionship.

Four beers and eight shots later, my lucky lady walked through the front entrance of the bar room. She was in her late thirties with black curly hair. She wore tight blue jeans showing off her nice ass. She had on a light jacket with a purple silk scarf draped over her shoulders. She wasn't the best looking I've ever seen, but attractive to say the least.

She walked to the opposite end of the bar and ordered a drink. The bar tender brought her a Bud Light as she smiled handing him some money. When he turned to register the change, she picked up the bottle and began guzzling. By the looks of it, she wasn't going to put the beer down anytime soon. She was just as thirsty as I was.

"My kind of girl," I thought sitting there watching wondering what was so horrific in her life that brought her to the bottom of a bottle?

Surely life couldn't be that bad. Then it occurred to me, *"Maybe her life is that bad. My life is in complete ruin and I have no choice but to drink my way out. There is no telling what life will bring. We all have our hardships and some are worse than others."*

When the bar tender brought her the change, she lifted the bottle from her lips. With the back of her hand, she wiped beer from the corners of her mouth. Picking her change from the bar top, she glanced in my direction. When our eyes met, she smiled tilting her beer in cheers. I exchanged the gesture by doing the same. It seemed we both had the same agenda in mind, get drunk and get laid. As if the two would make all our problems go away.

Standing from my stool, I pounded the last of my beer before gently setting it down on the bar. Strutting in her direction, I decided to buy her a drink to open the conversation. Pulling my wallet from my back pocket, I stopped next to her looking over towards the bar tender. When I had his attention, I ordered two Bud Lights and two shots of tequila. I didn't want to waste time with small talk, so I decided it best we get right to the point by getting completely and utterly trashed.

Thrusting her head to the side to remove the bangs from her eyes, she laughed before dropping her chin to her chest tilting her head in my direction. Looking into my eyes, she said, "So you're the lonely guy who thinks he can get into my pants by buying me a drink."

I chuckled as she lifted her beer to her lips holding a smile behind the rim of the bottle.

Shocked by her statement, I came to only one conclusion; be honest. Laughing I said, "Yah, that's pretty much it."

Shaking her head, she returned jokingly, "You guys are all the same. You think you can buy a girl a drink and she'll go home for a quick fuck."

Taking a moment to think, she then asked with a genuine tone of voice, "What kind of girl do you think I am?"

I was a bit embarrassed, but determine. Giving her the cutest face in the world I said, "I just came over to buy you a drink in hopes of having some fun."

Taking another moment to access the situation, she sized me from head to toe. Smiling once again, she said, "Well, you're in luck. You're pretty cute and I don't have a man in my life, so take a seat." We introduced ourselves as I laughed at her robust character. Her name was Sara.

The bar tender brought our drinks placing them on the bar in front of us. Telling him to keep the tab open, I grabbed one of the tequila shots and said, "Here's to good times."

With two fingers, Sara picked up her shot and banged it hard against mine. She returned, "Here's to good times."

In that moment, we threw back our drinks.

Slamming our glasses down, I ordered two more. We repeated the ritual.

An hour later, we were arm in arm like two drunken sailors. Our words were slurred and we were laughing our asses off. In the shape of a pyramid, shot glasses piled in front of us as the bar tender poured away.

Two hours later we were heading for my truck on our way to the RV Park. Sara was too drunk to drive, so she left her car in the bar parking lot. On the way home, we smoked weed from an old-school pot pipe introduced from Sara's purse as Red Hot Chili Peppers spilled from the vehicles speakers.

For the moment, all my problems had gone away.

We pulled into the RV Park stopping in the lot behind my camper. Sara had a small bottle of Jack Daniels in her hand which she kept tucked away in a travel bag she carried with her. The weed had me seeing double and I was in no condition to be driving. I was thankful for our arrival.

Exiting the truck we walked to the front entrance of my camper where I fumbled with the keys for a bit before I was able to unlock the door. With our bodies swaying back and forth, the two of us stumbled inside.

As we stumbled in, I stopped beside an overhanging cabinet which held my internal stereo system. Turning the power on, I watched as Sara clumsily took a seat at one of the booths surrounding the kitchen table. She had her weed pipe in one hand and her bottle in the other as Creedence Clearwater Revival played from the radio. After grabbing two shot glasses from the cabinet above the stove and two cold Budweiser's from the refrigerator, I took a seat in the booth apposite from Sara. Lining up the shot glasses, Sara poured in the Jack.

"Cheers," we said as our glasses clanked off one another.

We tilted back our drinks then slamming them down on the table wiping dribble from our chins. Sara sang the lyrics from CLR while I loaded the pipe full of fresh weed.

We passed the pipe back and forth as smoke billowed from its end. I coughed with each passing hit. The herb was good and I don't think I could get more fucked up than I already was.

We pounded beers while smoking bowl after bowl. Sara and I exchanged stories laughing at one another along the way. At one point we were standing in the kitchen in front of the refrigerator dancing as I watched alcohol spill from the tip of my beer splashing to the floor. I didn't have a care in the world. I was having fun for the first time in a long time.

Soon we were crashing in the wee hours of morning. Jack Daniels stained the table leaving rings in the paths of each shot. The ashtray was full of shorty's. One of the butts hadn't been completely extinguished, so it streaked the air with its presence.

Sara was with her back against the camper wall just below a sliding window. Her feet were stretched out in front of her along the booth seating. She had this weird disgusted expression on her face as she waved pot smoke from her eyes. I could see something was bothering her. I figured what brought her to the bar was about to be revealed. And by the looks of it, it wasn't going to be good.

After taking a hit from the pipe, she starred deeply into my eyes and said in a low tone of voice, "My father is all fucked up from Vietnam."

Not knowing how to react, I returned with sympathy saying, "Really? What happened to him?"

Her tone of voice escalated. She said, "He's just all fucked up. He has Post Traumatic Stress Disorder and he's schizophrenic. He has completely lost his mind. He's nuts...Fucking nuts."

Still not knowing what to say I returned, "That sucks."

With a harsh tone of voice, she went on by saying, "I have to take care of him and there is nothing I can do. He becomes very violent. Sometimes I watch him in the back yard crawling on the ground yelling god knows what. He acts like he's shooting people and throwing grenades. It's like he's reliving the war in his head. I tell him theirs nobody there, but he doesn't listen. My life is completely fucked because of him."

I shrugged my shoulders. I had no idea how to react to this situation. I picked up the pipe taking a hit. As the smoke left my lungs, I coughed from its strength thinking, *"We have some pretty good weed in Colorado."*

Sara looked at me completely disgusted becoming very hostile. She began yelling, "You don't know what I go through...and you don't know shit about Vietnam!"

Tears were pouring from her eyes. She began to scream, "Fuck you, you dumb mother fucker. You don't know anything about Vietnam."

I was taken back by her demeanor. The funny part, I really couldn't say anything. I wouldn't even know where to begin. She had taken a turn in a direction I was unfamiliar with. All I could do was sit there and watch her lose her mind. I even thought, "*Shit...You should see what I'm going through. Post-Traumatic Stress Disorder doesn't even chip the block. My head is completely fucked.*"

Sara was angry. She snagged the weed pipe from the table and threw it at me. Embers burst from my chest as the pipe bounced from my body. Jumping from the booth, she hurried to the refrigerator for another beer. She swung the refrigerator door open banging the cabinet wall making it rattle on its hinge. When she turned around, she began screaming again.

She kept calling me a dumb mother fucker.

Having enough of her shit, I rose from the table. In a non-aggressive manner, I walked towards her gently grabbing her shoulders making an attempt to settle her nerves. She wanted a fight. She wanted to vent all her frustrations.

In a cool manner, I said, "Calm down. It's okay. You don't need to freak out."

Punching me in the shoulder, she stood back from my grasp. She began shouting, "Fuck America. You don't know anything about Vietnam. Fuck you and fuck America."

The Elite were insulted by her comments. They began yelling, "Kill that bitch."

Even though the Elite were putting me through hell, I was on their side. She was defaming our country.

Stepping into her, I grabbed her by the shoulders once again. I said, "Calm down. There is no reason to be like this."

It was of no use. She was on a sick one and there was no way to settle her down.

The Elite continued telling me to kill her. Even though my brain was fucked, there was no way I was going to kill her. I still knew who I was before the brainwash and I still had my moral fiber. Just because my thoughts were screwed up didn't mean I was screwed.

Instead of following the Elite's orders, I went with a more rational approach. With soft eyes, I tilted my head to the side, smiled and asked for a kiss. For the first time since her erratic episode, Sara calmed down. Asking for a kiss had taken the fight right out of her.

Her eyes squinted as she gave the most repulsed expression I had ever seen. Her head turned to the side before she began shouting again. Facing me, she reached up to her mouth yanking a fake tooth from its hold. With her mouth open, I could see a dark hole just to the side of her two front teeth on the upper row. Never being in a situation like this before, I busted out laughing.

Seeing my reaction, Sara began yelling, "You think that's funny mother fucker? Do you want to kiss me now? Huh, do you?"

The Elite were hysterical. They couldn't stop laughing. Hearing them laugh had me in tears. I even began feeling like we were a team again.

Since I had always been somewhat of a clown, I went along with the script. I grabbed Sara by the waist bringing her in towards me. Casually I said, "Put that thing back in your mouth and give me a kiss."

Softening up a bit, Sara put the tooth back in her mouth. When she had it in place, she smoothed her tongue over the surface of her front teeth making sure it fit correctly. Peacefully looking into my eyes, she said, "Do you really want to give me a kiss?"

Smiling, I returned, "Yah, and I want to grab your ass too."

Sliding my hand over Sara's right butt cheek, I squeezed hard. She gave a slight moan placing her arms over my shoulders as our lips met. I have to say even though the tooth thing had me a little freaked out, she wasn't such a bad kisser.

We stood in the kitchen kissing for a while before we made our way to the bedroom. Sara, almost back to normal, was a pleasure to be around once again. Feeling bad for her, I decided we should have sex.

Still intoxicated, we crashed on top of the covers. Sara was wrapped in my arms laughing as we moved our hands over one another's body. Soon our shirts were off. With Sara breathing heavily, I worked my tongue over the nipples of her nice perky round breast. She had her legs wrapped around my waist squeezing hard. Continuing down towards her navel, I circled my tongue around Sara's belly button making her giggle with each tickle.

As I continued kissing Sara's stomach, she quickly brought her hands down to the button of her pants. With her pants unbuttoned and zipper down, Sara wiggled her way out of her jeans. Once the jeans were past her thighs, I sat up helping the rest of the way by freeing them from her legs tossing them to the floor. Now all she had on was a pair of red silk panties.

Sara had her legs slightly spread with her hand between her legs. She ran a finger over her vagina before pressing hard against her clitoris rubbing in a circular motion. Thinking her sexy, I watched as she played with herself.

Not being able to take anymore, I slid my hands up Sara's thighs pulling off her lingerie. Lying down with my head between her legs, I placed my lips around her soft pink clit. Sara moaned.

It wasn't long before I was taking my pants off. Completely naked, I rested my body on top of hers. Her silky lips gently caressed my penis as the two of us moved our hips around. Kissing once again, I slowly slid inside of her. Her warmth sent chills down my spine. Her nails dug deep into my flesh.

With my penis pinning her pussy, Sara arched her back yelling, "I'm going to come." She repeated herself three or four times before she came. I could feel her wetness.

Still awaiting my climax, I pounded faster and harder. Sara had a finger pressed against the bottom of her lip biting on her finger nail. With each thrust, I watched her head jolt towards the headboard.

She was panting...

She whispered, "Fuck me."

The sound of her voice brought me to my ends. Sliding out from her vagina, my penis contracted nutting all over her stomach. A good portion of my load shot over her left breast hitting her in the shoulder. Reaching down, Sara wrapped her hand around my cock messaging the remainder of the seamen from me. She had her other hand between her legs rubbing her pussy. I could tell she wasn't finished.

Within seconds I was deep inside her again. Wanting a different view, I rolled her over wanting to hit it from behind. She was on all fours as I rubbed the head of my cock smoothly over her satin lips. When she had enough of the teasing, I slid inside of her. She took a deep breath with the pressure. Her ass was pressed hard against my hips. Spreading her cheeks, I watched her vagina around me with each movement. She felt good.

We went at it for what seemed like hours. I was having the most fun I had since the elite had arrived. It was a little awkward at first knowing fifteen guys were watching me have sex, but I had gotten over it fairly quickly due to the large amounts of alcohol I had consumed.

Sara rose from the bed heading to the kitchen for another beer. I watched her perfect ass as she swayed toward the refrigerator. It seemed we had the same motive in life; alcohol was curing all of our problems.

On her way back, Sara grabbed the ashtray and the pack of cigarettes from the kitchen table. She had an expression of satisfaction; an expression showing I had fulfilled all her needs. Sitting on the edge of the bed, she pulled a smoke from the pack placing it between her lips lighting the end with a lighter. The cherry glowed in the almost dark room. The only light came from a small night light above the stove.

Sharing the beer, Sara began talking. She started off slow speaking of how much fun she was having. At the same time, I could see she was in deep thought by the gaze in her eyes; like she was reliving the night's events.

Then it was as if a horrible memory had struck her. Puffing on the cigarette, Sara squinted her eyebrows. Suddenly, she twisted her head thrusting backwards. I knew what was coming next. Sara was going to lose her shit again.

Before she could speak, I slid my hand over her thigh stopping between her legs. She was still wet from our moments in bed. With my thumb and finger, I pinched her clitoris. She made a soft noise. Putting her smoke out, Sara lay back in bed. Resting the remainder of the beer next to me on a ledge, I then brought my focus back to her. My intention was to distract her from her thoughts.

With my head on her shoulder, I rubbed her vagina. I don't think I could go for a third time, but I was willing to proceed if necessary.

My seduction was of no use. Sara decided she was no longer having fun. With a tight grip, she snatched my hand throwing it to the side. Shocked by the gesture, I removed my head from her shoulder reaching for the beer on the ledge. I wasn't one to put up with this kind of treatment, so I decided to work her over a bit.

Drinking from the bottle, I asked what was wrong. I had a smile on my face because I knew prying into her life was going to set her off.

"What do you care? You just wanted a quick fuck. You don't care about me," she said disgruntled.

I grunted at her outcry.

"I don't mean shit to you," she continued.

I have to admit, I wasn't planning on calling her ever again. She was a complete psycho; Bi-Polar if I had to make an assessment.

Laughing, I asked, "What do you mean? I thought we were having fun."

Not liking the fact I was laughing, she returned in a very harsh tone, "See, you don't care. All you wanted to do was fuck me. Fuck, fuck, fuck… That's all you want to do."

She wasn't making sense turning a hundred-eighty degrees in the wrong direction.

Pounding the rest of the beer, I crawled to the bottom of the bed. Bending over, I picked up my boxers stepping through the waist pulling them up over my legs. Sara, wanting a fight yelled, "Where the fuck are you going? You don't want to hear what I have to say?"

I had enough of her shit, but instead of losing my temper I returned, "I'm listening. I'm just grabbing another beer."

When I opened the refrigerator door, I scanned the shelves for a beer, but Sara drank the last. In the freezer I had a bottle of rum, so I poured myself a rum and coke. I could hear Sara in the bedroom dressing as she continually talked nonsense. Standing there, I had my head tilted towards the ceiling silently laughing. She just wouldn't shut up.

Back in the bedroom, I sipped on my drink. Again, Sara was going off about Vietnam. It was like I was living in some sort of military conundrum. Some kind of sick twisted bash I couldn't get out of.

The Elite were yelling the entire time she was having her tantrum. They would say, "Tell that bitch to shut the fuck up."

I understood where they were coming from. She just wouldn't let it go.

Between Sara losing her mind and the Elite with their yelling, I was stuck in the middle. All I could do was laugh in an odd way; half because I didn't know what to do about her situation and half because the Elite were shouting in my ears. All I could do was drink my rum listening as the two went back and forth. At one point, I wished Sara could hear the Elite. I wished she could hear what they thought about her. Shit, what a mess.

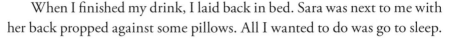

When I finished my drink, I laid back in bed. Sara was next to me with her back propped against some pillows. All I wanted to do was go to sleep.

With Sara going on about America and Vietnam, one of the Elite had had enough. He was so furious he began shouting, "Shut up bitch...shut the fuck up."

He kept repeating himself getting angrier with every word. He yelled as if she could hear him.

Turning over towards the wall, I talked into my pillow. I said to the guy now losing his shit, "Dude, she can't hear you. You're yelling for no reason."

He returned with anger, "I know, but she's pissing me off."

Shaking my head, I decided to try and get some sleep.

Sara began shouting fuck America again. She even leaned over in my ear yelling at the top of her lungs, "Do you hear me? I said fuck America you dumb mother fucker."

Even though Sara couldn't hear, one of the Elite shouted back, "Don't say that to him you dumb bitch. He's going to be one of ours."

Sympathizing with the Elite, I had an idea. Whispering into my pillow I said, "Don't worry about it fellas. If she says it again, I'm going to piss on her."

"Fuck yah," the elite shouted back.

"Piss on that bitch."

Sara had gone on for close to five minutes. She just wouldn't shut the fuck up. I expectantly waited for the words to leave her mouth, but somehow she was able to veer around the topic. I continued telling the guys, "If she says it again, I'm going to piss on her."

Then it happened. I was lying there almost asleep when Sara said the words. She was smoking on a cigarette while mumbling over the filter.

"Fuck America and fuck this country," she said.

I smiled saying to the boys, "That's it. She's going to get it now."

Pulling my boxer shorts down to my thighs, I rolled over pulling out my penis. Acting like I was cuddling next to her, I puffed up the comforter. I wanted a direct stream of piss towards Sara's leg. Pinching the tip of my penis to build some pressure, I let it rip.

As I pissed on her, I could hear the flow of urine bouncing off her denim jeans. It felt so good to pay her back for the remarks she made about our country.

My actions had the Elite hysterical. They were cracking up in laughter as one of them yelled, "He's one of ours."

It took Sara a few moments to realize what was going on. First, she went silent. Then, she reached under the covers feeling her thigh. Next, she slapped me on the shoulder yelling, "You dumb mother fucker. You pissed all over me."

With my face berried into the pillow, I was in tears holding back laughter. I didn't want her to think I did it on purpose. Slapping me on the shoulder once again, she shouted, "You fuck. I'm soaked in piss. You did that shit on purpose."

Thinking she was on to me, I began mumbling some words. I told her I wanted a burger with extra cheese and some fries. I was trying to act incoherent to the situation.

Sara wasn't having it. She pushed me over onto my back. When I rolled over, I could see the wet spot on her jeans.

She yelled, "A burger with extra cheese, you fucker. You pissed all over me."

The Elite couldn't stop laughing. One of them turned to the commander and said, "I can't believe you want to leave this kid here. You wouldn't want this kid with you?"

The commander grunted in return.

Sara was on a rampage. When I saw she was freaking out, I tried to calm her by saying, "Relax, I didn't mean it. I was passed out."

"Bullshit," she retorted.

"You had that thing out. You did that shit on purpose," she continued.

I was lying in a puddle of my own piss and I didn't care. Along with Sara's leg, my bed was drenched. Sara threw back the covers revealing my lower body. When she realized my shorts were around my thighs revealing my penis, she went into attack mode. For a second, I thought I noticed a smile cross her face, but it had quickly vanished when she decided to hit me in the shoulder a few times with a closed fist.

I kept telling her to relax. She wouldn't listen. She began yelling, "Take me to my car you dumb mother fucker."

I had to agree with her. Getting her out of the camper was the best decision of the night. She was a complete lunatic.

As she rounded up her belongings, I put on some pants with a sweatshirt. Sara was perturbed. The quicker I could get her to the car, the better off I was.

As we were leaving, Sara straight armed the door banging it hard against the side of the camper. The neighbors must have heard her yelling because I could hear laughter coming from the camper window in front of us. It was the perfect scene from a movie; two drunken people fighting in the trailer park. It made me think what my life had come to; hanging out with crazy people. I had to wonder if it had something to do with the Elite fucking with my head. Thinking it had, I shrugged deciding to make better decisions in the future. The problem was making proper decisions while under severe brainwash was a very difficult task. My mind wasn't right.

Sara complained about the piss on her leg the entire way to her car. A few times I tried reinforcing the idea of it being a complete accident, but Sara wasn't buying it.

"You had that thing out," she would continue to say.

With no argument, I kept my mouth shut.

When we arrived at the parking lot where Sara's car was parked, Sara jumped from my ride slamming the door closed behind her. She did not say good-bye. Instead, she simply tramped her way towards her car in disgust waving her hands around like the worst possible scenario in life had just occurred.

I had no feelings toward her. Instead, I Lifted my foot from the brake pedal stomping on the accelerator kicking up cinders speeding away from the lot. I didn't want to look back. I wanted no reminder of the night's events. Sara was definitely a complete disaster.

When Sara was out of site, one of the Elite said, "It's about time you got rid of that bitch."

I had to agree with him. With pride in my voice, I returned, "That one was for you guys. Nobody is going to say fuck America and get away with it."

After the night with Sara, it seemed I was back in the good graces of the Elite. They were still hesitant with conversation, but they weren't telling me to kill myself as much. Actually, it was weird in the way things were going. The Elite wanted me with them, but the commander did not. We were in a three way battle.

CHAPTER 11

D riving two hours for work every day had become quite the hassle, so I
decided to move to Aspen. With my parents already having a condo
in the downtown area, I was set to make the move immediately.

On a Saturday afternoon, I packed my belongings before trailing my
camper to a local storage center where I would be keeping it. As I cranked
the extension leg freeing my camper from the hitch of my truck, I found
myself solaced from the upcoming moving adventure. Living in an RV
Park had taken its toll, so I was relieved to have a place of my own once
again.

Before leaving town, I stopped by my parent's house to grab a few
essential belongings for the condo. After a bit more packing, I sent my
farewell even though I would be seeing my parents every day at their office
which was directly below where I would be staying.

"Don't get in trouble up there," my father had warned.

I laughed knowing I had this knack of getting myself into a pickle;
especially in a party town like Aspen.

I left town around three o'clock in the afternoon as the sun was over
head floating west as I drove with a grin on my face as I thought about all
of the thrills ahead. I could go snowboarding, hiking, mountain biking
and camping. Then there was my most favorite, hanging out with all my
old buddies from town; nothing but good times.

On route 82, just before getting into Aspen, I crossed over a bridge
where I could see the mountains of Maroon Bells on my right. Seeing
the majestic snowcapped peaks always had this soothing effect bringing
about a sense of curiosity. Every time I gazed upon them, I felt as if I could
conquer the world; a truly breathtaking site to see.

Continuing on 82 down Main Street, I watched as on-goers strolled the vibrant city streets. Mothers, daughters, friends and fathers weaved through the many store front arches. The elders watched with glee as their little ones skipped with joy. Everyone was so full of life.

Anxious to see more of Aspen's spirit, I drove further down Main Street passing my turn. Veering off onto a side street, I headed for Ajax Mountain passing restaurant after restaurant and pub after pub. The sight brought many fond drunken memories as my mouth watered with the sensation of a nice cold Budweiser.

After a quick cruise around town, I pulled into the lot behind my condo reversing into place for a more efficient unloading. Stepping from my vehicle, I glanced across the street towards the front entrance of my favorite Sushi restaurant in town. Once again, my mouth was full of sensation as I conceived the taste of a good Sushi roll washed down with a shot of Purple Haze Saki. Swallowing, I couldn't imagine anything better.

Grabbing a duffel full of clothes from behind the passenger's seat, I headed up the stairs to the second floor towards the front entrance of the condo. With my key in place, I turned the door's knob pushing it open as it slightly squeaked on hinge. Stepping through, I was instantly hit by the scent of freshly stained wood from a recent remodel.

Once inside, I was awed by the many artworks hanging from the walls. My most favorite were the reproductions of Italian and French posters advertising the best cafes from the period.

The living room was furnished nicely with brown swede couches and end pieces constructed of wood which almost but not completely matched the coffee table. Lamps provided a gentle ambient atmosphere in the dark hours. The floors were wide planked pine strewn with Asian throw rugs surrounded by walls of brilliant Italian plaster. For such a small place, I couldn't think of anything much cozier. It definitely had a touch of my mother's fecundity.

The guest area balanced the condo's character with a queen sized bed arranged in the center of the room. With the many pillows and fluffy comforter, it warmed the room nicely.

Dropping my bags near the closet door, I jumped on the bed stretching my legs far and wide. Extending my arms toward the headboard, I grunted in approval. I felt as if I could lie there forever.

After a quick relaxing break, I went down to the parking area to remove the rest of my belongings from my vehicle. Normally I hated moving, but this time I didn't mind since I had very little to unpack. Plus, I was living in one of the most congenial places in America making the event much more exciting.

I couldn't wait to get around town for a drink, so as soon as I finished sorting through my possessions I headed over to Mato's for a beer and a roll. My friend, Michael, was a Sushi Chef at Mato so I was excited to see if he was working.

Anxious to see Mike, I walked through the restaurant with a broad smile. Passing the bar on my right, I then headed around the corner where Mike normally stood behind a Sushi bar preparing fish. He was one hell of a chef and it was always a pleasure to enjoy his delectable creations.

As soon as I made the turn into the next room, I was struck by Mike's presence. It had been a long time since we had seen each other and I have to admit it was always nice to see him.

Mike usually dressed casually, but he was now with his chef whites and hat to match. He was around five-nine in height with reddish blond hair. When he was around town having fun, he usually wore a smile. When it came to making Sushi, Mike was all business.

I stood in front of Mike for a few moments before he noticed my company. While at work it was hard to get a smile out of him, I watched as his lips formed the gesture.

"What's up buddy," I said with cheer.

He shook his head as if trouble just entered town. He then responded by saying, "What are you up too? I haven't seen you in a while."

He had a mischievous grin on his face and I knew it was all directed towards me. With this expression, we both had a good laugh as the two of us remembered all the late nights and good times we had partying with one another.

Pulling a stool from under the counter, I sat in front of Mike watching as he prepared for the nights agenda. A menu wasn't necessary since Mike always knew the perfect meal to serve, but he did ask what I wanted to drink. Of course I ordered a double rum and coke tall.

Signaling for a waiter, Mike placed my order before going to work on a Sashimi Roll. He was an artist in the true sense. His fingers moved fast mended with precision as the dish came to life gleaming with colors of red, white, green, pink and purple. Adding a finishing touch, he finished the tender meat with a blow torch. As Mike seared away, my nose was overwhelmed with its delightful aroma.

With the brainwash continually rounding my brain, I was eager to get some alcohol in my veins. When the waiter arrived, he set my drink down in front of me along with a set of chopsticks and a white cloth lap towel. As soon as the glass hit the bar top, I had my drink in hand ordering another before the waiter had time to walk away.

Within minutes, Mike reached over the counter setting a plate of perfectly rolled Sushi edged with a brilliant wasabi green and the colorful pink of ginger. I couldn't wait to dig in.

When the first bite hit my mouth, I was embellished in flavor. Each color brought a sensational set of both texture and savor as I sat their overwhelmed by his masterful talent for food. It seemed I couldn't get enough.

By the time I finished with my roll, the waiter had placed another drink in front of me as Mike fancied another plate of fish. I pounded my drink before eating and soon found his second edible was just as artistic and tasteful as the first.

After my third roll, I was in heaven. My stomach was stuffed and I had a nice buzz from the stiff drinks. Mike and I caught up on old times and I was well on my way to an entertaining night in Aspen.

Saying good-bye to Mike, I left Moto's around 8:15. I had over seven drinks in me and the night was still young. I turned left out of Moto's and then another left onto Hopkins Street. Just around the corner down a flight of concrete stairs lie a Bar and Restaurant where my buddy John worked. I hadn't seen him in a while either, so I thought I would stop in for another drink to see what was happening for the night.

Down a short entrance just past the front door, Johnny stood behind the bar pouring drinks for a couple of Aspen's finest ladies. He had this genuine smile on. The one he kept solely for the hottest women around town. He was a classic in his own mind.

At the time, Johnny and I hadn't known each other for very long, but I have to say I valued his friendship. He was an all-around good guy.

Best of all, he knew how to have fun. He took life as it came and he never looked back.

I pulled a stool from beside the two ladies before Johnny looked up to see who I was. When our eyes met, he engraved the same look Michael had. He wore a devious grin from the many late nights partying with one another; a look only a true friend could provide.

Johnny's hand came over the bar top meeting mine.

"What's up buddy," he shouted thrusting his head back with an act of humor.

Pulling away from our grasp, he pointed his finger at my chest switching over to an expression of thought then pounded his fist into his hand before saying, "Double rum and coke tall. Bacardi if I remember correctly."

I gave him the all-knowing nod of my head and returned, "With a slice of lemon."

When I had a drink in hand, Johnny and I discussed my return to Aspen. It seemed he was excited for my return constantly keeping a drink in front of me while we shared the many stories which had passed since our last visit together. He filled my ears with town gossip of who was still hanging around and where they could be reached. We laughed as he read off a list of names and I was happy to discover many of the people I hung around still resided in the area.

It wasn't long before the two of us moved our attention towards the two women who were sitting next to me. They were new to town, but had been living there long enough to know Johnny on a regular basis. He introduced them as Lauren and Jessica.

Lauren sat closest to me wearing a pair of faded jeans and a yellow top. She had long blonde hair, gentle blue eyes and bronze colored skin. She had an athletic build and a small perky chest. She had a quiet smile which revealed her perfectly sculpted white teeth and her personality matched her appearance making her easy to fall for.

Jessica was much like Lauren except she had dark hair above green eyes. She was athletically toned to the point of being muscular and showing off her pleasant but strong demeanor. She had on a pair of black tights with a purple top which matched her dark hair perfectly. Even though she was more than attractive, my eyes were on Lauren. Something about Lauren made me feel comfortable inside.

Right away, Lauren and I hit it off. She was funny, caring, soft and best of all she was smart. After a few minutes of talking, it was as if Lauren and I had known each other our whole lives. We got along great.

What seemed like minutes turned into hours. The bar filled with eager patrons ready to get the night started. Those who were hungry occupied the tables on the outer edge along the window ordering food from a select menu which was filled with delicious plates. Those who were ready for a drink scrambled around the bar ordering whatever concoction their taste buds desired. The atmosphere was lively as Johnny and his bar-mate, James, poured drink after drink. With Johnny occupied, the conversation was left between the two ladies and I.

I just ordered another double rum and coke when Lauren and Jessica informed me they were heading over to Eric's, another hot spot in town which was just a few blocks from Elevations at the base of Ajax Ski Resort. I was bummed to hear they were leaving since Lauren and I hit it off so well. I was shortly relieved when she invited me to join them.

Even though I was excited, I didn't want to seem overzealous. Instead, I told her I was going to finish my drink and maybe later I would make my way in their direction. To my surprise, she gave sad eyes and said, "Okay then. Maybe we will see you over there."

I smiled returning, "You will."

Her eyes brightened and I could tell she was into me. As my face flushed a bit, I hoped she didn't notice. And she didn't. Reaching over with her arm, she rubbed my shoulder with her hand saying, "good-bye."

I touched her hand with mine and said, "I will see you in a bit."

She smiled turning away. As she turned, I couldn't help but see her well-proportioned ass immediately thinking how perfect she was in every way imaginable.

When I finished my drink, I ordered another before saying farewell to my old time buddy, Johnny. As we shook hands, I told him I would meet with him later in the week for some drinks. He gave me his sly smile and said, "Alright my man, I will see you soon."

Leaving a twenty dollar bill on the counter for a tip, I headed for the door.

On the walk to Eric's, I thought about Lauren the entire way. I kept thinking how nice and sweet she was; how she smiled and how she warmed my heart. Excited to see her, I hurried to the bar.

Upon my arrival at Eric's, I was greeted by the door crew who wore all black outfits. They checked my identification for age before letting me enter the establishment. Down a concrete flight of stairs, I turned right towards the entrance of the Martini Bar. Outside, the patio area was packed with people of all ages. Some stood with drinks in their hands while others sat around circular tables under umbrellas. Even though a majority of them were in their twenties and thirties, a good many of them were in their forties and fifties. The diversity made for a comfortable ambiance.

As I walked through the main entrance of the Martini Bar, I was shocked to see they had remodeled since my last visit. Cozy brown couches with fluffy throw pillows set around black wooden tables were shadowed by gray stone pillars and modernistic art work stretched across dimly painted walls. The patrons were just as characteristic as the atmosphere with their fall attire, bright smiles, and colorful dazzling drinks. The scene made me thirsty.

Making my way towards the bar, I sifted through the different clicks of people in search of Lauren. Finding she was nowhere in sight, I squeezed through groups of people huddling around the bar top patiently waiting for drinks as others chatted to their nearest friend.

When I had the bartender's attention, I ordered two double rum and cokes. I ordered two because I didn't want to wait in line for a while. I paid him his money telling him to keep the change before walking towards the stairs where there was a large room above displaying wall to wall pool tables. Lauren didn't seem to be the type to play pole on a night out, so I quickly scanned the area making sure she wasn't around. And she wasn't. Filing through a group of pool players, I weaved my way towards a hallway leading into the Cigar Bar which was another piece of Eric's and more like Lauren's style.

Walking through the doors of the Cigar Bar, I noticed the lights were dim and the conversations were quiet. Small plumes of cigar and cigarette smoke swiveled in the air directing their way towards the exhaust fans high above. Guests sat on top of leather couches talking to one another and I could see a small group of patrons surrounding the bar area.

Just to my right, Lauren sat with Jessica on a set of leather reading chairs stuffed in the corner of the room. Her eyes sparkled off a table lamp to her left as I stood there for a minute observing her beauty. When she turned in my direction, our eyes met filling here with a smile. Taking a second to break her conversation with Jessica, she invited me over with a wave of her hand.

Jessica took a moment to see what caught Lauren's attention. I could tell by her expression she was just as happy to see me standing there; the signature of a true friend. She was showing her approval for Lauren's interest by accepting me into their lives by issuing an extravagant smile. If I had any doubts or nervousness with the situation between Lauren and me, they were quickly swept away by Jessica's trust in me.

I sat on a brown swede love seat just opposite of Jessica next to Lauren using the armrest of Lauren's chair to settle my elbow. The three of us talked of places we had adventured to in our lives as well as the areas we grew up in. They explained how the hotel industry brought the two of them to Aspen and how eager they were for the winter's ski season. I listened attentively speaking of previous years and how those years had been great for snowboarding and this year like the rest would be just as exciting. I didn't want to add I had missed out due to a prison term from addiction issues, so I immediately dismissed the thought even though it made me feel dishonest. Instead, I blocked the thoughts of incarceration. I then pondered over speaking of my experience with the Elite and how they were trying to coerce me into committing suicide, but soon realized the story would only make me look crazy even though it was really happening.

Thinking of the Elite was a mistake. The thoughts brought on a bout with brainwash. Instantly, my brain was infiltrated by thoughts of murder. I put my head down trying to block the visuals, but the more I tried to exit them from my brain the worse they had become.

My mouth began to water. I felt as if I was going to vomit as people were being massacred. Blood and guts filled my visual screen. Women were screaming as men shouted for help. I had an automatic rifle in my hand and everyone who was in my way was either going to be shot or was in the process of being shot. I began to laugh as I pointed my rifle at a man's head who was now below a bar top screaming for mercy. He had on a blue tie over a white shirt. His pants were khaki a brown belt and brown shoes to match. He was handsome with dark skin and dark hair. He was going to die.

I aimed for the center of his forehead and pulled the trigger. His head splattered popping like a pumpkin. His arms and legs flailed as his life ended. I shot him again.

Confident he was dead, I raised my head in the air and began with and evil howl

When I finished howling, I lowered my rifle as shots rang from my weapon once again. I could feel the guns vibration; its power running through my forearms. A woman in her thirties ran towards the front entrance of the bar. I saw her beauty upon my arrival. She had on a red dress which fit perfectly around her tender curves. Her blonde hair danced with her step as she ran wobbling on her high heels. I aimed toward her torso. I couldn't wait to pull the trigger.

The gun whispered death as a bullet whistled through the air impacting her chest. The tip of fury raging jerked her body toward a bar table knocking it over as she rolled onto the floor. With blood pouring from her side, she tried to move in an attempt to free herself. I felt no mercy. Instead, I pulled the trigger to end all her pain and fear. Her head lunged forward on her shoulders as brain matter splattered the wooden floor. Finally, she was dead.

There was blood everywhere as the floor crawled with the wounded... stilled by the dead. Those who dodged the may-lay ran for cover as those closest to the exit ran for freedom. I tried picking them off one by one. I was successful leaving only the lucky ones to escape.

My body was slumped over as my head bobbed back and forth. I could hear Lauren's voice while feeling her hand gently rubbing my back. Speaking softly she said, "Boo...Boo? Are you alright?"

Slowly, I turned my head to face her. Her hand was on my back rubbing in soft circular motions.

I had drool dripping from the end of my lip. I lost track of time and suddenly everything in the room became quiet. All I could hear was Lauren's voice as she tried bringing me back to life; back to reality.

As soon as I saw her face, I jumped back in my seat. She had blood all over her. Just as soon as the visual arrived it had disappeared. I wiped the saliva from my mouth rising from my chair.

"I have to go," I said to her.

Jessica didn't know what to think. She sat there utterly baffled by the presentation. I was too drunk to be embarrassed and too confused to explain myself. The Elite had taken control of my brain in a very serious manner.

As the Elite watched me stand from my chair, they laughed uncontrollably. One said to their commander, "He made it through another episode. He's not going to kill anyone."

The commander grunted in disapproval. One thing was for sure, he either wanted me to kill somebody or he wanted me to kill myself. I wasn't going to give him either.

I had tunnel vision leaving Lauren behind. I stumbled tripping over peoples feet as they shouted, "Hey, watch your step buddy."

I pushed some to the side while stepping through small groups doing everything I could to get out of there as fast as possible. I didn't care. All I wanted to do was get home where I felt most safe; away from the scene and away from the fright; away from all those who surrounded me.

When I was back outside on the patio area, I stopped leaning my butt against a brick wall with my head bent over my knees. I coughed spitting from my mouth still drooling as I watched strands of saliva swivel towards the ground.

I was in bad shape…

After catching my breath and wanting to get out of there, I continued through the crowds making my way for the concrete stairs. I was almost there, almost away.

Scaling the stairs one by one, I reached the top where I bumped into a security guard. He put his hands around my shoulders and said in a calm manner, "Are you okay buddy? It looks like you had too much to drink."

I did have too much to drink, but that wasn't the problem. The Elite were the problem.

Looking over his shoulder, I could see the street lights. Their glow sought the ground as a halo of purple circled its frame. Visuals of the murdered filled my brain. It was like a bad night on LSD.

"I just want to go home," I said to the security guard.

"I just want to go home."

Wanting to get me home safely, he asked if he should call a cab. Only living a few blocks, I declined the offer thanking him pushing passed his grasp heading for the street. I was off-balance from the alcohol and my brain was completely fried. All I could do was follow the street lamps as their wicked glaze entered my eyes guiding me home.

Away from Eric's, I turned down a side street anxious to get home. I had my hands pushed hard against the sides of my temples with the feeling of short buzzed stubble against my finger tips from a high and tight fade. Ten steps from the corner, I stopped with a ringing in my ears. One of the Elite noticing my frantic yelled, "Just kill yourself and we will go away. All you have to do is kill yourself Boo."

With rage in my voice, I looked straight to the sky towards the satellites and shouted, "Fuck you, you dumb mother fuckers. It's never going to happen. I will never kill myself or hurt another human being as long as I live. You bitches will never get the best of me. I will not die."

The elite laughed before a man of about forty years of age with the deepest most gruesome voice I had ever heard said, "You're going to die."

His voice was fearsome, but I wasn't scared. Instead, I laughed with my head still raised in the air. Digging deep into my throat, I hacked a loogie spitting in his direction. A moment went by before the man decided he didn't like the display of disrespect. In his deep voice he said, "I'm going to kill you."

Even though his voice was sadistic, I didn't care. I simply returned, "I will be waiting for the day."

What came next was fearsome. He had a laugh created from a dark deep evil; a laugh of massacre; a laugh of horror. I couldn't believe my ears. This was a man of death. It was then I knew they truly meant to kill me. They weren't going to let me live knowing what I knew. I had all of their secrets.

Suddenly, the street turned into an insect farm. Everywhere I looked, I could hear the sound of crickets. The trees chirped with birds. The bushes squeaked with squirrels. No more than three feet in front of me, the sound of a Bald Eagle. Then the oddest sound of all. It was that of an ocean Seal barking with order. Barking as I lived an internal nightmare.

I began walking again. The noises followed with every step. The street lights glared through the branches of trees reflecting off each leaf. With the sounds of crickets, my mind was brought to that horrible moment inside the cigar bar. Instantaneously, my mind filled with its blood and terror.

I stopped thinking, "*I just left the women of my dreams behind.*"

I was raged. I was disembarked. I couldn't believe what was happening to me. I couldn't believe I just left Lauren sitting there with no explanation. I wanted to tell her everything. I wanted to tell her I had the ability to hear through spy satellites and this Elite crew were trying to kill me because I discovered too many of their secrets. I wanted to say I had discovered a life beyond normal; that I had discovered Pandora's Box. A box that has yet to be revealed to the public and because of this I was sought out to be killed.

This secret being the secret of all secrets; a secret of my own before this Elite crew stumbled across me. It's a secret I cherish only to be discovered by another telepath like myself.

I wanted to tell her everything and I wanted her in my arms. I wanted her to say everything was going to be alright.

I soon found myself at the base of the stairs leading towards my condo door. I grabbed hold of the railing pulling myself along the way. Opening the front door, I ran from the crickets and birds to the safety of a cupboard for a bottle of rum. When I opened the cabinet door, I found the Elites key system worked just as well indoors as it did outdoors when the sound of birds filled the inside of my cabinet space. I smiled thinking how cool their technology really was.

Reaching inside the cabinet, I pushed aside a few bottles of alcohol before discovering I was out of Rum. Instead, I had to choose between Gin and Vodka. Liking the taste of Gin, I went for its handle. With the brainwash bombarding my brain once again, I quickly unscrewed its top raising the neck of the bottle to my lips and began pouring alcohol down the back of my throat. It tasted so good.

When I had ingested enough of Gin to keep my mind off the brainwash, I reached to my left and opened another cabinet door grabbing a glass from the top shelf. I poured myself a drink adding some ice finishing with a touch of tonic and a lemon wedge; the perfect match.

Walking over to the couch, I reached below the television turning on the stereo grabbing a book of CD's and began flipping through my selection. I froze at Pigs on the Animal Album by Pink Floyd. I felt it necessary and appropriate for the time.

Opening the wheel of the stereo, I placed the CD next to a random selection of disks already set in the player. I pressed the button for disk number 5 watching the wheel contract then turned the volume three-quarters of the way up while boosting the base; in my mind, the only way to listen to Pink.

Taking a seat on the couch, I guzzled from my drink as the cool ice froze my lips, The beginning of the song echoed through my ears as my head rested against the soft swede couch cushion. Starring toward the ceiling fan as its aggressive wings broke the air, I gazed upon it's shadows dancing its way to oblivion. With nothing but pink to keep the minds wonder, I entered a dream...

A dream like no other...

A dream resulting from pure mental torture...

I was looking through a tint of glass beyond the propeller of a World War II fighter plan. The engine roared as the fire of machine guns filled the air. Bullets streamed in death towards the may-lay of enemy fighters weaving through the air.

Both sides were fighting for their lives with the Germans outnumbered and losing. The ones bombarded by gunfire streaked through the sky uncontrollably. Cascades of black smoke marked their line as they plummeted towards earth. Tension was in the air as the smell of burning oil whipped across my face.

To my right a fighter plane engulfed in flames. Bullet holes riddled the planes aluminum side as dark oil from the engine rippled across the shining metal tearing away into the sky. A man of Italian decent was behind the controls screaming for his life. He couldn't hold on.

Soon, flames from the damaged engine overcame the cockpit. Terror was in the man's eyes as fire swept over the hood stretching towards him with the streaming wind. His face began to melt with every second of exposure. His skin bubbled then burst into colors of red and yellow; black with burnt tissue. With no other option, he reached between his legs for his service pistol. A sense of calmness surpassed his fear. Before sticking the gun to his head, he gazed into my eyes sorrowful for his life's ending journey.

In those moments, time had frozen. Our planes went into slow motion. I could see each swoop of the propeller as its sound muffled my ears. With our heads facing each other, the Italian nodded his head saying farewell. He raised the pistol to the side of his head and pulled the trigger.

The loud pop of the firearm batted through the wind. Instantly, his head rattled to the side as his body slumped forward shifting his steering out of control. His plane veered in front of mine as he descended to his grave below. He was gone forever; gone to a place unknown.

I wondered if he had family who would miss him...

When I looked ahead, I reacted to an enemy fighter approaching in my direction. I had only seconds to make my move. I turned a hard right missing his wing by only inches as our planes almost collided. His engine roared clearing overhead. The sign of Germany staring me down in the shape of a silver iron cross. My heart jumped in my chest as the reality hit home. I had nearly died. It was close, but not close enough.

A set of cumulonimbus clouds in front. I banked a hard left seeking sanctuary from the almost near fatal crash. The clouds were thick with moisture making it hard to control my aircraft. I bounced with the turbulence as my wings bent on end. Visibility was near nothing and all was still except for a quiet whistle from a chilling breeze. The war of gliders had seized to exist. My mind was at ease. I was now all alone with no other soul around except for my own. I was lost... lost for those to wonder.

Steering away from the turbulent moisture, I maneuvered my aircraft acrobatically spinning in circles diving towards earth solaced from the deadly skies above. My sight expanded into prairies lined with colors of green, brown and yellow just as I leveled the aircraft above the tops of white flowers. The turbulent winds swayed each blossom with the speed of my propeller.

With the tires of the planes landing gear just above the ground, I landed on an old overgrown dirt road. Dust kicked with the violent drafts as the plane settled along the roads surface skipping once then twice before straightening itself out.

Stepping on the brake pedal, I brought the WWII aircraft to a stop before hitting the switch to stall the engine. With the propeller in its final stages of rest, I unstrapped myself from the seat raising myself from its bond jumping to the wing of the craft. My boots made a clunk against the aluminum structure. I stood there for a moment looking out observing the beauty of the tumbling hills of Germany.

As I stood there captivated by the sight, I tuned into the sound of Pink playing in my ears. Suddenly the desolate area rumbled like an earthquake. The wing danced to the seismic rhythm knocking me off balance. The plane's wing shook as I fought to catch my footing. The ground rattled with the fierceness of a stampede.

There must have been thousands of them. Just over the horizon as the sun's descending day brought fire to the sky, I watched as a haze of brown filled the air below. In the distance, I could hear their hooves tearing across the ground. Pink was making their presence.

Then, over the furthest hill I saw them. They came with fury attacking like Trojan warriors moving in a current of wind. When one turned, they all turned. They were heading straight for me. All I could do was gaze upon them as they triumphantly came forward. I wasn't scared. In fact, I stood in tranquility amazed by their fierce power.

It wasn't long before I was surrounded by them. There were hundreds even thousands of giant pigs. They moved around the plane with unknown speeds as I stood on top of my shiny thrown looking down upon a wake of pink. Their faces were mean and grueling. They had no cause. They were eyes of terror. The plane shook with thunder in their passing. The noise was overwhelming. And just as quickly as they came, they had gone.

I woke the next morning in my bed. I had no idea how I had gotten there. My head hurt and all I could do was think of the amazing dream I had from the night before. Then it hit me. I was late for work.

I rolled over to check the time. When I moved, I noticed there was something wrong. I had this wet feeling around my crouch. Realizing what had happened, I reached below with my hand to check the sheets below. They were just as soaked as I was. Instantly, I became embarrassed knowing the Elite were watching. In that instant, the room filled with crickets. The nightmare was starting all over again. The Elite chanted in a childish tone of voice, "You pissed yourself, you pissed your pants."

It wasn't long before one of them yelled in excitement, "Kill yourself bitch, you're dead."

I wanted revenge. I was humiliated. I was enraged, ready to strike at any moment. I wanted them to pay for what they were doing to my head. I wanted them to pay for every torturous relenting moment.

With the sounds of crickets, my mind sunk into a realm of brainwash. I began reliving the visuals from the night before; nothing but death and murder. I couldn't stand it, but I was determined to live. I was going to survive.

I jumped from my bed shaking the thoughts. The more I tried to get rid of them the worse they had become. It was impossible to get the thoughts out of my head. It just kept getting worse and worse.

I ran into the bathroom stripping my shirt from my body. My pants were soaked with urine, but I had no care. When I passed the hallway leading from the living room to the back bedroom, I stopped in my tracks. In the middle of the hallway on the hardwood floor laid the bottle of gin. It was empty and on its side. My glass was not far away. Spotting the floor, puddles of water remained where cubes of ice once lay. Finishing off the disastrous portrait, I squeezed lemon not far from the glass. I laughed at the site shaking my head thinking, *"Another rough night those fucking guys."*

Desperately wanting a shower, I blew off the scene continuing through to the bathroom. Standing in front of the mirror, I gazed across to my reflection where I noticed a large gash above my left eyebrow. Pissing my pants wasn't the only fucked up event of the night, I had bumped my head as well. I didn't need stitches, but the wound was deep. Dried black and maroon blood surrounded its edges. This wasn't the worst part. I hit my head so hard the bottom of my eye was green and yellow. Always the worst when you had to go out into public. Cuts like this made me feel like somebody kicked my ass. In a way, somebody did.

I touched the wound with the tip of my finger. The area around my eye was sore as I cursed myself for the blunder. Life hooked up to the satellite wasn't getting much better. In fact it sucked.

Telling myself to forget about it, I kicked off my pants and jumped into the shower. A steam bath fixture was placed on the side of the wall so I turned the knob. Within seconds hot steam poured from the brass outlet. The warmth from the shower combined with the steam had my body fully relaxed. The tension from my bones and muscles dissipated as I stood there leaning against the stone tile wall. My head pounded from a hangover and all I could do was think of how fucked up life had become. I was hurting and I didn't know how much more I could take.

I don't know how long I was sitting there, but when I opened my eyes I was sitting on a stone bench towards the back of the shower. Hot water beaded against my legs as the moist air filled my lungs. With the haze, I could hardly see my hand as I wove it like a wand in front of my face. I was mesmerized by the solitude and even though I could hear the Elite voices as they talked to one another, I felt alone. In those moments, I was at peace.

Rising from the bench, I turned off the shower and steam bath. I still had a headache and feeling nauseous as I opened the glass door reaching for my towel. I was in tough shape. Depleted of all nutrients and dehydrated I walked over to the sink twisting the knob watching as water swirled around the basin. I waited a couple of seconds making sure it was nice and cold before cupping my hands for a drink. With my hands against my mouth, I couldn't get enough as I took gulp after gulp.

My stomach rumbled and I farted. The Elite laughed. My mouth began to water. I ran for the toilet lifting the lid as quickly as possible. Vomit gushed from my insides splashing around the bowl. I gagged... I coughed...I threw up...I repeated the process.

My stomach was beginning to protrude from my mouth. All I had left was yellow bile as I leaned over the toilet dry heaving. I cursed myself for getting so wasted. I cursed the Elite for their purpose.

After drying off and putting some clothes on, I decided to take the day off from work to recuperate. I called the superintendent, Tim, to let him know I wasn't feeling well and it best I didn't come in for the day. He was okay with my decision. Hanging up the phone I walked into the kitchen for a drink. In my eyes a large stiff cocktail was the only way to kill a hangover.

Rummaging through the kitchen, I ended up with a cranberry and vodka; one of my favorite morning drinks since too much orange juice tended to give me acid reflux. With my drink in hand, I headed for the couch getting my day started by listening to music. I had Red Hot Chili Peppers in mind, so I spun the CD in the carriage setting the song list with the track to Otherside playing first.

Two drinks later, I was back on my feet and ready to go. Red Hot Chili Peppers was jamming from the stereo and all I could think about was partying. Partying was the only way to beat the system. It was the only way I could control my thoughts. It was the only way I could live on.

Four drinks later, I was out the door and on my way to another bar for cocktails. This bar was legendary in Aspen. As I walked the streets, the Elite filled the bushes with crickets and the trees with birds. The passerby's had no concern for the sounds since it was virtually impossible to distinguish between real and fake, but I knew they were there and that's all that mattered. Their sound triggered attacks of brainwash and the Elite were using it as a tactic sticking me inside my head. It worked.

As I rounded the corner heading for the brick walkway leading to the front entrance of the establishment, I fought the Elite the best I could. I fought every deranged thought that entered my mind. When I sought death, I dreamed of flowers. When I sought rape, I dreamed of the mountains. I figured if I could change the visuals to good instead of evil I would be able to conquer the lunacy in my brain. If I could beat my brain, then I could beat the Elite.

I opened the double doors of the Onion and headed into darkness. The scent of beer was in the air as I peered towards the bar. The stools were filled with fellow drinkers as I searched for my spot amongst the crowd. Down towards the end, a single seat pulled away from the bar with my name written all over it.

Walking along, I nodded my head to those who enlightened my entrance. I was greeted mostly by smiles except for those few who were more concerned with their current conversation. When I arrived at my chair, I pulled the stool a bit further from its resting place before sitting down. I was eager to order a drink, so I grabbed my wallet from my back pocket resting a set of twenties in front of me.

The bartender was skinny and tall with blond wavy hair set in a style from the eighties and more like a modified mullet. He appeared cheesy as hell, but when I had his attention he walked with confidence and a sense of coolness that could only be structured from many years skiing in the mountains of Aspen.

I ordered a double rum and coke tall with two shots of Patron on the side. The bar tender turned to pour my drinks and when he returned I paid him with the cash laid out in front of me. As he walked away to register the change, I grabbed the first shot of Patron and poured it down growling with the last bit trickling over my throat. The second shot went down smoother than the first and when I had finished I began working on the rum and coke.

I spent two hours at the onion drinking my life away. The Elite entered thoughts into my head and I did the best I could to block them with better visuals. Eventually my defense became useless and I went right back to raping and murdering people. The bar turned into another scene and all I could do was drink. It was the only defense I had.

This bar was one of those places where you could drink your dreams away and nobody bothered to intrude on your business. It was always a friendly crowd and if you wished to enter a conversation the table was always open.

On this particular day, I chose to stay to myself. I was having a rough time and I didn't want anyone seeing the inside of my head. The rape and murder scenes were too much for the ordinary human to handle and I was everything but ordinary. I even began feeling as if people could see what I was thinking; like I was being judged by my thoughts. It made me feel very uncomfortable being around people.

By four o'clock I was wasted. I was on my way out the door and on my way to see my favorite cocaine dealers. I hadn't done coke in a long time, but I felt the need for a pick me up. Keeping my balance, I pushed through the double doors of the bar and into the sunny side of Aspen. With the sudden brightness, I was blinded for a moment but recovered quickly. I didn't have a care in the world and that's the way I liked life on the satellite.

Pulling a Camel Cigarette from my jean pocket, I lit its end and began puffing away. When the red bricks of the mall ended, I turned left heading for Roberto's house. He lived on the second floor of an apartment complex on the opposite side of town. His home always smelled like a Burrito and he always had plenty of quality cocaine.

After a ten minute walk, I headed up a set of concrete stairs toward Roberto's front door. When I reached the top landing, I made a right passing door after door before making another turn. As soon as I rounded the corner, I was surprised to see Roberto sitting outside on a lawn chair. He was wearing tan cargo shorts and a wife beater with taco sauce dribbled down the front. He was on his cell phone talking to somebody in Spanish and by the sound in his voice it wasn't a pleasant conversation. When he saw me, his eyes grew with my unexpected arrival. Then his lips curled into a smile as he waved me over to a second chair on the opposite side of the door. In English in a heavy Mexican accent he said, "Take a seat Boo, I'll be one moment."

He began talking on his cellular once again.

Seconds later, Roberto was off the phone. Standing from his seat, Roberto stretched his arm with his hand out wide in front of me. Roberto pulled me from my chair and wrapped his arms around my shoulders in a bear hug. It was good to see him.

Roberto was a large man straight from Mexico. He liked his money, his food and his women all in the same order. He was a friendly guy and all business. The best part, we had been long time friends which meant the cocaine came at a very cheap price.

Since I hadn't seen Roberto in some time, we spent a few minutes getting reacquainted before he invited me inside for a beer and a line. Eager to except, I followed him through the door past the living room where a leather couch and a glass coffee table stood. A large television was on my right and just to the left hung a large painting of the Virgin Mary.

In the kitchen next to the refrigerator I noticed an old circular wooden dining room table with four worn out chairs scattered around its edge. On top of the table, aluminum foil with scrunched ends opened with a set of flour tortillas inside from the afternoon's lunch. They were a bit crusty and curled, so I knew they had been sitting for some time. Next to the tortillas, a bowl with hardened re-fried beans and an empty plate which had the remains of scrambled eggs which had turned green from standing too long. In the corner, a bottle of salsa laid on side next to a jar of pickled jalapenos. A handle of Tequila was stationed in the center with an array of empty glasses thrown about. The table as a whole was in disarray and by the looks of it, three people had eaten before leaving in a hurry. I laughed at the site.

Roberto opened the refrigerator door grabbing a set of Corona Beers from a metal shelf inside. He popped the caps using a bottle opener from a set of keys he had dangling from his pocket. Handing me the cold brew, we tapped the necks of our bottles in salute before swilling from the bottles end. The taste was refreshing as I thought how great Corona tasted; such a good beer.

Taking a seat at the breakfast table, Roberto pulled a large sack of cocaine from his right pocket. With his left arm he swiped a set of plates to the side clearing an area to lay out some lines. My eyes grew with excitement. I hadn't snorted a line of powder in a very long time and I was eager for the stimulating effects.

With four fat lines laid out, Roberto handed me a straw to snort with. Leaning over the table, I sniffed the powder moving the straw up the line with my head to the side in order to see. When I finished the first line, I immediately moved to the next switching nostrils. When I finished the second, I set the snorter down throwing my head back pinching my nose with my fingers. As the powder dripped to the back of my throat, I gagged from taste and potency. It was good... Real good...

Standing above the table, I watched as Roberto snorted his lines. I laughed while looking over his shoulder. I laughed because it brought back so many old memories, I laughed because Roberto was a lot of fun. I laughed because I was so fucked in the head there was nothing I could do. I laughed and I laughed. I laughed so hard Roberto turned around and looked at me. When he saw my face, he said with his Spanish accent, "You alright Boo, you fucking loco man."

Then, we had a laugh together.

Four beers and six lines later I was out the door and on my way home with an eight ball of cocaine in my pocket. The drug mixed with the alcohol had me high on life and I felt unstoppable. After cutting through a couple of alley ways, I found myself at the bottom stairs of my condo. A cool breeze whipped past my face and I was happy to be home.

Running up the stairs, I pushed through the front door heading for the kitchen where I made myself a drink. After pouring a vodka and tonic, I laid out three lines of cocaine and began snorting them immediately. The rush was intense. My head was ringing as my knees began to feel weak. I was on top of the world and nobody could stop me. Not even the Elite.

Eight lines and three drinks later I was lying on the couch listening to the extraordinary music of the Grateful Dead. I was high and in heaven. My thoughts were clear and concise. It seemed the combination of the two drugs had overcome the weakness of my mind. The drugs were working and they were working great. I laughed hysterically knowing I had finally evened the odds with the Elite.

With the stereo remote in hand, I switched to Sublimes, Steppin' Razor sound track. Dropping the remote on the coffee table, I laid out two lines of cocaine. I rolled a twenty dollar bill into a straw and snorted some coke. Throwing the bill to the table, I held my head back allowing the drug to drip down the back of my throat. When finished, I yelled at the top of my lungs. I yelled, "Fuck you fucking bastards... Fuck you."

The Elite grunted in disapproval. I laughed at their demise.

Jumping from the couch, I headed for the kitchen to make myself another drink. As I opened the refrigerator door, I was struck by the oddest occurrence. I couldn't remember what I was doing. I was lost for words and thought. I became dizzy as everything in the condo began to spin around the refrigerator. I held tightly to the open door.

Catching my breath, I stood drained from all energy. My ears rang as my stomach contracted. I felt as if I was going to vomit. I was sick and this was only the beginning.

The light in the refrigerator became black as an oval ring glowed through my eyes. I had the wah-wahs as all sounds in the condo reverberated through the air. It sounded like a helicopter overhead, but really I was falling out. All I could do was hold on.

Bending over, I gasped breathing heavily for air. My palms were sweaty and my mouth watered as I coughed. I was in bad shape and I couldn't explain why. Suddenly, I hit the ground with a thump. The refrigerator door slammed against my head. I was curled in a ball holding my stomach. I wanted to scream, but all I could do was lie there gurgling from my mouth.

I thought I was going to die…

The Elite were ecstatic. They shouted with glory. One said to their leader, "Hey commander, he's down."

Another said, "It's about time that fucking kid died."

The commander said nothing.

But, I wasn't going to let them beat me.

Fighting for my life, I rolled onto my side. Drool ran from the corner of my mouth dripping down the side of my cheek. My brain hurt as I kept thinking, "*This can't be happening. I'm* dying and *there is nothing I can do.*"

After a few minutes, the ringing in my ears stopped. My blood began to flow as my muscles regained strength. Not wanting to give up, I slammed my hand hard against the wooden planked floor yelling, "You mother fuckers. You're not killing me."

With all my might, I rolled onto my stomach with my palms pressed against the floor. Weak and disoriented, I pushed myself up. My elbows shook as my wrists took the pressure. Sliding my knees under my torso, I raised myself from the kitchen floor. Grabbing hold of the counter top, I steadied myself. Breathing heavily, I took a moment to regain my composure.

Shaking off the episode, I poured myself another drink. In the path of destruction, I cut out a line. I sniffed… I gagged… I laid out another line…

Ten minutes later I was coked out of my mind dancing on the living room coffee table with a fresh drink in hand and the stereo blasting. My brain moved fast with thought and there was no way to control it. I just kept going. I did line after line and drink after drink. The day turned into night and the night never ended.

At one point I was so wasted I fell from the coffee table landing hard on the floor. My head bounced with the landing as I crushed my shoulder beneath me. I laughed thinking to myself, "*This shits got to stop. It's got to come to an end.*"

I went on like this for three more days. I got drunk, bought more coke and tore the house up. My shit was a mess. I was out to lunch and there was nothing to stop me.

By the weekend, I had spent over six-hundred dollars on cocaine and alcohol. It got to the point where all I wanted to do was get high. My mind was racing and I couldn't control myself. Time was a blur as I figured myself lost, but not forgotten.

Friday night rolled around, so I called my buddy Brett to see what was going on. Brett was a childhood friend from Philadelphia and even though he graduated with my brother Jason, I had known him since the fifth grade. He is a tall guy with dark hair. He wears a five o'clock shadow by two in the afternoon and he is one hell of an outdoors man. He liked his weed and he liked lots of it.

While on the telephone with Brett, he mentioned his friend from Chicago who was in town and she had a couple of girls with her. He was meeting them at the Cigar Bar for a drink and I was invited if I wanted to go along. I gladly accepted the offer telling him to give me a call later in the evening. He agreed, so we left the conversation.

I spent the rest of the afternoon sobering from my cocaine binge. It was tough, but I had managed. Basically, I drank a fifth of Rum and passed the fuck out. I missed many nights of sleep from partying, so the rest did me some good.

When I woke, it was around six-thirty in the evening. I jumped in the shower, put a nice blue button down shirt on, a pair of jeans and a nice pair of black Doc Martins; the only dress shoe a man should own. I combed my hair by putting some water on my hand then brushed my teeth. While looking in the mirror, I decided I looked good.

Before leaving the condo, I poured myself a cranberry and vodka. I drank before pouring another. When I was on my third drink, Brett called to let me know he was heading over to the bar. After a brief conversation, I told him I would be there by eight-thirty. He laughed before saying good-bye then hung up the phone.

By nine o'clock, I had a gentle buzz and was on my way out the door heading over to the Cigar Bar. The Elite filled the streets with their sounds of crickets as I rounded each turn in the direction of the bar. Every time I heard their noise, thoughts of murder and rape entered my brain. My head would jerk in odd directions as I attempted to block the disruptive thoughts. And each time I jerked, the Elite would say, "Just kill yourself already."

I kept thinking to myself, *"It will never happen."*

When I arrived at the Cigar Bar, Brett was sitting in the corner with his friend from Chicago. Next to her sat her two friends. I laughed because they were sitting on the same chairs Lauren, Jessica and I had sat during the night I had to leave due to the severe scene of death. The Elite picked up on it too because one of them said, "I can't believe he went back to that place after what happened last time."

They all laughed before one of them said to their commander, "You're taking this kid in. You're never going to get him to cut himself."

In response, the commander grunted. I knew I was tough and I also knew the man was right. I was never going down. I was never going to give up. I wasn't going to kill myself.

Brett stood from his chair to shake my hand as I walked up. He introduced me to his friend who then introduced her two friends. All three of the girls were cute, but the shortest of them I found myself most attracted too.

She was short with brown hair, green eyes and a nice figure. She had a cute smile and an easy personality. Deciding she was most fun, I sat in a leather arm chair alongside her. Immediately, our personalities met as the conversation began to flow. I found she was fun, exciting and full of life; exactly what I needed for these troubling times. She was perfect for the night's activities.

Her name was Erin and she was hard to resist. Her smile made the attraction that much greater. After a couple more drinks, Erin sat at the edge of my chair rubbing my leg telling of her life long story. We laughed at funny tales. In the end, we had met our physical stimuli. The feelings were there and the only option was to finish off the night by going home with one another.

In the middle of this exchange, my kidneys were full. I had to take a leak. Breaking the conversation, I excused myself as Erin scooted to the side letting me through. I headed to the doors of the Cigar Bar making my way towards a bathroom which was tucked in a small hallway just short of a stairwell. Of course there was a line and of course there were three people in front of me.

I was in the middle of telling the Elite to go fuck themselves when the restroom door opened. To my surprise Franky, and old buddy of mine, appeared from the Restroom. I could tell he was up to no good by how big his eyes were and the way he pinched his nose. With my stinking thinking taking over, I thought of how good a line of coke would taste. Wondering how much cash I had in my pocket, I stopped myself thinking I had enough for an eight ball.

"Franky," I said grabbing him by the shoulder as he came closer.

He gave me this look as if he didn't recognize who I was before it hit him. A smile appeared as he yelled, "Marx, you fucker what have you been up too?"

He had a thick British accent which killed me every time he spoke. The reason his accent killed me was because it formed his personality perfectly. He was quite the character.

Taking a step to the side away from the crowd, I asked if I could buy some of what he was holding in his pocket. He scrunched his eyebrows taking a moment to think. Without hesitation he reached into his pocket handing me a large bag of cocaine. In his British accent he said, "Give me a hundred for that and I will just get some more. I got the guy with me so it's no problem."

I reached into my pocket sorting through a bunch of twenties before I had five of them in my hand. We shook as the money went from my hand to his. Without counting to make sure it was all there, he stuffed the cash into his right pocket.

"Thanks mate," he said mischievously.

He gave me a grin telling of where he would be if I wanted to come over and hang out. I had my own party to deal with, so I just said I'd stop by later to see how everyone was doing. As we parted, he slapped me on the shoulder saying, "See you around."

I nodded my head knowing I would see him since I was back in town.

In the restroom, I took a leak before railing out a line. I rolled a twenty into a straw and sniffed. By the taste, I could tell the shit was good. I also knew I wasn't going to need much to get high. I packed the drugs into my wallet before flushing the toilet one last time to make the timing look good since I didn't want anyone knowing what I was up too. Then I left.

When I opened the door, I gazed upon those eager to use the lavatory. I could always tell those who were most eager to piss because they always moved and swayed in line. The thought made me laugh as I passed by knowing I too was glad for the relief.

I stopped by the bar purchasing two drinks before heading back to Erin. She was sitting in my chair when I arrived and I could tell she was eager to see me by her brightened smile as I approached. Still wanting to sit next to me, she moved to the side so we could both fit. I handed her one of the drinks and we started right where we left off with comfortable conversation.

Many drinks later, the night had come to an end. We paid our tabs then headed downstairs for the exit. The courtyard was packed as we weaved through traffic making our way to the outer stairwell. Erin and I stayed back from the others having our little conversations as we cut the corner towards my condo.

Once inside, the girls sat around the bar counter-top as I poured drinks for the five of us. When we had our drinks made, I lined out a pile of cocaine for us to enjoy. With straws in hand, the girls snorted off a couple of rails each. When they were finished, Brett and I had our way with the white substance. By no means did the two of us hold back. We went rail after rail and rail after rail. By the looks of things, it was the start to a good night.

Erin and I were sitting on the couch as the band 311 pumped through the stereo system. She had her legs across my lap as I rubbed her free hand with my own. She was comfortable to be around.

It wasn't long before the Elite realized what was going on. I was out of my head and having a good time.

"That bitch is a COP," one of them had said.

My ears straightened with the word COP. Instantly, I became paranoid of the situation. As Erin spoke, I began judging her way of speech. I watched her lips move to see if there was any disguise in word play. I searched her brain for any means of deceit. The only problem, my telepathy didn't work very well. I was hearing thoughts about every three minutes which was not enough to get a full read on whether she was law enforcement or not. I figured the guys were full of shit, but the way the drug worked I was already deep in thought about her being a COP and I was definitely becoming paranoid and skeptical.

Not wanting to ruin a good thing, I tried not listening to Elite. I stayed with the conversation blocking out all paranoia.

Then one of the Elite said, "Look at his eyes, it's getting to him."

Instantly, I concentrated on my eyes trying not to show any signs of concern. This only made things worse because the drug began making my eyes twitch. Soon, I found myself blinking uncontrollably. It was very annoying.

Noticing what was going on, Erin reached over and touched my chin. She said with concern, "Are you alright, your eyes are blinking a lot?"

Her soft touch said it all, I knew she wasn't a COP and I also knew she cared for me.

"I'm fine," I said softening my glare.

I went back into teddy bear mode. Our bodies came closer as she wrapped her arms around my neck giving me the sweetest kiss ever; just a peck on the lips, but the one that started the infusion.

With Brett and the other two girls out in the kitchen, I decided it was time for Erin and me to hit the bedroom. I stood from the couch with Erin's hand in mine pulling her towards me. Placing my hands on her hips, I asked if she wanted to lie down. She was more than willing, so a smile appeared as she said, "Yes. That would be good."

As we passed the kitchen, I noticed Brett was pouring another round of drinks. I figured the three of them would be occupied for a while so there was no reason in bothering to tell them where we were going. I assumed they would figure it out.

In the bedroom, I walked over to the nightstand and laid out a couple of lines. Erin did hers then I did mine. Afterwards we sat on the edge of the bed talking for a bit. She was quite a spontaneous women and it was one of the qualities about her I adored so much. This was what made her so likable.

Soon we were kissing. She was cuddled next to my body with her lips wrapped around mine and her thick warm tongue felt amazing. Before we knew it, we were naked under the covers. She was on top rubbing her soft vagina against my penis. It felt so good.

Just as I was beginning to get hard, one of the Elite yelled, "She's got AIDS. We heard her talking to her friend earlier."

Instantly, all arousal had vanished. I couldn't get a boner to save my life. I knew the elite were joking, but the thought kept making me think. With the thought of AIDS and the effects of cocaine, getting a boner just wasn't happening. Not wanting Erin to see my demise, I rolled her over onto her side and began kissing her once again. I had my hand between her legs rubbing gently as the two of us embraced one another. I so wanted to be inside of her, but I couldn't. It just wasn't working.

A couple of minutes later, Erin noticed there was something wrong. I wasn't taking the night any further.

"What's wrong," she asked.

I sucked up my pride and returned, "I did too much coke and I don't think I'm going to be able to get it up."

Erin started laughing. Reaching across with her arms, she pulled my head closer and whispered, "That's okay we can have fun another way."

She angled her body towards my genitals straddling her legs around my head. Soon her soft tongue was wrapped around my penis as I pressed my lips around the tip of her clitoris. I could hear her breathing thinking, *"She's quite amazing."*

We went on in this manner for what seemed like forever. I wasn't able to get aroused, but it was quite the sensation. At the end of the night, Erin rested her head against my shoulder and went to sleep. I was pissed I couldn't please her better, but I figured she didn't mind so much. It was just nice to have a warm body cuddled next to one another.

As I laid their thinking for a moment, the Elite became a nuisance. They began laughing saying, "Yah fucker, you couldn't get it up."

I had to laugh because it was true, but at the same time I was a little embarrassed. Not wanting to get into an argument and not wanting to wake Erin I said, "Whatever. Shit happens."

Two more hours had gone by and I still couldn't sleep. Gently sliding away from Erin, I walked to the end of the bed grabbing a pair of boxers and some pajamas from the dresser drawer. Turning my head towards the bed, I could see Erin peacefully sleeping. I smiled thinking how cute she looked snuggled under the covers. With my right foot, I prodded my toes under the pair of pants I wore from the night before and swung them in the air grasping them in my hand. Reaching into the pocket, I pulled out the last of the cocaine pouring it onto the table not bothering to set it into lines. In the other pocket, I pulled out a bill and rolled it up. Bending over the pile of cocaine, I sniffed its contents then threw the bill on top of the dresser.

What I was thinking, I don't know. I bet I snorted close to a gram of shit. My heart started racing and all I could think about was a drink. That's exactly what I wanted. I headed into the kitchen to pour myself a double rum and coke tall with a touch of ice; a lot of fucking alcohol and a splash of coca cola.

With a couple of gulps down, I started feeling better. I had quite the rush going and I was beginning to feel paranoid. With the Elite continually sticking thoughts into my head, I had bad visuals. Emotions wouldn't go away. If the Elite created paranoia, then I would be paranoid for months on end. And now, now I was paranoid and the drugs weren't helping.

I started looking out the windows seeing if anyone was watching. Even though the Elite were around, it felt as if somebody else was there. It felt as if all eyes were on me. I couldn't control the feelings.

Noticing my actions, one of the Elite yelled, "They're trying to kill you."

Not knowing what he meant by the statement, I had to think. I knew the Elite were out for me to commit suicide, but I couldn't imagine who else would be out to physically kill me. Knowing I had knowledge of some pretty crazy technology and secrets, it could only mean one thing. The Agency was out to get me.

"*But they couldn't be,*" I thought to myself.

The agency was supposed to take me in. They were on my side and these guys are just pissed because I called the commander's wife fat. There had to be more to the story. There had to be a clue. Something else was going on and I wanted to get to the bottom of it.

Next to a leather reading chair a wicker basket filled with old newspapers were stacked high. I grabbed the top three papers which were the latest. Shuffling through, I arrived at the crossword puzzles and began filling them out. According to old movies, the agencies always put code in the puzzles. It was a long shot, but definitely worth a try.

Between the intensity of drugs, alcohol and the stresses of brainwash; sweat began dripping down the sides of my face as I frantically moved my way from puzzle to puzzle. It wasn't long before I had six newspapers strewn about the floor working on all six at the same time. I had my laptop next to me as I looked up word after word filling in the blanks. I was going insane and I was no longer in control of my life. The elite had taken over my brain.

Hours later, the living room was in disarray. There were newspapers all over the couch, the arm chair, the floor, the kitchen counters and everywhere the eye could see.

I drank...

I sweat...

I filled out crossword puzzles.

I was in a craze. I couldn't stop because it was stuck in my head. I needed to know what was really going on. Why was this happening to me and why were these guys trying to kill me? The obvious was there, the technology. But, there had to be something more.

It wasn't long before I was caught with my insanity. Erin came out of the room and walked into the living room. She stood at the end of the kitchen peering into the living room with a look of sheer terror. Her mouth was on the floor as she looked at me in utter confusion.

I was lying on the floor with ink all over the palms of my hands filling out the puzzles at a rapid pace. My hair was soaked with sweat and at one point I even noticed I was shaking a bit. I didn't care. I was on a mission and I wasn't quitting.

Without saying a word, I went back to work leaving Erin standing there in utter astonishment. When she turned around to walk back down the hallway she said, "Oh my god, he's fucking crazy!"

She was right. I was crazy and only because somebody was fucking with my head.

Minutes later the girls passed through the living room heading out the door. I was embarrassed, but too fucked up to care. It was quite obvious by the expressions on their faces they were scared. More so knowing they had just spent the night at my place.

When they were gone, I went back to work. Brett was still in the back room sleeping and I knew he wouldn't care how I was acting. Brett new what fucked up and shit happens meant. He was and still is a good friend. He knew me as a person and would never question what was going through my head. It seemed like he always understood.

The puzzles had no clues. I had wasted my time with them. By three o'clock I was passed out in bed with my shoes, pants, and a t-shirt on. The house was a mess and empty glasses once containing rum and coke were standing on every dresser, table and counter in the house. Few had spilled over and the house was silent except for the occasional passing construction truck with its loud exhaust.

Around midnight I woke from my drunken cocaine slumber. Brett was gone and I was left to clean the house. I went for a drink before making my way to the shower to wake myself.

Life was rough and these guys weren't going away. From the time I woke till the time I passed out, I heard their voices and they never had anything nice to say. They would simply say, "Kill yourself." I was in a bad position, but the war was not over. I was determined to win.

Weeks went by as I found myself in the same routine, get drunk and get high. I was walking around a complete mess. The Elite kept telling me to kill myself as they entered horrifying thoughts into my head. I was brainwashed, paranoid and wasted at all times. They even said I had a hit man after me, but I quickly dismissed the thought by sleeping by my front entrance with a sleeping bag, a pillow and the door wide open. Nobody came to kill me, so I no longer had the thoughts.

*

My parents opened an office in Carbondale Colorado. It was under construction for most of the summer but was now open for business. The layout was much nicer than their old office and there was a lot more space.

It was a Thursday night when my parents and I met for dinner at an excellent Restaurant in the downtown district of Carbondale. During dinner, I tried to keep my head on the best I could. Sometimes it jerked with the violent thoughts. I had a form of brain turrets that just wasn't going away anytime soon. Brainwash was a mother fucker and that's the best way to put it. With my parents around, I had to make sure I was keeping steady. It was tough, but I was able to manage. Alcohol usually made the head spasms go away, so rum was the choice drink of the night.

After dinner, I decided I had two much to drink to make the drive back to Aspen. Always keeping a sleeping bag and pillow in my car for such occasions, I decided to shack up for the night at the new office.

Since my truck was already parked in the front of my parent's office, I took a short trek down a couple of blocks to where I was parked. Grabbing my gear from the back cab, I entered the building seeking a good spot to set my belongings.

After walking around for a bit, I noticed the place was silent of television and music. I quickly found myself bored and unable to find comfort. Wanting another drink, I decided to head over to the liquor store for a bottle of rum.

On the way to the store, the Elite had the streets filled with crickets and frog noises. They were really annoying with that shit, but at the same time I couldn't help but think how amazing their technology was; sound lasers, who would have thought?

Upon entering the liquor store, I began scanning the shelves for the rum section. After a quick aisle search, I found my product of choice, Bacardi Silver. Nothing in the world tasted better. My mouth salivated. I even grabbed two lemons from a basket as I walked towards the counter to pay for my demise. Handing over a twenty dollar bill from my billfold, I smiled at the cashier with an expression saying, "Only if you knew how fucked up my head is and how fucked up I'm about to get."

In return the cashier smirked telling me to have a great night.

"Oh, I will," I said as he handed me the change.

"I'm going to have a really good night."

With my change in pocket and a brown bag of Bacardi with two lemons stuffed at the top perched under my arms, I exited the store. I was pissed my life had come to this. I had a drinking problem before the Elite showed up and now I had a really bad drinking problem on my hands.

When I turned the corner to head back to the office, I drunkenly weaved between two pedestrians; a well-dressed couple. No more than three feet behind them, I yelled into the dark starry night towards the satellite. At the top of my lungs, I screamed, "You fucking pussies are never going to kill me...Never."

The elite laughed as one of them said, "We're not going to kill you. It's the pressure. You're going to kill yourself."

"Fuck you," I yelled back.

I was livid. Continuing to walk, I listened for the Elite's noise, but the air was silent. They weren't playing their game and I wondered why?

When I arrived back at the office, I aggressively pushed through the office doors making my way towards a small kitchen tucked in the corner of the room. I opened a cabinet door grabbing a large glass searching the smaller drawers for a cutting knife. Once I found a knife, I went to the freezer for a couple of ice cubes. Then I realized something, I forgot to buy coke to mix with my rum.

"Fuck," I yelled.

"It's always something."

Deciding I didn't need coke as a mixer, I unscrewed the top of the bottle and began guzzling its contents. The alcohol burned the back of my throat. I gagged almost vomiting in the sink. Taking another pull from the bottle, I coughed as the vapor steamed my lungs.

"This was no way to live my life," I kept thinking to myself.

"I had to get these guys away from me."

Soon, I was hammered standing in front of the sink holding on for whatever it was worth. My body swayed from side to side. I gripped harder with my hands trying to steady myself. I needed a pick me up. I needed a line.

Pulling my cell phone from my pocket, I called a guy from work who lived in town and who always had a sack for sale. We had also been friends for a long time. I contacted his number pressing send waiting for him to answer. Within seconds, I heard is voice speaking in a heavy Spanish accent.

"Boo, how are you," he said.

When I spoke, he noticed I had been drinking. He began laughing before saying, "You loco man. Too much drinking."

I laughed at his comment.

Ten minutes later, I met my buddy in front of the office. He pulled up in a red Chevy truck with tinted windows. He had a smile on his face knowing I was on a mission to get fucked up; a mission of destruction. We talked for a brief moment before he handed over the bag. I paid a hundred bucks for three grams even though I knew it was overweight since we had been friends for so long.

He thanked me for the business and I thanked him for driving over. We shook hands before he pulled away. As he turned his truck, he said, "You careful buddy. No trouble."

I waved as he continued down the road happy to have a handful of rejuvenation.

Back inside the office, I poured the bag onto the kitchen counter. I lined up six rails laughing at myself; laughing because I was on an evil path. A path I wished for no other human-being; a path of death and self-destruction.

I rolled up a bill and snorted four of the six lines. Once they were down, I finished off the other two. I washed them down with a chug from the bottle. Instantly, I was awake and feeling good. I had strength and determination.

"You're never going to beat me," I said to the Elite.

"You're never going to beat me."

I spent an hour drinking rum, snorting coke and talking shit to the Elite. I wanted them mad. I wanted them angry.

When I was tired of talking shit, I decided to look on the internet for some music to play. While I was looking up music, I found porn instead. I loved porn. I was drunk, high and delirious. I said to the Elite in an evil cry, "I'm going to beat off, drink and do drugs until you're out of my life."

That's exactly what I did.

I put some porn on the computer, turned up the volume and listened as two girls went at it. It was hot and I needed another line and a drink. I went to the kitchen railing out four more lines. When I was finished snorting, I grabbed the bottle and drank profusely. I was in a craze.

Walking back to the computer where the porn was playing, I grabbed my sleeping bag and pillow. I laid out a bed on the floor turning the computer screen so it faced where I had my set up. Next, I got under the covers pulling my pants down around my ankles and began stroking away. I laughed at the Elite as they grunted in disgust.

"We don't need to see all of that," they shouted.

I could tell they were fooling knowing everyone masturbates. Either way, I didn't care. The girls on the screen were hot and the drugs had me going. I was horny.

A half hour into it, I realized I wasn't going to get aroused. It happened again. Something about that drug made it impossible to get a hard-on. I was determined to finish and I wasn't going to quit. I was going to bust a nut at no cost.

An hour later, I was still at it. The Elite were making fun of me, but I didn't care.

"You're not going to get it done," they shouted.

"You did too much of that shit," they continued.

I knew they were right, but I wasn't going to give up.

Three hours later, I had a whole new set of girls on the screen and it wasn't getting much better. I just kept stroking. I lost track of time. My mouth was dry and I could barely swallow. My eyes were watering as sweat poured down my cheeks. I was into it.

Then it started to happen. I began to get a boner. I yelled, "I told you fuckers I was going to get it done."

The elite began to laugh as one of them said, "This kid's funny as shit. I don't know why we're not taking him in."

The others agreed.

I had a full boner and it felt good. I was rubbing away with a bottle of lotion at my side which I picked up from the bathroom during a short intermission. I slapped some more lubrication on that puppy and life was good.

The Elite were in tears. They couldn't believe how long I had been going for. It must have been close to six hours.

Suddenly one of them burst out into laughter. I couldn't imagine what was so funny. Then I caught on as soon as I heard a set of keys enter the front door.

"*Holy shit*, somebody is here," I thought to myself.

I jumped from my jerking spot in full out confusion. Knowing I had to turn off the computer, I went for the monitor first. Then I realized I had a pile of cocaine laid out on the kitchen counter. I didn't know which way to turn and I didn't have much time. I figured the porn was more embarrassing, so I stuck with shutting off the monitor since the computer was on the other side of the desk.

Then the door opened. My pants were around my ankles and the sleeping bag was in the same location. Quickly, I reached down in time to cover myself with the sleeping bag. In the other arm, I had the computer monitor tucked under my armpit. The girls were moaning and screaming with desire from under my arm. I had no time to fix my situation. I was busted.

In that instant, the door flew open and the hottest girl who worked for my parents walked through the front entrance. We were twenty feet apart from one another. She had blonde hair, a hot body and huge breast. It couldn't have gotten much worse. I stopped dead in my tracks. She looked at me in surprise. The worst part, I was holding the monitor as screams of orgasm shot through its speakers.

The girls of porn moaned. They shouted in ecstasy. All you could hear was, "Oh yah, fuck me. Fuck me harder."

I was so embarrassed standing there with the monitor in my hand. The girls kept on shouting.

Tracy looked at me, assessed the situation and began to laugh.

"You alright there," she asked?

I didn't know what to say. I was in complete shock. She listened to the girls and began to smile before saying, "Looks like you got your hands full there. I'm going to head back to my office while you handle that."

I nodded my head as she walked by. When she was at a good distance, I stood there turning my head over my shoulder and began talking to the Elite.

I said, "You assholes, you didn't tell me she was coming."

We were all in tears from the situation. I was humiliated. It was the first time in my life I had been busted jerking off. The worst part, she was hot.

When Tracy was back in her office, I placed the monitor back on the desk and the sleeping bag to the floor. I pulled my pants around my waist buttoning and buckling. Next, I turned off the monitor and set the computer back to its normal settings.

As I put everything back in its place, I was shaking my head in laughter. It was just like the Elite to not warn me of a horrible situation. But I have to say, it was funnier than shit. They got me on that one.

When I had my sleeping bag and pillow in order, I walked to the kitchen grabbing my bottle and drugs from the counter. I wrapped the cocaine in a dollar bill and shoved it into my pocket. Without saying good-bye to Tracy, I headed for the door. I threw my gear into the cab of my truck and jumped behind the wheel. In my truck, I laughed at the scene inside before saying to the Elite, "Thanks fellas. That was awesome."

After that night, I decided I needed a change of scenery. My head was fucked and people were beginning to notice. I had to find a place where I could be my own person and nobody would know the difference. I needed a place where I could live free from judgment. I needed a place where I could go crazy.

CHAPTER 12

I decided college was the perfect place to go crazy and lose my mind. I could get fucked up as much as I wanted and I would fit right in. College provided three things in life. It provided smart, weird, and party all in one. There was a crowd for everyone.

Since I knew all of the Elite's secrets and all of their satellite technology, I decided to find a space technology program which would best suite my needs in bringing an intimate threat to the Elite's existing spy gear.

Like I said in the beginning of this book, I know all of the Elites technology and secrets and this technology is so phenomenal it's to the point of being out of this world. They were trying to kill me for this technology, so I wanted to bring it to the public. Being able to mimic bird, insect, and animal noises through a satellite laser for the Elite to communicate in war was just the beginning. The technology gets far more powerful.

The problem the Elite had with me, I know how to build this technology making me an even greater threat.

I walked into my parent's office a few short days after Tracy caught me beating off. My father was at his desk working on the computer as I sat in a chair directly across from him. He tilted his head down enabling him to see over his bifocals and said, "What's up?"

I returned, "I'm going back to college, so I'm packing my shit and heading down to the Junction house to get things organized."

When the news hit him, a smile appeared at the corners of his lips. Being the coolest dad in the world, I knew he would be excited for me.

"Okay," he exclaimed!

"Do you know where you're going," he continued?

I had not, so I shook my head saying, "No."

He then said, "Well, you better get on the computer and figure it out. I'll be down in Junction in a few days, so we can talk more about it."

I was glad for his support in my decision. We shook hands before I left the office.

Immediately after leaving, I drove back to Aspen and began packing for my new adventure. In two hours, I had the truck packed and the house cleaned. Before leaving town, I filled up at the local gas station and wasn't mad I was paying five bucks a gallon. I used to hate it, but today wasn't the day to hate.

*

When I arrived in Junction, I picked up a bottle of rum at the local liquor store down the road from my parent's house. As soon as I arrived at the pad, I threw my bags in one of the guest rooms before walking to the kitchen to make a drink. This time, I remembered to buy the soda.

The Elite couldn't believe I was readying to leave town. I knew they were still in Colorado because I overheard one of the guys say they liked the Olathe Sweet Corn, the best corn ever. This made me believe the Elite were hiding out somewhere in Montrose Colorado. It wasn't far from Grand Junction and it was even closer to Olathe.

They kept saying, "You're not leaving, you're staying here."

I would answer, "Nope, I'm going back to school."

When one of them had enough of the nonsense, he said, "You will fail and we will make sure of it."

I knew school would be tough with the Elite around, but I was determined to show them what I was made of. I not only planned on going back to school, I planned on getting straight A's. That's right, a 4.0 with the worst brainwash known to man. I figured if I could do it, the agency would be proud.

Just to be a wise ass and to answer the man who said he would make sure I failed, I said, "I'm going to get straight A's and shove that technology right up your fucking ass. You really don't know what type of kid I am. I'm going to find a space technology school and build all of your shit and release it to the public. Your gear is now mine."

165

The guy grunted as one of the younger guns said to his commander, "He's going to do it commander. You better pick this kid up."

The commander said nothing...

I sat down in front of the computer and within a half an hour I knew where I was going. I wanted to be somewhere warm and close to home, so I chose Arizona for the place to be. I had a friend whom I grew up with who attended the University of Arizona. I wanted to be close to her, so I chose Tucson. The most exciting news, they had a space technology program.

I stood from my chair, chugged my drink, grunted through my throat and said not too loudly, "I'm going to Tucson Arizona bitches and I'm going to build your shit."

The Elite began to laugh. I saw their humor most of the time, but they were really wearing on my nerves. Sometimes they were fun to have around and at other times they sucked.

*

After a little research, I found I needed a 3.0 from the Community College in Tucson Arizona to transfer into the University. I also needed to establish a year of residency to achieve instate tuition making things more affordable. These factors set me back a year in transferring into the University, but I was willing to put forth the time and effort. The reason being, I wanted to beat these guys and I wanted to beat them good.

I found a Community College online. It was a few blocks from the University and I was able to obtain cheaper tuition through the Western Undergraduate Program. Basically, since I was living in Colorado I could get the same tuition prices in Arizona since both states participated in this program. All I had to do was get my ass down there and register before the spring semester started. Not a hard task since my plan was to leave for Tucson Arizona after the weekend ended.

My parents drove down to the Monument that Friday after work. We met at an Italian Restaurant downtown. I had a file full of papers to show them where I was going to school and what courses I would be taking. I had all the documents for the Western Undergraduate Program as well and a map of the route I would be taking to get there. I figured the drive would be twelve to fourteen hours from Junction to Tucson.

After dinner, we headed home. As I drove, I found myself excited for the change in life. I was excited for college and a new beginning. I was really fucked in the head and I needed a change of pace. I figured school might straighten me out a bit. But what was most important, I thought if I left town the Flite would shut down the satellite.

The next morning, my father and I pulled camping gear from the shelves in our garage. When we finished: I had a cooler, Coleman Stove, tent, backpack, tarp, rope, water jugs, pots, pans, dishes, cups and dish racks all lined up in the driveway next to my truck.

The site was wonderful. My plan was to camp all the way to Tucson and stay in one of the National Parks when I got there until I found a place of my own. The weather would still be nice and I wasn't going to have to worry about hefty hotel prices; just me, my gear, my bottle of rum and the desert. Life would be good.

I had my truck packed and ready by twelve in the afternoon. My mother had lunch ready for us and I could tell during lunch my parents were excited for me. They knew I had a tenancy for partying, so the change would be good for me.

Sunday, we relaxed around the house. I drank Corona beer to keep the Elite at bay and I made sure I didn't get wasted so my parents wouldn't get on my case. It's how they were with me. Alcohol ran in the family genes and there was nothing I could do about it at the moment. The Elite were a very annoying crowd and it was the only way I knew how to deal with them.

Monday morning my parents headed back to Aspen for work and I had plans to be on the road around 9:00 am. I had a bit of a hangover, so I actually didn't leave the house till eleven o'clock. Once I was on the road, I stopped by the liquor store for a fifth of Bacardi. In the parking lot, I unscrewed the cap and got my day started. With my brain in sheer horror, Rum was the only way I could maintain.

With a couple good gulps of Bacardi in me, I decided to hit the bar to say good-bye to a couple of waitresses I used to party with. Upon my arrival, Karen must have seen me in the parking lot because as I walked into the bar she had a double rum and coke tall waiting for me along with a clever smile. Taking the seat in front of my drink, I said, "Hello," before explaining to her how this would be my last good-bye for a long time. I told her of my plans to head to Tucson for College and she was sad to hear I was leaving.

I didn't get out of the bar until 6:00 pm. I was wasted and full from every flavor chicken wing you could possibly imagine. Fumbling with my keys in the parking lot, I had trouble unlocking the door before getting behind the wheel. I started the engine, hit the roof for good luck, told the elite to fuck themselves and drove away.

I was on Route 70 heading towards Utah when the commander started talking through the satellite. It had been a long time since I heard his voice, so it was quite the shock. He said, "I can't believe this kid just left us here."

The words made me wonder if the man really wanted me and this was some sort of game.

"Maybe they are here to train me for the Agency," I thought to myself.

I quickly brushed off the thought deciding to send a little comfort their way. I said, "I'm not leaving you here. We're still in the United States. I'm just going to school for a bit. We will still be together."

The commander grunted and I knew he was upset. I couldn't care because of what he was putting me through. I also decided school was a positive thing since these Elite members were supposed to be the smartest and best trained in the world...

Around 10:00 pm I was in Utah somewhere between the desert and the mountains. I was taking the long route to Arizona because I had a friend In Las Vegas I wanted to surprise. As I drove through the winding road, I found myself in White Dear National Forrest. Observing the signs for camping, I decided to pull off the road for the night setting up a quick camp.

It was pitch dark when I turned into the campground. I drove around for a bit searching for the most primitive campsite possible. Since it was nearing winter and summer had since passed, there was not another soul in the area. I was all alone.

I reversed my truck into my spot. Shutting off the engine, I grabbed the fifth of rum I had stored behind the seat and began drinking straight from the bottle. My buzz was wearing off which meant the brainwash was beginning to enter my head tenfold. When I finished with a few gulps, I opened my door and walked to the back of my truck where I had my gear stored. Lifting the hatch, I reached in and grabbed my tent from its storage area. I had a bed mat and sleeping bag next to the tent ready to go.

The moon was almost full, so I had enough visibility to find a flat area to work off of. But after a few moments, I decided I was going to need more light. In the side pouch of my vehicle, I had a flash light I kept for emergency purposes. When I went to turn it on, I quickly found the batteries had died and I was now shit out of luck.

"Fuck," I cursed myself.

The elite began to laugh. I didn't have the time or the patients to deal with their shit, so I blew them off for the time being.

I needed a fire. With no flashlight in hand, it was going to be tough. I began scanning the area the best I could. After a few minutes of searching, I discovered the summer campers had picked the area clean. I was going to have to get to higher ground if I was going to find what I was looking for.

I took a small trek around some rocks before I found an opening in a set of trees just above the rock face. I wasn't scared, but I also didn't want to get attacked by a mountain lion or bear. Making as much noise as possible, I yelled as I blazed a trail.

After a short climb over some boulders, I reached my destination. The only problem, between the thick foliage and the rock face I wasn't able to see shit. I was left dragging my hands along the earth floor in search of wood.

Within seconds, I found what I was looking for. A dead branch poked me straight in the chest.

"Fuck," I cursed myself as pain shot through my body.

I was lucky it wasn't an eyeball. Taking a moment to feel around, I discovered the branch was part of a fallen pine tree with plenty of bare barked wood to build a fire from. I broke off as many thick branches I could carry and headed down the boulders.

Getting down was much harder than the way up. I found myself slipping and falling on my ass most of the way. One time, I even had to throw the wood down in front of a set of boulders enabling a decent to lower ground. I lost a couple of branches on that one, but I wasn't worried since I had enough in my arms to start the fire.

Once I was back at the site, I quickly broke the branches into smaller pieces arranging them inside the metal fire ring in the shape of Tee-Pee. With some paper from a notebook I had stored behind the driver's seat, I crumpled a few leafs sticking them between a few lose branches. Taking a lighter from my pocket, I ignited the paper setting the wood aflame. I was lucky the wood caught sending a wave of fire into the air along with a light plume of smoke.

After a brief moment, I decided I was going to need more wood. I left the camping area one last time and scaled the rocks for more wood. Since I wasn't planning on staying awake for much longer, I figured another load of some good thick branches would do just fine.

When I had a good pile of wood going next to my fire, I had enough light to get my tent set up with some sleeping gear inside. I was excited to get some sleep under the stars. But of course, I had some drinking to do.

Driving my truck in reverse, I maneuvered my vehicle closer to the fire. I popped the hatch of the 4-Runner one last time and sat in the back with my legs dangling over the bumper. With my bottle of rum in hand, I drank straight from the bottle. It sucked, but it was what I had to do. The Elite, never for one second, let up on the brainwash. They put thought after thought into my head.

The next morning, I woke early to the sounds of birds filling the canyon walls. It was always an amazing event in life to awake in this fashion. The tent was moist, my sleeping bag was moist and the fresh pine from the trees and burnt wood from my fire filled the air. I stretched, let out a sigh and said to the Elite, "What's up fellas? Another good day of disastrous brainwash awaits us."

The few who were up early laughed at my comment. One turned to his commander and said, "I can't believe you want to leave this kid here."

The commander returned, "I don't want him with us."

This time, I grunted. I said, "You're never going to find a kid like me ever again."

The boys laughed once again. One of them said, "You're right we won't. Keep your head up and keep fighting. We want you. We don't care what the commander thinks."

I smiled at the thought. In return, I said, "I like the way you think Matty."

Matt busted out laughing.

He asked, "How did you know my name?"

I returned, "It's something I can do, but it's not always correct."

Matty laughed once again.

I had a way to analyze people's names through their voices. I wasn't always correct, but 98% of the time I was. I didn't want these guys knowing at first, but I figured now was the time to let them in.

Once I was out of the tent, I rolled up my sleeping bag, threw it in the back of my truck and began breaking down my site. Taking a few moments to gaze around the park, I found myself in awe. The park was beautiful. The sandstone rock formations were amazing and I had no idea from the night before what the morning sites would bring. The greens from the pines colored the landscape perfectly and I could think of no other place I would like to be at this exact moment in time. It was absolutely breathtaking.

In twenty minutes, I had the 4-Runner packed and was ready to go. I took a couple large gulps from the bottle before hitting the road. I didn't know when I was going to run into another liquor store, but I was running low on liquid fix. I needed more alcohol.

Driving from the camp, I took one last gaze into the Parks heart of life. It took my breath away one last time. As I was leaving, I decided I would remember this place for the rest of my life. It was spectacular... I planned on returning someday.

I headed down Route 70 with what was left in the bottle tucked between my legs. I was on my way to Vegas excited to see my friend Lindsey whom I've grown to love from our times in Aspen together. She worked at a large Casino in Vegas, so I figured I would stop in and say, "Hello."

Forty minutes later, I bumped into a liquor store. I grabbed a fifth of Bacardi and a sandwich from a convenient store. I gave up on mixers since I was driving, but decided on a Sprite chaser. I ate my sandwich in the parking lot before guzzling from the bottle.

When I hit the turnoff for Route 15, I knew I wasn't far from Vegas. The sun was hot on my arms and the taste of Bacardi was on my lips. All I could think about was seeing Lindsey and playing a few hands of Texas Holdem.

Hours later, I pulled into a Vegas parking in what looked like an old fifties diner. Lindsey had not a clue of my arrival, so I was excited to surprise her. Searching through my contact list, I dialed her number. After a set of rings, I was disappointed that there was no answer. Sitting in the parking lot, I chugged from the bottle making sure nobody saw. I was drunk to say the least and my head was turning in thought.

The Elite...

The Elite did their thing...

They brainwashed me.

"Kill this and fucking rape that," they would say.

That's what I heard all day long as pedestrians crossed in front of me and everyone or anything I came into contact with. Kill and rape. That's all it was. That's all my head could think of.

An hour later, I had finished half the bottle before dialing Lindsey's number one last time. Again, there was no answer. I was upset to say the least, but couldn't blame her since she was unaware of my arrival.

Ten minutes later, I was in the parking area of a Casino. I was drunk, I was pissed, I was brainwashed, and I was in need of a shower. I didn't care. I came to Vegas to play in Vegas.

I drank from the bottle then sparked a large joint I had rolled for the occasion: I puffed, I drank, I puffed and I drank.

Leaving my vehicle in a cloud of smoke, I walked toward the entrance of the Casino like something out of Hunter Thompson's, Fear and Loathing in Las Vegas. Passing security, I headed straight for the card tables. The chronic had me tripping and the alcohol had me stumbling. One thing was for sure, as long as you weren't bothering anyone in Vegas you were okay in Vegas. You could get as fucked up as possible and nobody cared. All they wanted was your money. That's what they were there for, win or lose.

I was in the perfect place, I liked cards and I liked to win. I bought two hundred dollars in chips before sitting down at a five-ten table. I got a grim smile from those who were doing well and a nod of head from those who weren't. I could always tell who was losing by the expression on their face. They had the look of defeat and catch up; panic was more like it. Those who were winning showed not a care in the world. They were the ones having fun.

You, the new guy, you were fresh meat. All eyes were on you and one thing was on each of their minds, *"I'm going to take your money."*

They gave you the stare, the smile and the look of prey. They wanted one thing and one thing only. They wanted your money.

I got my first hand of cards and it was one hell of a hand. I had pocket queens. I loved pocket queens because they always won for me. I made my bet in order and watched as the fellas threw in their chips. Poker was anyone's game, so the calls meant nothing.

On the flop, I hit a third queen. When the bets were made, I just called hoping some sucker would bet for me. And he did. The man to my left went all in. The second highest card on the table was a jack, so I figured he had an open ended straight or maybe pocket kings or pocket bullets. There was no flush draw, so I was safe with two more cards coming. I had my man.

One other player called with chips to spare. I figured him for a low three of a kind since the queen was the highest card showing. Everyone else folded.

On Fourth Street, I was still looking good with a two of spades hitting the board and no help to either player. I made a side bet with the man still holding chips. He had dark hair and a dark complexion and I could tell he thought he knew what he was doing. He called.

The River Card came and it was a six of hearts. I was the winner. My hands shook a bit from adrenaline, so I took a moment to calm down before pushing all my chips forward. If you knew poker, those who had the winning hand always took a moment to push. But if you knew poker, sometimes pushing too fast makes the opponent think you're bluffing; the act of acting as if you have a strong hand. With this hand, I decided to take my time. When the time was right, I went all in.

My opponent took his time in calling. I had the board beat and the best hand smoking. It didn't matter how long he took, he wasn't going to win. I was excited, but I wouldn't show it. He made the call. He matched my two hundred dollars. I smiled as I watched him flip his trip Jacks. I shook my head as if I lost then revealed my cards, trip Queens. Nothing could beat it. The man couldn't believe his eyes as I was awarded a few smiles from the table acknowledging the presence of competition. I now had five-hundred and sixty dollars sitting in front of me.

I went on like this for hours. I won most hands leaving the ones I needed to behind. I was hitting card after card and hand after hand. When finished, I left the card table with fourteen-hundred and eight-five dollars. I was a happy man and the Elite were astounded with my play.

Leaving the table, I cashed my chips in before heading to the bar. I ordered a double rum and coke tall with a dice of lemon. I quickly took the drink to the neck before going for another. After my third one, I decided it was time to leave. As I was getting up from my stool, my phone rang. It was Lindsey. I was excited for her call, but I was also ready to hit the road. Deciding I still had time, I answered her call.

Lindsey sounded good on the phone when I answered. She was cheered hearing I was in town, but sad to inform me she was stuck in the office for the rest of the night. She would not have time to meet up. I was okay with it. We took a moment to talk before I hung up. It was good to hear her voice, but I was ready for a change of scenery.

I walked out of the Casino and into the parking area heading towards my truck. I unlocked the door and jumped in. Grabbing my sack of weed from inside the console, I rolled a joint the size of a cigarette. I sat in my truck for a moment puffing thinking, "This shit has to end."

I was fucked up all the time and I felt like shit 90% of the time. These guys were really getting to my head and it had to stop.

I pulled out of the parking lot blazed to no end. I had the rum between my legs drinking steadily as I turned back onto the 15. My plan was to continue into Arizona from Vegas stopping at the Grand Canyon for the night to camp. I hadn't been there since I was a child, so I thought it would be a great sight to see once again.

It was about a 280 mile drive from Vegas to the Grand Canyon. Not a long drive, but at least a five hour one. I had a fresh bottle of Rum in the back seat and I was still working on the one between my legs. The best part, I was hammered and the chronic had me twisted. My thoughts were a bit under control and that's how I liked it. I was ready for the trip.

I pulled into the Grand Canyon State Park around 9:30 in the evening. I drove to the Park Ranger booth handing the man the desired amount to enter the park. He gave me a ticket for my windshield and I was on my way.

I followed the signs for the campground as I entered the main area of the park. I made a right down a winding road until I came to a brown cedar sided shack. I parked my vehicle before walking toward the main window where I discovered a sign stating, "Closed for the night."

There were directions in paying for a site as well as maps for desired camping areas. I pulled a random site tag from a sheet of paper and was on my way in search of the number on my tag, 500 hundred yards away and around a bend, I found the site matching my ticket. It was the perfect spot. It was nice and flat between a set of pine trees with plenty of space for privacy. I pulled my truck in so my headlights were facing the area I would be setting up camp and got to work.

Within a half an hour, I was all set. I had my tent set up with a sleeping bag, pillow and mat ready for the night. I had my Coleman stove lit with a piece of salmon and some potatoes cooking in a skillet. My bottle of rum was in front of me along with a small glass of soda. There was a bit of ice left in the cooler, so I was even able to mix myself a drink. It didn't get much better than this. What was most important, the Elite were taking a break from brainwashing me. They were quiet except for the small sounds of crickets placed randomly around my campsite. For once, the sounds were peaceful and I liked them.

I had a couple of drinks before I ate. As I gazed upon the stars, I realized how powerful and beautiful life could be. Sometimes, one just has to take a look around. Camping always made me feel so alive providing a will for adventure; a will for survival.

After I ate and drank a bit, I cleaned up camp heading to the shower to wash after two long days of driving. It felt as if I scrubbed an inch of road scum and party from my skin. I was dirty and gross, so the shower was quite the relief. I must have spent forty-five minutes standing there soaking under the shower head holding myself in my own arms. I was excited to get to Tucson, so thoughts of college and a better way of life filled my brain. I was a ticking time bomb on this satellite and I never knew when I would finally explode.

As soon as I left the shower, I brushed my teeth and changed my cloths before heading back to camp. It was a great feeling to feel so fresh and smell so good. I threw my towel over the back of my truck putting my things away in their proper order. My dirty clothes were stuffed in a canvas laundry bag that I placed beside a cooler. I shut the hatch, left the towel on top of the truck to dry then headed to bed. I was silently asleep in no time at all.

I didn't wake once throughout the night. In the morning, I rose bright and early with a bit of a hangover. I was excited to see the canyon in daylight, so I quickly made breakfast from eggs, cheese, salsa and tortillas.

Once I finished eating, I tore down camp and packed the truck only leaving what I needed to shower and get ready after a short hike down the switchbacks of the canyon. When I was satisfied there was nothing left to do, I jumped in my truck driving over to the main hotel area where I found parking. Just beyond the parking area, the Grand Canyon.

Leaving my truck, I walked to the edge of the Canyon. The sun was showing bright from the east as leveled clouds whispered through the air. As I stood their peering over the edge, I was in wonderment of Earth's creations. My mind froze with the astonishing formations reflecting before me; colors of green, purple, tan and red; colors of pastel inks. Down below, the Colorado River appeared as a mere meandering streak.

Walking along a shallow stone wall topped by a wooden post rail, I made my way towards a trail head where I began descending down a series of switch backs. I didn't plan on going far, just far enough to have some peace. When I found my spot of interest, I sat on a series of rocks with my feet over the edge. It was silent except for a gasp of wind echoing through the canyon walls. A breeze swayed the branches of Junipers as I listened into the massive depths of the canyon.

Next to me, two chip monks in chase. I laughed at their friendship. Not a care in the world. They were simply living their lives as animals. I was jealous over their way of life.

An hour went by before I decided it was time to go. For the first time in a long time, I didn't feel the need for a drink. I wanted to be sober and free from all the chaos. I wanted to be free from myself. I wanted to be free from the Elite.

Once I was back in the parking lot, I took one last glance towards the canyon. I raised my arm in the air waving my hand saying good-bye to the astonishing site.

"I will see you again someday my friend," I said to myself.

"I will see you again."

I showered before hitting the road and mapped out my course with a road atlas. I figured it would be a five hour drive before I arrived in Tucson if I drove straight through. I pulled out of the Canyon campground thinking how a few more nights here may do me some good. After some short thought, I decided getting on the road was more necessary. I needed to be in Tucson and that's all there was to it.

*

I arrived in Tucson around 4:30 in the afternoon, a little longer than I had expected due to a long lunch break and a seat at the bar. Sober, brainwash had torn me a new asshole and I wasn't able to deal with it well. I was sick in the head and that's the best way to describe it.

I pulled into an old mom and pop gas station figuring I could get some good directions to a nearby campground. The air was hot with the sun's fierce brightness. Beads of sweat formed at my hairline as I walked toward the front entrance of the station. I was drunk and I was a mess.

I opened the door and headed straight for the cash register. Behind the cash register, a gentleman in his early sixties stood swatting flies. He was a little overweight. He wore an old white and blue striped button-down shirt from the seventies and a pair of khakis lightly stained from tinkering in the shop. In his breast pocket, he had a set of pens.

I pulled a Slim-Jim from the rack to my right placed it on the counter and began a short conversation with the man. I wanted to know where I could find the best camping in town. He smiled at my youth before tilting his head in thought. He said with a bit of a country in his slang, "That would be Ray's Campground just over Gates Pass. I recon this is the place to be."

I smiled knowing he had directed me in the right path. His eyes sought past memories from the campground and I could see he was reliving his youth. Grabbing a notepad from next to him, he pulled one of the pens from his shirt pocket and began drawing a map for direction. When he finished, he pointed outside toward the main road telling which way to turn before heading towards the mountains. He used the map he drew guiding me through step by step filling in a few land-markers here and there on the paper.

When he stopped talking, I was confident with his direction. I thanked him by shaking his hand. I paid for the Slim-Jim, grabbed my directions from the counter and headed out the door. Before I left, I pulled up to the pumps and filled my truck. Once I was done refueling, I drove to the nearest liquor store and picked up a bottle of Rum, a two litter of Coke and some ice for my cooler.

Out of the liquor store, I backtracked in the direction I came from turning down the proper road following the directions the man from the gas station had written down. After a short drive, I found myself at the base of the mountain winding my way through a desert landscape stilted by Saguaro Cactus resembling giant clay animated Gumby characters. They were an amazing site to see.

Shortly afterward, I passed a stone outbuilding set above a giant stone wall overlooking a canyon ravine. There was a parking lot to the side, so I decided to pull over and roll a joint before continuing on. I had an ounce of chronic for the trip that I had barely touched since my departure from Colorado. When I opened the bag, my vehicle filled with its aroma.

I rolled a joint and I smoked it. It was the second best brainwash reliever.

The whole thing with brainwash was caring about my thoughts. If I showed care in what I was thinking, it ate me alive. The more I care about my thoughts, the more it hurt me on the inside. It changed my thought pattern. It changed who I thought I was as a person. It won't make me act on my thoughts, but it definitely made me think bad thoughts. It made me believe I was weird and people were looking at me strangely; like they could see my thoughts and this is who I was. I had to keep my moral fiber and remember who I was before the brainwash. I had to push through and move on. I couldn't quit and staying alive was the only choice I had to survive.

I pulled out of the parking lot blazed, but not confused. I turned right heading towards the pass and soon found myself descending as I crossed over to the other side. The view was amazing and all I could think about was a new life in Tucson Arizona.

As I came over the pass, I noticed a small town down below to my left. It wasn't your average looking town. It appeared to be something out of an old western movie. I decided it was a place of interest and I would definitely be checking it out someday. I later discovered they called the town, Old Tucson. It was now a museum and once a Hollywood movie set where they shot films.

When the road came to a Tee, I turned right according to the directions. After turning, a couple of elderly ladies were on my left fiddling around a horse trailer. They waved as I passed by, so I eagerly returned the gesture.

I turned left according to the signs leading into Ray's Campground. As I pulled in, I noticed a tan ranger station on my left. The door was closed and I wasn't sure if anyone was around. I hopped out of my truck and checked the front door of the office. As I expected, it was locked. There had to be a Ranger around, so I decided to drive around in search of him.

No more than two hundred yards away, around a campground circle, I found the man I was looking for. He was a Mexican guy in his mid-fifties with bushy hair. He wore a tan park shirt tucked into a pair of blue jeans. Patches were sewn at the shoulders and he had the look of a caring man as he walked towards his vehicle.

I pulled alongside of his truck and waited as he approached. Our smiles were brought together as I sat their watching for his arrival. When he was near, I asked, "Do you have some sites available?"

He took a brief moment to size my character before returning, "Sure we do. Why don't you meet me over by that shack and I'll get you signed in."

I was happy for his response. Putting the truck in gear, I drove around the circle as the man hopped into his vehicle. Along the way, I picked out the perfect site. I chose one with a Pavilion over top of a long picnic table. It was exactly what I needed to protect myself from the sun during the long hot days in the desert.

I put the site number to memory and continued on towards the shack. When my vehicle was parked, I walked to the entrance of the front office waiting for the man to show. Within minutes he was unlocking the door letting me in. We walked towards a glass case as he rounded its edge on the other side from where I was standing. Inside the case, bones from different desert animals lined its walls along with a variety of dead woods which when dried resembled the skin of a leopard. The notation read, "Cholla Wood."

He asked which site I preferred.

I answered with a smile on my face, "Site 21."

"Good choice," he returned.

As he filled out the forms, I took a moment to glance around the room before stopping at a poster on the left hand wall. It was a poster of everything poisonous in the desert. What caught my attention most was a picture of a Brown Recluse. I've heard nothing but bad stories about those little guys. The bacteria they release had the ability to eat your flesh alive. The thought made me shiver as I put the appearance of the spider into memory.

When the man finished, he had me sign a form of agreement. When I finished signing, I handed him the desired amount for the site in cash before he handed me a list of park rules and regulations.

After glancing over the rules, I was given a tag for my site. I nodded my head thanking him as he reached over the counter to shake my hand. He introduced himself as Jim. He then said, "If you need anything I will be around during the day until 5:00 pm."

I thanked him once again before heading out the door.

I backed my truck into my campsite making it easier to unload my gear. In forty-five minutes: I had the truck unloaded, a kitchen set up in the picnic area under the pavilion, my tent erected on good level ground and a nice cold rum and coke in hand.

After an hour of drinking, I decided to cook dinner. I threw some coals on the grill and rolled a couple ears of corn in aluminum foil with a little butter. In the cooler, I had hamburger meat that was still a bit frozen in the middle. I made two burgers setting them on the grill when the coals were ready.

When my meal was finished, I ate in peace. There was a light breeze coming from the west and the sun was heading in the same direction. Besides Jim, I was the only soul in the campground. At that moment, I was at rest. And after the long drive, I couldn't think of a better place to be then the desert of Tucson Arizona.

After dinner, I sat for a while absorbing my surroundings. Once again the Saguaro Cactus had my attention with their tall bodies and long arms. What was most attractive about them, a type of bird nested within its rotten hollows.

"A home for everyone and everything," I thought laughing.

I cleaned up my mess and waited as the sun descended from the blue skies. I was halfway finished with my second bottle of rum and I was wasted. Sitting there in my lawn chair, I rolled my head from side to side. I wasn't going to make it much further into the night, so I decided to get some sleep.

Raising myself from the chair's comfortable grip, I stumbled towards my tent. I unzipped the tent door, popped off my sandals and collapsed on top of my sleeping gear. There was no need to get under the covers because the desert was one crispy place. When I passed out, my sleep was unremembered.

The next morning, I woke with a hangover. The Elite were talking as one of them said, "He's up."

With his voice, I could hear a group of soldiers sitting in front of the satellite feed. They said, "Get up pussy you have shit to do today."

I laughed at their humor thinking, "They are right, I have shit to do."

I put on my sandals and walked straight to the cooler. The only way to get my day started was by catching a buzz. I made myself a rum and coke before sitting in a lawn chair. After my second drink, I made a quick breakfast of some eggs and tortillas. I cooked on the Coleman stove and it worked beautifully.

After breakfast I walked to the shower. The campground didn't have a shower of their own, but Jim was kind enough to lend me a key to a private shower used only by those who volunteered and researched in the desert. These researchers were usually from the college and were not around during the summer months.

By 11:00 am, I was shit, showered, shaved and buzzed. I threw my towel over my tent to dry and hit the road leaving the camping area behind. I drove back over Gates Pass and down the road towards the city of Tucson. I had never been there before, so I thought it would be nice if I drove around the area finding my bearings.

In about 20 minutes I was familiar with the town. I drove down the main streets turning here and there until I had my bearing. Next, I pulled over and asked a man in the parking lot of a gas station where I could find Pima Community College. He directed me up the road a bit to my destination.

I pulled into the college with a smile on my face. There were new buildings along with some old, but all in all the place was in good shape. I walked through the front entrance of the student center and headed straight toward the front desk where a sign read, Admissions. After talking to a lady standing behind the counter, I had an appointment to see the next available counselor.

Within a half an hour, I had all the proper material to start the spring semester. She even gave me the address for a specific website to sign up for financial aid. I was well on my way to a great start.

Leaving the college, I decided to head over to the liquor store to pick up some supplies so I could celebrate for the night. I also decided it wouldn't

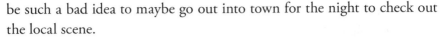

be such a bad idea to maybe go out into town for the night to check out the local scene.

On the way back to camp, I had the windows down with a nice breeze blowing across my face. I was happy for a new start in school and I was even happier I was away from Colorado and my parents. I didn't want them around because I didn't want them knowing what I was going through and how bad my life had become; they would never understand.

My life was tough and my actions spoke more than the truth. I was on a mission to get fucked up. I was on a mission to best these guys. There was no way I was going to let them win. It just wasn't happening.

I pulled into camp and began drinking right away. Once I had a good buzz, I rolled a joint puffing on its end. I was high, drunk, and beside myself. I quickly found there was nothing to do, so I decided to go on a hike where I discovered lots of Cholla Wood, cacti and lizards.

Forty minutes later, I was back at site with another drink and another joint. The Elite were quiet making little comments here and there about how well I camped. More often than not, I heard, "I can't believe were leaving this kid here."

These statements left me confused once again. It seemed they were trying to take me with them and at the same time they were also trying to kill me. I guess they figured if I killed myself they would be released from the pressure. They wouldn't have to make the decision of taking me in or not. I would be dead and out of the way.

I ate dinner, drank and smoked weed till about 7:00 pm. It was too early to go out, so I decided to hit a local dive bar until the night got started. Downtown and around the corner from an Irish bar, I found a local spot with shuffleboard and pool tables. It was perfect and the crowd wasn't so bad either. Here many of the women were my speed, so I decided I liked the place.

After a bunch of drinks and a bunch of shuffleboard, I found myself fitting in with a small group of locals. They had no idea what was going through my head, so I made sure not to talk to myself since it seemed I did a lot of that. I was used to the solitude of the Elite and me, so at times while in public I found myself being stared at as I talked to what seemed like nothing.

"It's a shame a boy so handsome ended up like that in life," I would hear.

It was embarrassing, but there was nothing I could do. It was the nature of the program I was on and I had no choice but to go along with it. There was no sense in explaining myself. And if I did, nobody would have believed me anyway.

The group of girls I played shuffleboard with informed me of a band playing at a bar called the Motel. They gave me directions telling tales of good times. They wouldn't be heading in that direction this evening, so I was sad to leave them behind. But, I also decided this was a new town and there would be plenty of time to bump into them at a later date.

I headed over to the Motel to see what was going on. It was a short drive from my current location, just over the train tracks on the other side of town. It was a white building with a large metal sign reading, Motel. Due to the large amount of cars in the designated parking area, I had to park down the street in temporary parking. It was so late I didn't think anyone would mind.

Before leaving my vehicle, I took a couple of rips from my bottle before heading into the bar. I walked through the front entrance into a very unique seating area where I heard loud music coming from the bar to my right. Walking over: I passed the bouncer check point with flying colors, paid my cover charge of ten dollars and walked through the doors.

Upon entering there was a bar to my right. I ordered a double rum and coke from a hot dark haired girl with tanned skin. I paid my bill before heading to my left up a couple of stairs toward the staging area. The music was a little heavy for me, but the crowd was having fun.

After my third drink, I found myself in the crowd dancing and having a good time. I had been there close to an hour when I had an awkward occurrence. This pretty blonde girl dressed in a mini skirt and a tight white top walked over to me. Stopping in front of me, she reached out with her arm, pinched my nipple giving me a Titty-Twister.

I was shocked and I didn't know what to say. The Elite were dying. One said, "Did you see that. That chic just pinched his tit."

Still not knowing what to say to her, I quickly spun around so my back was facing her and said to the Elite, "Watch this one."

As soon as the words left my mouth, I spun back around. I reached out with my arm and pinched her nipple giving the same amount of pressure she gave me and twisted. It was at this moment I figured the name of the band was Titty-Twister. Why else would a girl just come over and twist my titty? I was confused.

The look on the girl's face was that of disgust. She quickly swatted my arm away and stepped back saying, "What the fuck asshole."

I was stunned to say the least. This wasn't the reaction I was expecting and at the same time I guessed the name of the band wasn't Titty-Twister.

With squinted eyes, I observed her disapproval before saying, "You did it to me first."

But, she didn't care. She yelled, "I'm a girl."

"Well, you shouldn't go around grabbing guys boobies," I returned in a calm manner before turning around to walk away.

The Elite and I were cracking up. It was the funniest most awkward situation I had ever come across in a bar.

Who the hell gives you a Titty-Twister when they don't even know you?

I went home wasted that night and I barely remembered getting to bed. It had been a long day of drinking and I had to wake early in the morning. I had to find a place to live.

The next day, I woke around 10:00 am. I went through my usual morning routine of drinking, showering and cooking breakfast. I didn't know where I was going to start my search, but I did decide it wouldn't be too hard in finding a rental since I was living in a college town.

*

I spent two weeks searching for my pad. It wasn't as easy as I thought. I wanted my own place and it had to be clean and affordable. It sucked. It was actually depressing. It felt as if I was never going to find the right home to live in. I drank and I drank a lot.

On my third week, I came across the perfect place. It was an adobe cottage two blocks from the University and it was in excellent condition. I called the number on the sign and made arrangements to speak to the owner. We spoke for a brief moment before he decided to meet me with a key to show me around.

Ten minutes later, a well-dressed man showed with a key. He let me into the cottage and as soon as the door opened, I knew this was the place for me. The walls were freshly painted. The floor was a red stained concrete.

The kitchen was brand new. The bathroom was completely remodeled and the back bedroom was the same as the rest of the house, perfect.

It didn't take long to decide. I said to the gentleman, "What do I have to do to be in by today."

He smiled before saying, "Just come down to the office and I will have my secretary get you set up."

We shook hands making a deal.

I was out of his secretaries' office in a half an hour with a fresh set of keys in hand. I had a smile on my face from ear to ear and I couldn't wait to move in. I was excited to say the least.

After leaving the office, I drove back to camp and rounded up my belongings. I said my good-byes to the park ranger whom I had become friends with over the weeks. He was a great guy and I will never forget him or the hospitality he provided.

When I arrived at my new home, I quickly unloaded my camping gear into various closet spaces around the house. I made a bed in the back room out of a sleeping bag and a bed mat. It was going to be harsh living conditions for a couple of days. I needed to furnish the place. In the end, I figured it was no different than camping.

After everything was put away, I jumped into the shower thinking how good it felt to have my own bathroom again. The last three and a half weeks seemed more like a year. The time was very draining and I was glad to finally have some settlement in life.

My refrigerator was empty except for a bottle of rum, coke, bottled water, a few condiments and a couple of steaks. I needed to go grocery shopping, so it was the next task on my agenda. I loved to cook, so of course while I was at the store I filled my cart with some very creative cooking items for my recipes.

I made an early night of the day. I didn't feel much like going out, so I rolled a couple of joints and sat in a lawn chair in the middle of my living room starring at blank walls drinking rum and coke. I had the Elite around, so we kind of bullshitted throughout the night until I was tired enough to get some rest. It was usually a one way conversation with them, but at least I was able to make them laugh.

When I would ask them, "Why don't you guys ever talk? And why don't you ever say something nice so we can have a good time together?"

They're response would be, "You're not over here yet. Besides, we don't even like you."

I knew they were lying because if they laughed at my jokes then there was some sort of love between us. I didn't care how they were acting towards me I wasn't going to give up on them. I wanted to go with and be a part of them. I wanted to be a member of the Elite.

The next day, I lay in bed until around ten o'clock. I was still tired from the night before, but I was excited to head over to the furniture store to purchase new furnishings. I jumped into the shower, changed my clothes, made breakfast then headed out of the house as fast as I could.

Twenty minutes later, I found a nice furniture store just outside of town in the opposite direction from where I was camping in the state park. There was a large sign outside reading, Clearance Sale. I figured it was the perfect place to be.

I walked inside and the first item catching my eye was a set of green couches which would fit perfectly in my living room. Along with the couches, a wooden coffee table and set of end tables which matched perfectly. Since it was a package deal, I decided to buy the end lamps as well.

Next, I needed a bed. Walking over to the sleep center, I decided on a light cherry stained frame, foot board and head board along with a comfortable pillow top mattress which had a little less firmness than I was used too.

As I lay on the mattress, a sales man came over asking if I had any questions. Standing up from pure heaven, I said, "I'll take this mattress with that bed frame over there."

The gentleman smiled saying, "We can do that."

He pulled a small ordering pad from his pocket and began writing down tag numbers. When he finished, I brought him over to the couch set where he began writing down more tag numbers.

While the salesman wrote on his pad, I noticed a set of throw carpets along the back wall. Walking over, I spotted two that caught my eye. One was green in Oriental fashion and one was burgundy done the same way with a small difference in design. When the salesman was finished with the couches, I had him throw the rugs in as well.

Satisfied, I paid for my merchandise ordering same day delivery. I couldn't stand living without furniture for a long period of time, so the faster it arrived the better off I was.

Leaving the furniture store, I drove over to Target where I bought all my kitchen and bathroom accessories. I had pots, pans, silverware, spatulas, bowls, can openers, dish rags, wash clothes and towels. Just about everything you could think when moving into a new home. I even bought a cool clock to hang on the wall along with a few prints of some abstract art. I was hooking it up.

By the end of the day, I spent a little over seven-thousand dollars. By 7:30 at night, the furniture movers had all my furniture in the house put together and set in their proper spaces. The place looked great. I had the cable guy coming over the following day and my TV ready to be hung from the wall. It wasn't going to get much better than this.

*

The new semester wasn't starting for another six weeks. This gave me plenty of time to do absolutely nothing. While waiting, I received my acceptance letter to Pima in the mail along with a packet to register for classes.

After a week of sitting at home, I was going nuts. I didn't hang out with anyone. I wasn't doing anything adventurous. And all I could hear were the Elite's voices as they forced thoughts into my brain.

The brainwash was phenomenal. The TV was even starting to brainwash me. Everything exciting on TV had to do with murder, rape and suicide.

You don't realize it, but all we watch is brutality and killing. This brutality made my imagination that much greater. I thought about death all day long and the thoughts weren't leaving my mind. The Elite made sure they stayed well planted freaking me the fuck out.

I had to get out. I had to do something exciting. I liked palm trees and I liked them a lot. One night, I packed my truck with a small camping shovel, a flashlight and a blue Rubber-Maid tub. My plan was to drive out into the desert and dig up three palm trees. I must have been out of my mind, but at the time I was unaware of my behavior. I had trouble controlling myself to begin with and the brainwash was making it that much worse.

On the way to the desert, I stopped by the liquor store. My mind was fucked. I had been sitting on the couch watching people get killed for the last week. I opened the front door to the store and walked in. I passed a cute girl with long legs and blond hair. She had on a pair of white shorts showing off her tanned legs. She smiled as I walked by and all I could think about was taking the wine bottle next to me breaking it on one of the shelves and stabbing her in the fucking neck.

As scary as the thought was, it made me laugh at what my mind had become. My thoughts were that of murder and rape, but deep down inside I had control of myself. I still knew right from wrong.

I snatched a bottle of Bacardi from the shelf. When I walked toward the cash register, a skinny Mexican guy stood behind the counter. I took one look at him and all I could think about was sticking a knife right through his eyeball. I could see the blood trickling down the front of his face. I could see the white of his eye wrapped around a skinny blade. When he talked, he talked with a blade protruding from his eye socket. When his head moved, the blade moved along with it. It was an eerie visual.

I looked at him and laughed. In return he gazed upon me strangely. I could tell he knew something was wrong. It must have been written across my face. On the inside, I was of pure evil. On the out, I was kind and gentle. In reality, I was fucking crazy trying to hold onto sanity.

Shaking off the thoughts, I paid the man and headed for the parking lot. I opened the door of my 4-Runner, stepped in and immediately started drinking from my newly purchased bottle. For a second I thought I was drinking blood. The harsh burn on the back of my throat instantly dismissed the idea. The brainwash was getting worse and there was still nothing I could do.

Pulling out of the parking lot, I headed for the desert. I needed to find a place where nobody would catch me digging up three or four small palm trees. I had to be in the middle of nowhere.

Thirty minutes later, I decided I was in the middle of nowhere. I hadn't seen a car in quite some time and I figured I would be off the side of the road far enough where nobody could see me or see what I was up too.

When I was satisfied this was the safest place to dig, I grabbed my bottle from the front seat and began drinking. Wiping dribble from the corners of my mouth, I stepped out of my vehicle heading towards the hatch to grab the shovel and flashlight.

I had a grin on my face as the Elite cracked up.

"This fucking kid," they would say.

I walked out into the desert with bottle and shovel in one hand flashlight in the other. Every few steps, I stopped and drank like there was no tomorrow; like today was the last day on earth. I cursed and I laughed. I looked up towards the stars. I screamed, "Fuck you. I'm not going to die."

I was a raging lunatic. I was crazed and in a daze. I was living the ultimate twilight zone.

A hundred yards out, I stumbled across a palm tree where its seeds laid root. There must have been eight baby palms in a twenty foot radius. They were only about two foot high, but they were perfect for my home. I put the bottle on the ground along with my flashlight angled towards my working area. With my shovel in hand, I quietly began digging under the sand.

I drank and I dug. I didn't know what I was doing or why I was out there. All I knew, I wanted palm trees in my house and the thought was stuck in my head; Palm trees, Palm trees, Palm trees...

It's was all I could think about.

An hour later, I had three palm trees standing in the bucket in the back of my truck. My hands and knees were dirty and my palms were bloody and blistered from digging. I let out a crazed laugh as I looked at my new trees sitting in the back of my truck. All I could hear were my thoughts as they said repeatedly, "*Palm trees, Palm trees, Palm trees...*"

I had lost the plot. I had lost my mind...

Driving home, I smiled while drinking from my bottle. I had sweat drying on my forehead as I tasted its salt against my lips. The city lights streamed across my view as I thought of another world; a world more normal than the one I was living in; a world with the perfect utopia unlike my own.

I turned down the drive leading to my cottage. As I pulled in, I noticed a neighbor on the other side of the fence who was not part of our village community. He did not look normal.

He was a tall man with blond hair. He had on a white shirt stained with dirt. I could see from the light emitted from his head lamp he was sweating. He had a look to him that could only say one thing, drugs.

I was wasted and in need of a fix. The thought of getting high slammed my brain and it wasn't going to leave until I scored. I jumped out of my truck and headed towards the fence. Noticing my approach, the man starred straight at me. When I got a little closer, he said, "What's up man? You look a little worn out."

I was and it showed, if only he knew the whole story and the whole truth.

"Yah," I returned.

"I just went into the desert to dig up some palm trees for my living room," I continued.

The man looked into my deviance. He smiled before saying, "Out in the desert stealing plants are yah."

We both began laughing. I was relieved to see he was with good humor, but I still had to ask the almighty question. The question making guys like this run away if they didn't know you personally. I needed a bag of coke and I needed it now.

Leaning over the fence getting a little closer, I asked, "Do you know where I can get some powder?"

The man popped his head back and began to smile. From the look he gave, he knew exactly where to get what I wanted. He too leaned closer to the fence. He said, "I can't get coke, but I can get you some crystal."

I knew crystal. I had some roommates a while back that smoked it. I dabbled with it here and there while I was living with them, but never really liked it. With my limited resources for drugs in town, I was left with no choice. Crystal it was.

"That's cool, how much can you get," I returned?

The man answered quietly, "I will have to call my buddy, but he has whatever you need."

Nodding my head in agreement, I pointed to my front door saying, "I'll be over at my place if you want to stop by later. I guess I'll take fifty dollars' worth."

The man agreed while reaching over the fence to shake my hand. He said with a sly smile, "I'm Tommy."

We shook hands as I introduced myself.

After the conversation with Tommy, I said good-bye then walked back to my truck where the palm trees lay in the tub. I was proud of them and

I couldn't wait to get the trees into some pots. Grabbing the tub from the back, I walked inside my cottage. I didn't have pots for them yet, so I took them into the bathtub and filled the Rubber-Maid with enough water to cover the roots. I figured they would be fine until tomorrow.

Placing the Palm trees in the living room, I decided it was time to get cleaned up, so I jumped in the shower. As I stood there cleansing, I watched as a wake of brown dirt from my body found its way down the drain. I laughed at my insanity. I laughed because I just spent an hour in the desert digging up palm trees for no other reason except for the fact they were stuck in my head.

I got out of the shower, dried off and put some clothes on. I was excited for the dope man to come over and I honestly couldn't wait.

Walking into the kitchen, I opened the refrigerator door and made myself a double rum and coke tall; just the way I liked it with lots of ice, very little cola and lots of alcohol. I drank about half of it before filling it once again to the brim.

I took a seat on my new couch admiring my new surroundings. Everything I purchased fit nicely and I didn't have one single complaint. Ten minutes later, there was a knock at the door. It could only have been one person, the dope man.

When I opened the door, I was surprised to see another man with him. He dressed about the same as Tommy, not so well. I let them both in taking seats on the smaller couch next to me. I could tell by the looks on their faces they weren't there to chit chat, so I got right to the point. Reaching into my pocket, I grabbed a couple of twenties and a ten throwing the stack on the table.

The new guys name was Mike. I could tell he had been to prison because I had been there a few times myself. He was hardened the way prisoners are. He had the look.

Mike pulled a small glass jar from his inside pocket and poured out a large pile of crystal. The pile was more than I was paying for, but shit I wasn't going to complain. When he finished, he screwed the lid to his jar and grabbed my money from the table. He wasn't there to talk, so he just said, "If you need anymore get hold of Tommy and I will come over."

I nodded my head in agreement and thanked him. We shook hands and the two of them were out the door.

After the neighbors were gone for a minute, I cut out two lines with a card and rolled a bill into a straw. I snorted both lines, one in each nostril. My nose burned. It burned and it burned really bad. That's just how that shit was. It tore you up.

Ten minutes later, I was flying. My buzz had worn off and the drugs had kicked in. I wanted to do more. I went into the kitchen and snagged the aluminum foil from a cabinet drawer. I tore off a sheet and folded it the way my old roommates taught me. I folded the foil so there was a canal running down its center. Sitting back on the couch, I pinched a pile of speed and dropped it on the crease of the foil. Taking a lighter from my pocket, I melted the pile and began running it back and forth along the canal until I had a nice streak of speed to smoke.

Taking the guts of a pen apart, I had my straw. I angled the straw just over my stream of speed. I lit the speed from under the foil at one end watching as smoke vacuumed through the straw into my lungs as I inhaled. It tasted like shit, but the affects were spectacular. I was on top of the world.

I smoked the foil and then another before I was satisfied in having enough for a while. The Elite didn't say a word. They were neither disappointed nor happy with what I was doing. It was as if they were letting me make my own choices. They never told me to stop doing something and they never encouraged me either. If I had to guess, I would say they were happy I was ruining my life. The reason being, they wanted me dead.

Forty minutes later, I was sitting on the couch bugging out. The speed was way worse than the effects of cocaine. It sped my thoughts so fast it was fucking annoying. The brainwash was a hundred fold. I didn't care because it felt better than being drunk all the time. I was tired of being drunk, so the speed was a nice change. The only problem, the brainwash was that much more intimidating.

The house was quiet. My hearing was on supersonic. I heard every crack, blip, creak, drop, and bend throughout the cottage. It was actually starting to bug me out. It felt like somebody was always staring at me. It felt like somebody was trying to break into my home. It felt like somebody was trying to kill me. I was a fucking mess.

I tried not to care, so I smoked some more. When I was feeling too high, I drank to calm down. From the Elite's responses to my actions and how my eyes were reacting to the drugs, I could tell they could see the shit was bugging me out.

I stayed up all night drinking and doing speed. When the sun came up, I just kept going through the dawn. Before I knew it, it was night again. The problem was, the pile of speed Mike left wasn't going away, I still had about half of it in front of me.

By eight o'clock in the evening, I had been sleep deprived, starved, drunk and high for quite some time. I was beginning to hallucinate. The noises throughout the house were becoming more profound. I was wigging the fuck out.

At one point, I had all the lights off in the house as I stood in front of the blinds peeking out through the windows. In the front of the house, all I could see was the driveway. In the back of the house stood a fence no more than five feet away leading into another neighbor's back yard. I was a fucking mess. I was hearing shit and worst of all it sounded as if voices were coming from every direction; voices unlike the Elite.

Then it got worse. In the middle of bugging out, I heard one of the Elite say, "He's got the agency on him and they want him dead."

The words pierced right through my body. My mind went wild as I began to think. It could only mean one thing. I was doing drugs, so I wasn't trusted with the information I had. I was carrying all the top secrets on earth and these people wanted me dead for them.

Sweat began pouring down my cheeks. I was doomed and soon a dead man.

Then it happened. I was standing by the front window peering out when I heard a noise from my bedroom. There was a side door in the room and it sounded as if somebody was trying to get in. Instantly, I panicked. The drugs raised the level of paranoia. I didn't know what to do. My reaction was to grab a weapon to defend myself.

Creeping into the kitchen as quietly as I could, I grabbed a sharp cutting knife from the cabinet drawer next to the sink. Next, I thought of all the points of entry throughout the cottage. If somebody was coming through the back door, my best point of attack was to stand in front of the refrigerator and get them as they came through the bathroom which connected from my bedroom to my kitchen leading into the living room. It was the only way an attacker could get to me and it was the shortest

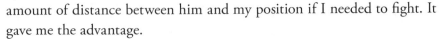

amount of distance between him and my position if I needed to fight. It gave me the advantage.

As I stood there with knife in hand, the intensity of the situation escalated. I was waiting, I was listening, I was building fucked up shit in my head and I was getting ready to explode.

There was nothing, not a sound nor a word. I just stood their freaking out with sweat pouring down the sides of my face anxious to beat the man who was coming through that door. My heart was racing.

When all was quiet, I was hit with the oddest sound; a loud clank against the side door. My heart jumped through my chest. I whispered to the Elite, "Fuck this I'm out of here."

I said it like we were friends. I said it like I trusted them. Why, I don't know?

At that same moment, I ran into the living room snagging my keys from the coffee table. It was dark, but I knew where I had placed them. In the same motion, I went for the front door. As fast as I could, I unlatched the bolt opening the front door and ran for my truck. I didn't think anybody would shoot me in public, so I felt a bit safer. In reality, I wasn't. I had a Hit Man after me. The worst part, I was so fucking high I couldn't tell the difference if the situation was real or not. For the moment, I was going to have to assume it was. The clank against the back door was real and that's all that mattered.

As fast as lightening, I put my key into the driver's side door of my vehicle. I ducked my head so I wouldn't get shot; I started the engine, threw it into gear, reversed and then sped away. At twenty miles per hour, I screeched the tires making a right without stopping at the end of the drive. I was heading for the main road into town where there would be lots of people and lots of lights.

With adrenaline pumping through my veins, I thought, "*This bastard isn't going to kill me. I was going to make sure of it. If he was, he was going to have to do it with a hundred people watching.*"

I raced down street after street. I turned here and there making sure nobody followed and I also made sure to stay in public view. I was a fucking wreck. My heart was coming through my chest and I was on full paranoid mode. I wanted to get away.

At one point, I dialed 911. When the guy answered, he sounded like one of the Elite. I quickly hung up the phone thinking, "*These guys took over my cell phone too.*"

What made things worse, they had a Hit Man after me.

I was stopped at a stoplight. It had just turned red. I didn't like stopping my vehicle. I felt like somebody was behind me readying a bullet for my head. I tried using the frame of the trucks body to shield all angles from a direct shot. I didn't want to die.

While I was waiting for the light to turn green, one of the Elite said, "That agent is taking a shot."

With his words, I stepped on the gas blowing through the red light and out into traffic. I made a left hand turn speeding down the road. There was no way some motherfucker was going to get the best of me. I just wasn't letting it happen.

The problem was, I was hooked up to a satellite and in all reality there was no getting away. These guys would know my exact location at all times. No matter how fast I ran I would never get far enough away. I was a dead man and there was no escape.

I drove around for hours letting the drugs wear off. When I finally calmed down, the Elite began to laugh. Nobody took a shot at me and I was still alive. Most of all, I needed to get home and off the streets where I could relax. I needed a shower and some rest.

It was about 7:30 when I was finally able to lay down. I drank some rum to kill what was left of the high and I even smoked some weed to make myself tired. In the living room, a pile of speed sat on the table waiting for my next drunken adventure. I was an idiot to say the least.

I woke up around 7:00 in the evening. I went straight to the refrigerator and poured myself a drink. The brainwash was back in full force. The worst part, I had to learn how to defend myself from its affect all over again.

In reality, the only way to get used to brainwash was to take it on sober. The reason being, your body and brain got used to the stress and effects on a sober level. Drinking was cheating. It made you not care what you were thinking and when you didn't care there was no stress. See how it works. My best bet was to actually deal with the brainwash sober. The only problem was I could only take so much before I exploded and went out drinking. There was only so much I could humanly take. It was viscous.

I went weeks drinking. When I drank, I got hooked to the speeds affects. It was almost as if I had become addicted to the drugs paranoid effect. It had become a game of cat and mouse. The Elite played off of it and they played off of it well.

They were using their key system to create any noise imaginable. Since I could here through their radio, they could make a noise on their end and send it anywhere in my house. It didn't have to be an animal or insect noise anymore. They could bang their foot on the floor and send it through the laser and target any area. See what I'm saying? They figured out how to use what was around them to make noises which seemed real around me. It sucked. It threw the dynamics of the game in a whole new direction. Now, I couldn't tell if it was them or somebody else.

I drank, I got high and I became paranoid running around town like a chicken with its head cut off. At one point I was laying on the floor in my bathroom. The Elite had me thinking somebody was going to shoot at me through the bathroom window. The drugs had me so fucked up it was unreal. I was delusional.

Laying on the bathroom floor in such a panic, I actually felt as if somebody had killed me. I believed I was a ghost and everything was different. I sat up and began to cry. I even began to believe the Elite were ghosts and the reason they were in my life was because they were waiting for this moment to happen to take me away. It was the most unusual feeling I had ever experienced in my entire life. I had felt death.

The Elite played me like a fool. They used the paranoia from the drugs to intensify the brainwash. They played the game well. They had me believing death was real.

*

I had enough of this shit and this lifestyle. I couldn't take anymore. I needed to go home where it was safe. I needed my parents. I needed to tell them what was going on. I needed to tell them the whole story and the whole truth. The question, would my parents believe me?

I packed a bag full of clothes and hopped in my truck for the twelve hour drive home. I was taking a route from Arizona up through Flagstaff Utah on into Colorado. It was quicker than going through Vegas and I needed to get home as fast as possible.

I drove smoking weed the whole way. I didn't want to show up wasted on rum because I wanted my parents to believe me. I rolled into town just past 7:00 pm. I stepped out of my truck and stretched for a moment before thinking, "*This is going to be interesting.*"

My parents had no clue I was coming home, so the surprise was going to shock them.

I opened the front door with my duffel bag in hand. As I shut the door, my mother came around the corner from the living room. The look on her face said it all. It said, what are you doing home?

I didn't know what to say at first. I stood there taking a moment to realize she was my mother and everything was going to be okay. My composure didn't last. I dropped my bag on the floor and walked into her arms and began crying. I took her off guard. She didn't know what to say or how to react. I just stood there crying, holding on as tight as I could and I didn't want to let go.

When I stopped weeping, I stepped back and said, "I have people trying to kill me."

She couldn't and wouldn't understand. Her expression was that of complete and utter confusion. The first words to come out of her mouth were, "Whose trying to kill you and why?"

Taking a moment to gather my thoughts, I began with the story by saying, "An Elite crew was sent to train me for a government agency. These people discovered I had the ability to hear through the same frequency as their spy satellite system. In the process, I've discovered many of their secrets. In fact, I have discovered all of their secrets.

I continued, "There's a Commander of this Elite crew who came to train me who doesn't like me. We don't get along at all. He had been using his satellite technology to brainwash me. I can't explain why or how it's brainwashing me just know it's getting bad thoughts stuck in my head and they're not going away. I've been drinking heavily and doing drugs trying to stop the torture. But, I have had enough and I can't take it anymore."

I then began crying all over again. It was the best I could explain the situation.

My father came into the living room from the garage. I explained the same story to him as well. He was in shock. He couldn't believe the words coming from my mouth. He even called me crazy.

"You're on drugs and you're crazy," he said.

My mother figured the same thing. She figured I was crazy and going delusional; that I may have been on drugs and I was going nuts.

Ten minutes later there was a knock at the front door. I blew it off because I didn't care. My mother came from her bedroom to answer the door. She was in tears. When she opened the door, to my surprise two uniform police officers walked into the living room. They were about the same height and build except one had blond hair and the other had black. A dispatcher's voice spoke through their radios as they both reached for their hip to turn down the volume.

The officer with dark hair looked at me and spoke. He said, "What's going on Boo?"

I immediately spoke my story. I got halfway through before the officer decided I was crazy and it was time to detain me. He told me to turn around bringing the sound of handcuffs from his belt. I couldn't believe what was happening. I wanted to run and get away, but I had no choice. My parents were present and it was best I just leave with the officers.

My mother was crying. She had tears like I had never seen before. She looked into my eyes and said, "Boo, these guys are here to help. Don't fight them. They are going to take you somewhere where you can get help. You need medication because you're going crazy. You're delusional and you don't even know it."

As she spoke, I thought, *"Great Mom. You called the fucking cops. What the fuck is wrong with you?"*

I couldn't believe she turned me in. When I thought about it, who would ever believe this story? If I wasn't living it, I wouldn't have believed it either.

There were two cruisers outside of my parent's house as one of the officers walked me to his car. I was placed in the first cruiser parked in the driveway. Even though I didn't have anything to say, the officer was very polite with me. He simply stated, "I'm taking you over to the Mental Health Clinic to get you checked out. You're probably going to be there for a couple of nights, but don't worry they're going to get you taken care of."

As the officer drove, I rolled my head back and breathed heavily through my nose. I kept thinking, *"This can't be happening. I can't believe my mother turned me in."*

We pulled into the Mental Health facility shortly after leaving my parent's house. I wasn't happy to be there, but I didn't mind either. I just wanted to get some sleep and forget this night ever happened. I wasn't mad at my mother for turning me in because I understood why she did it. She thought I was going crazy and needed help.

I was led into a side room behind a locked door. The officer removed the handcuffs giving me a light smile. He took a moment to look at me before saying, "Good luck Boo. These guys will take care of you."

I knew he was trying to be nice and was only there to help, so I thanked him. He smiled before patting me on the shoulder. As he turned to leave, I watched as he left the room. The door buzzed open then locked with his exit. There was no escape. I was trapped in the mental ward and God only knew when they were going to let me out.

A nurse gave me a set of blue scrubs to wear during my stay. I was also given a pair of tan socks with padding on the bottoms of the feet for traction. No shoes or shoe laces were to be worn in the facility as a patient. They said it was for my safety. They didn't want anyone getting kicked in the head with a shoe and they didn't want anyone hanging themselves with a lace.

Once I was dressed, I was asked a series of questions. The main question asked over and over, "Are you thinking about suicide or harming others?

I laughed at the statement. I definitely wasn't going to kill myself and hurting others was absurd even though I'd been known to get into a fight or two during my day.

I shook my head, no. The nurse informed I would be seeing the psychiatrist in the morning and for the time being they had a room for me to sleep in until the doctor's arrival. She took a short pause and continued by saying, "You'll be under twenty-four hour suicide watch until he gets here."

I blew off her statement and said, "Just show me to my room and I will be fine."

She smiled before answering, "Alright then. If you need anything just let us know."

I agreed and was led into a room right around the corner.

The room was painted white. The floor was made of ceramic tile and in its center a thick plastic mat for sleeping. Just before entering, the nurse handed me a pillow and a cotton blanket to keep warm. It wasn't much more than the standard prison issue, but it would do.

I walked over to the mat, threw out my blanket and laid my head to rest on top of the pillow. As I lie there staring at the ceiling, I couldn't believe where I was. I couldn't believe I was in a mental institute. The worst part of the whole situation, I wasn't crazy. Everything that was happening was real; hard to believe, but very real.

I must have fallen asleep because around 1:00 am I woke to the load noise of a yelling man's voice. When I started to understand what he was shouting, I began to laugh. He yelled, "You're all going to die. They're after me and they're going to kill you next. Fuck the CIA and fuck America. They're coming for us. I'm dead! I'm dead! I'm dead I tell yah!"

Next, I heard the nurse's voice who led me to my room in the beginning of the night. She said in a calm gentle voice, "Tim, you need to get away from the window and get some rest."

Tim didn't care. He yelled while pounding on the reinforced glass. He yelled, "Fuck you bitch. They're going to kill you too. They're in my head. They're going to kill us all. They told me they are."

I had to see what Tim looked like and what all the commotion was, so I raised myself from the mat and headed towards the door where I could see. When I peered down the hallway, I watched a man in the same blue scrubs as myself. He was short and skinny with long gray hair sticking straight into the air. His fingernails were dirty and I could see he had completely lost his fucking mind. He was certifiably nuts and it showed.

He kept banging and screaming. His words were confused and in an improper order. He was a raging lunatic in the ultimate sense. He spit from his mouth with every word. He paced back and forth before going into another rage. He cursed and he threatened...

He was my neighbor in the mental institute...

I couldn't watch anymore. It was a good show, but I just couldn't watch. The nurse was on the other side of the glass telling him to lie down, but Tim wasn't having it. His brain was imbalanced and there was no stopping him now. He was on a full force mission of crazy. He wasn't letting up and he definitely wasn't going to sleep anytime soon.

When I had enough of watching Tim's frenzy, I walked back to my mat to lie down. Once again, I stared at the ceiling thinking, "*What a fucking place.*"

Tim was on a sick one. He was yelling and screaming. The nurse kept telling him to get away from the window, but after a while she had given up.

Tim, on the other hand had not. He was determined to lose his mind.

After twenty minutes of lying there listening, I had enough of Tim's shit. I rolled my head to the side and began yelling myself. I began yelling at Tim.

I yelled, "Just shut the fuck up and go to fucking bed."

Tim wasn't listening. He kept going on with his rampage. I was going nuts. I couldn't take it anymore. Tim needed to shut the fuck up.

"Shut the fuck up and go to fucking sleep Tim," I shouted once again. I kept repeating myself in the same loud volume over and over again. "Just shut the fuck up," I would say a bit crazed myself.

My head was shaking. I was beginning to spit from my mouth just like Tim. The man was driving me absolutely fucking nuts.

After one of my bursts, Tim shut the fuck up. It was like magic. My mind was instantly at ease. I couldn't believe it worked. I laid there laughing. I laid there at rest.

I heard a shuffle of Tim's feet down the hall. He remained quiet and it seemed he had enough of himself. Then, he surprised the shit out of me. He was standing in my doorway. I looked at him and he looked at me. His pointer finger was in the air as he began going crazy once again. He slobbered and drooled. He yelled the best he could.

In his raspy voice, he shouted, "There going to kill you. It's the CIA and they're going to kill you. They're taking all our money and they're not telling us things. We're all going to die. They're poisoning us. They took control of our brains and we're all going to die."

I was cracking up. Tim was going nuts at my door. I thought, "*If only he really knew? If only he knew it was really possible.*"

The only part he had wrong, it wasn't the CIA. Right now in my situation, it was somebody else. I laughed because he was right; delusional in his head, but real in mine.

I listened to Tim for about three minutes before I was at my ends with him. I couldn't listen anymore. Snagging my pillow from under my head,

I threw it at Tim hitting him in the forehead. His head shot back on his neck. His greasy hair folded to the side. His mouth closed and for the first time in the night, Tim appeared to be thinking clearly. He looked at me sounding like Froggy from the Little Rascals and said, "I'm going to get you for that."

I burst out laughing. The man was so crazy he was hilarious. I said to him in return, "Just get away from my door and shut the fuck up."

Tim turned around without saying a word and walked away. Halfway down the hallway he went into his CIA spiel again. It was sickening to hear him go. He was never going to stop. As he walked away screaming, I yelled one more time in hopes of stopping the man. I yelled at the top of my lungs, "Shut the fuck up Tim. Just shut the fuck up. Go to sleep and shut the fuck up."

Within minutes, a man was at my door. He worked in the facility and I could tell he was a little upset with me. He said, "Boo, there are people here with severe mental disorders. You can't be yelling at them. Tim hasn't taken his medication and this happens often with him. As soon as his medication kicks in, he will be better. You have to promise you won't yell at the other patients anymore."

I wanted to be left alone, so I agreed with the man. All I wanted was for some sleep and this nightmare to be over. Seeing I was calmed down, the man left the room.

The next morning, I woke early. A different nurse from the night before led me into a room where I was able to eat breakfast. My meal consisted of cold cereal, milk, a banana and a box of juice with a straw sticking from the top. It wasn't much, but I was full when finished.

Next, I was brought into a doctor's office where an elderly gentleman with white hair, a white coat and tan pants sat behind a desk. He wore glasses pressed hard against the bridge of his nose and by his expression he took his job seriously.

Taking a seat in a wooden chair, I began with my story. I told him how I had the ability to talk through an advanced satellite system. I told him how it was brainwashing me. I told him who was behind it all. And most of all, I spoke of the misery it had caused in my life.

When I finished with my story, the doctor asked a few questions while scribbling in his note pad. I figured he was writing down I was a man of delusion who heard voices. Maybe I was paranoid schizophrenic and I had all sorts of problems which needed dealing with. Most important, I was fucking crazy and my mind just wasn't right.

When I left his office, I was led into a large room where large comfortable fold out chairs rested. The type of chairs where you pull a lever and a foot rest appears from the bottom. I was given a blanket and a pillow to keep myself comfortable.

Upon sitting down, I counted a total of ten chairs. Four of those chairs were occupied by crazy people just like me. Two of the chairs were occupied by women and the other three by men. The woman closest to me was in her mid-twenties. She wore multicolored hair completely shaved on one side dyed pink and green on the other. She had her blanket tightly wrapped around body as she sat there laughing at herself. I later discovered her name was Jenny.

The next chair was occupied by a man named Tommy. He had short curly brown hair. He was of medium build and from where I was sitting I would guess he stood around six-three. He had a blank stare on his face interrupted by unknown laughter. I would say he lost his mind a long time ago.

On the other side of Tommy sat a woman with fuzzy blond hair and makeup which was all over her face in all the wrong places. She looked like something out of a bad clown movie. She mumbled when she spoke and by the sound in her voice I would have to say she smoked at least two packs of cigarettes a day. Her name was Shelly.

Then there was our winner of the night, Tim. Tim was quiet as could be. His hair was wet and freshly combed. He sat in his chair without a blanket wrapped around him and he appeared to be steady as an arrow. The reason I say this, the night before I noticed he had a bad case of the shakes. Today, he was looking sharp and steady. I laughed at the wonders of modern medication.

The last seat was filled by an unknown man who slept. Because he was sleeping, I was yet to discover his mental awareness. I figured it was a good thing he was sleeping. Why? Because the less craziness I had to deal with, the better off I was.

Twenty minutes later, Tommy came from the restroom with a puddle of piss down his leg. I couldn't believe my eyes. I knew right away things were going to get interesting. Immediately Jenny, the girl with colored hair, looked at Tommy and said, "Hey Tommy, you pissed yourself."

I was cracking up. She said it so nonchalantly it became a classic.

Tommy spoke like a child at all times. He looked her straight in the eyes even though it seemed he was gazing to the left a bit and said, "No, no I didn't. That's not piss."

Just as the words left his mouth, a male staff member opened the office door and said, "Hey Tommy, you pissed yourself."

He must have seen James through the glass window connecting his office to the room where we were sitting. I could tell the man didn't want to laugh, but at the same time I could see he thought the situation funnier than shit.

Tommy wasn't having it. He said to the man and kept repeating himself, "It's not piss. It's not piss."

Jenny turned her head toward Tommy one more time. Looking at the wet spot on his pants she said, "Yup, that's piss."

I was dying. I couldn't stop laughing. I was living the ultimate movie and I couldn't get enough of it. I wanted more. I simply wanted to see more.

It got better. Shelly, the women with fuzzy hair and fucked up makeup looked over at Tommy.

She said, "My husband used to piss himself just like that and that's piss man. Why don't you go and clean yourself up?"

I was rolling in laughter. The show continued.

Tommy threw his arms by his sides in a temper tantrum. He continued to speak like a child. He yelled frantically, "It's not piss. It's not piss."

The man in charge was trying not to laugh, but couldn't hold back. He went back into his office and grabbed a fresh pair of scrubs for Tommy to wear. When he re-entered the room, he tossed the scrubs towards Tommy.

Tommy let the scrubs hit the floor. He was still yelling, "It's not piss."

Shelly had enough. She said, "Pick that shit up and go change your pants Tommy."

Jenny kept saying, "Tommy you peed yourself."

I couldn't stop laughing.

Tim didn't say a word and the guy sleeping remained silent.

Tommy quickly snagged the scrubs from the floor and walked into the other room. When he returned, he still had piss all over the front of him.

Jenny took one look and said, "You still got piss all over you. Go change. That's gross."

Tommy wasn't having it. He walked over to his chair, sat down and covered himself with the blanket. He just sat there marinating in his own urine without a care in the world. I was amazed.

The girls kept on him. They told him he was nasty and needed to change. They were on him and they wouldn't quit.

Tommy just ignored them rolling his eyes here and there as he became very dramatic with his facial expressions. When the girls became too much for him, he closed his eyes feigning sleep. And after a while the girls let the situation rest.

I stayed in the chair room for the rest of the day. Every now and then, a newcomer would join the room blessing us with their craziness. By the end of the night, we were led to separate rooms where I was able to lie down on a regular mattress with sheets, pillow and a blanket. While lying there trying to fall asleep, I couldn't help but think how much the place reminded me of the Aspen County Jail; nice and cozy for an institution.

The next morning, I was taken to a large room with a full kitchen surrounding a long rectangular table. Jenny, Tim, Shelly, Tommy, the guy sleeping and about five others I haven't met yet were all sitting at the large table eating breakfast.

Pulling the nearest chair from the table, I thought how fucked up the situation was. My own mother had me committed to the psych ward. I still wasn't mad, I just thought, "*If she only knew the truth about what was really happening.*"

I also thought, "*We're going to have a good laugh about this someday.*"

I ate breakfast before sitting on one of the couches opposite the kitchen table. There were about four couches in all and I now owned one of them. I didn't want to talk to anyone. I just wanted to sit there in thought. When I wasn't thinking, I was turning my shoulder to talk to the Elite. They were laughing so hard they had me laughing as well.

I kept thinking, "*What a fucking mess.*"

By 11:00 AM, the patients were coloring with markers. There wasn't much going on besides a couple of counselors watching the clients making sure one of them didn't kill themselves. I guess they figured me somewhat normal, so they left me alone.

I went two days like this. I drank juice from cardboard boxes and watched adults act like children while drawling pictures of whatever came to their lunatic minds. One guy must have really liked death because all of his pictures had somebody being slaughter. The counselor tried to evaluate one of the drawing's with the man and all he could say was, "I want to fucking die."

On the third day, I was standing next to one of the counselors. We were talking and I had made a comment about her hair. It was kind of wild with black and blonde streaks. In her mind she said, "You little shit."

With her thought, I busted out laughing and said, "I'm not a little shit."

She blushed. She looked at me and said, "You really are telepathic."

I returned, "I am. I'm not crazy it just doesn't work that well. People's thoughts are fairly quiet, so I usually only hear the louder thoughts. I actually hear radio waves better. That one works really well."

By 2:00 in the afternoon, I was in the psychiatrist's office talking with the doctor. I had previously told him I was telepathic with the ability to hear through radio waves. I told him how I was being brainwashed by an Elite military group and how it was affecting my brain. He didn't believe me at the time, but now he was looking at me in a whole new light.

He said, "Boo, now this story is really happening or it isn't.

"Is this stuff really happening to you," he continued?

I didn't want to say yes because I just wanted to get out of there. Instead, I said, "No it's not real. I just made it up in my head."

By the expression on his face, I could tell he knew I was lying. He shook his head before writing on his tablet. He then said, "I'm going to release you today, but I want you to talk to one of our outpatient counselors when you leave here. She's in the building next to ours."

I agreed to speak to the counselor before shaking his hand. I thanked him for his help and gave him a reassuring smile that said, "This is all true and I can't really talk about it."

He looked at me nodding his head as if to say, "I know. We just found out you really are telepathic."

A half an hour later, I was given my street clothes to change into then led out a door where I signed a set of release papers. I said my good-byes to the staff and walked out the door.

Across the way in the building next door, I walked through a set of double doors. I went to the front counter and said to the receptionist, "I have an appointment to see Heather."

The receptionist tapped on her keyboard for a moment. She scanned the screen and said, "Take a seat over there and she will be right with you."

I thanked her, walked over to the waiting room and sat down in a chair.

Heather was prompt. Within minutes, she poked her head from a steel door and called my name. I followed her through the door down a hallway to her office taking a seat next to her desk. When she sat, she leaned back in her chair folding her hands on her lap. She took a deep breath, stared at me from behind a pair of glasses which made her look both sexy and smart at the same time and said, "Do you have something you want to tell me?"

Not wanting another night in the nut house, I returned, "Nope, everything is fine."

She took a moment to assess the situation. She then said, "Are you sure you don't want to tell me something; something about the military maybe?"

I looked her straight in the eyes and said, "No mam, I think I'm okay and everything is fine."

Heather wasn't buying it. The whole town heard of a real telepath, so I'm sure she had heard as well.

She then said, "My father is an active member in the Pentagon. I can give him a call and let him know what's happening to you. Do you want me to call him?"

I didn't want to get the guys in trouble. I thought about saying yes to the phone call, but I just didn't want the situation to go in that direction.

After some more thought, I returned, "No mam, everything is fine."

Heather took another deep breath and spoke once again. She said, "Boo, we believe this is really happening to you and we want to help."

I just couldn't sell the guys out. I knew if I told her it was all true and these militants were trying to kill me, it would all be over. The nightmare would end. I would have my brain back and this insanity would come to an end. What bothered me most, was telling on the Elite. I really didn't want them going to jail. I'd rather fight through this than see them in trouble.

I looked at her and said, "I'm going through some weird things in life, but I'm going to be okay."

I could see Heather was upset. She truly wanted to help, but I wasn't letting her. I stood from my chair and thanked her saying I was okay. Before I left, she said, "Boo, if you ever want to talk about this or if you want me to talk to my father for you I'm here."

I thanked her one last time, before leaving her office. I couldn't do it. I couldn't sell out.

*

My parents picked me up from the lobby of Heather's office. We drove home as my father asked of my stay in the loony bin. I laughed brushing it off. My mother explained how she was sorry for turning me in and I reassured her it was okay. The three of us then decided to go for something to eat, so we ate at my favorite Italian Restaurant.

I spent two more days with my parents before driving back to Tucson. I didn't drink or smoke from the pipe the entire way. The brainwash sucked, but I was dealing with it for the moment. Instead, I took some time to reflect on my situation in a sober manner.

The most fucked up part, the Elite began working my brain over even harder after my stay in the nut house. They began telling me I was crazy and I was a murderer and a rapist. They were calling me a monster.

For them to say this about me hurt and it hurt really badly. They knew what they were doing to my head and now they were trying to make me believe it.

When I got back to Tucson, I started drinking heavily again. The brainwash was simply too much to bare. I was a wreck and that's all I can say.

Along with the alcoholism, I continued with the drugs. I was buying crystal in small amounts from the neighbors and the shit continually made me paranoid. While I was going through these paranoid frenzies, the Elite worked my brain over so severely I was snapping constantly losing my shit. They were determined to make me commit suicide and they weren't giving up.

*

School started with the Spring Semester and I was a hot mess. It was hard to concentrate and all I could do was drink and smoke weed to calm my thoughts.

At night I drank and tried studying to the best of my ability. When I read books for my Western Literature class, I couldn't remember what I was reading. I was lost of thought and comprehension. I didn't want the Elite to succeed, so I was determined to do my best. I was determined to finish with honors.

A month into the semester, I was holding tight. My grades were steady with A's and B's across the board. It took me three times as long to study, but I was doing well with it. I was putting in the time and effort.

The Elite couldn't believe it. For how fucked my brain was, the Elite just couldn't believe my grades. They kept saying to their commander, "You're not leaving this kid here. We're taking him with us."

At times, I could hear them yelling at the commander. The guys were beginning to get pissed. Some would even say, "It sucks what we're doing to this kid. He's a good dude."

They couldn't believe what was going on themselves. And they were starting to get angry with their commander. When I say angry, I mean angry.

The problem was, the commander wanted me dead, so they had to follow his orders. No matter how upset they had become, they continually tortured me through brainwash. Their mission was for me to die.

*

Some days the brainwash was worse than others. I was in my math class one day and this day was one of those really bad days. The thoughts started off really slow and just kept escalating turning into sheer horror.

A really hot girl named Samantha sat directly in front of me. She always wore tight outfits showing off her perfectly rounded ass and large breast. She had brown hair with a sort of punk rock look to her. She was funny, sweet and tough all in one. Her smile was the best and the two of us got along great. I even tutored her in math on occasion. We had become good friends.

This day was not such a good day. I was checking out Samantha's ass when the Elite picked up on my observations. One of them said, "Just fuck her and get it over with."

The guys were laughing. With how bad my brain was working I went into sex mode. I began imagining myself having sex with her. This wasn't a bad thing since she was hot, but it wasn't a good thing either because of what comes next. The thoughts you can't control.

My mind had Sam bent over the desk completely naked. I was inside of her as she gasped with every thrust of my hips. Every now and then she would glance back towards me showing the sexiest smile ever.

Then it happened. One of the Elite yelled, "Kill that bitch."

The thoughts went to kill. I was fucking Sam and punching her in the back of the head at the same time. She was screaming as I continuously beat her to death with my dick still inside of her.

Sweat began dripping from my forehead. The walls of the room caved in. My vision had dark shadows as I began looking around the room. I had a knife in my hand. I was running around the room stabbing people whenever I had the chance. I stabbed them in their sides and I stabbed them in their necks. I was going for jugulars. I would go kill someone than go back and fuck Sam. While I fucked her from behind, I imagined myself slicing her throat. There was blood everywhere. Students were lying on the floor screaming holding their wounds and all I could do was fuck Samantha's bloody body as she screamed. Sometimes in pleasure while other times in fear.

I got sick to my stomach. My vision crossed back over. The room paralleled normal, but I had not. I was going to vomit. I grabbed my books from my desk stuffing them into my back pack and stumbled to the door. I held onto the wall most of the way for balance. My equilibrium was off. When I made it to the door, I wrapped my hand around the knob stifling into the hallway.

For a brief second, I could see Samantha's expression. She was in shock. She couldn't understand what was going on. She was confused. I was saddened by her reaction. I was saddened because I liked her.

I walked slowly down the hallway toward the end. Sitting on a bench, I had to regain my composure. I had my elbows on my thighs with my hands pressed hard against my face. I vomited. I vomited orange bile all over the floor.

I coughed...

I spit...

I puked again...

I went to the Liquor store bought a bottle and went home. That's all I have to say.

*

Spring break rolled around and I had to get the fuck out of town. I needed a new view on life. I needed a change of scenery. I felt a new and exciting place would change everything; as if it would make me happy or something.

San Diego was seven hours away from Tucson. All I had to do was hop on Route 8 and head out of town. I packed a bag full of clothes along with a standard set of toiletries. I had a headache, a hangover, a dry mouth and a thirst for alcohol.

I pulled out of my drive around ten in the morning. I quickly stopped to check my mail then drove around the corner. The windows were down with a nice breeze and the radio was at a subtle volume playing David Gray.

Before leaving town, I bought a fifth of rum. I rolled two joints in the parking lot of the liquor store smoking one of them when I got back on the road. My mind was at ease with itself. I was excited to hit the beach and even more excited to swim in the ocean.

I drank rum and smoked weed the entire trip. I rolled into San Diego around six in the evening. I was wasted upon my arrival. I followed the signs for Ocean Beach since I had never been to San Diego before. It was the closest beach off the route taken.

I needed a hotel, so I drove around from hotel to hotel shopping for prices. The Ramada Inn gave me a sweet deal for the week. I paid the lady at the front desk before she had me fill out some paperwork giving me a key to my room. I was tired. All I wanted to do was shower and take a nap.

Hopping back into my truck, I drove around the hotel parking lot in front of my room number. I grabbed my bag from behind my seat and headed inside. When I opened the door, it was a relief to see a nice clean bed. I dropped my pack on the luggage rack, jumped in the shower then went to sleep.

I slept all the way till morning. I woke in a dark room with the sun's rays peeking through the curtains. Rays of light streaked the floor and across my bed as the thought of spending the day next to the ocean entered my mind.

I was showered, drunk, high, and fed from a continental breakfast by 10:00 am. I had a bathing suit rolled up in a towel along with an extra set of boxers to put on after my swim. At 10:30, I arrived in the public parking area of Ocean Beach by Tower 5. Just beyond where I was parked and out in the ocean, were a group of surfers waiting for their next set of waves. It was a beautiful site.

I changed into my bathing suit from behind the wheel of my car. When I stepped out from my vehicle, the sun was warm with a cool breeze. The smell of a salty ocean was in the air and all I could think about was body surfing a fast wave.

I crossed the sandy beach passing the guard tower on my right. A little further over, dogs ran wildly. A sign read, Dog Beach. I smiled as dogs splashed through the water. Some shook their fur with spits of water rain-bowing against the sun's light. It was a great day to be at the beach.

I threw out my towel along the sand. I popped out of my sandals taking my shirt off rolling it into a ball. Walking down to the water's edge, I listened to the rumbling waves crash hard against the ocean floor. The event was exhilarating.

Without thought, I walked straight out into the ocean. The water was freezing to say the least. My balls were tucked tight to my body in an attempt to warm themselves. My teeth clanked and I could not control the clatter. Instantly, I dove into the ocean swimming as far out as I could go. With all the brainwash, my mind was suddenly at peace. In that instant, I had forgotten all that had happened. I was rejuvenated with a new sense of life. I was free.

I spent an hour in the ocean riding waves to shore. Sometimes I got pounded to the ocean floor and other times I lost my suit around my ass cheeks. All in all, it was an exciting morning. I was having fun for the first time in a long time. Something I had been missing, but had not forgotten.

After the beach, I dried off and changed my clothes. I was in desperate need of drink, so I decided to walk into the shopping district to see if I could find a fun bar to hang out in. I needed somewhat of a dive.

I found exactly what I was looking for in a few short blocks from where I was swimming. The bar had a large front window open with stools lined on the inside looking out into the street. The parking area in front was lined at the curb with custom made choppers and the stools inside were occupied by a bunch of bikers out having a cold beer after a days' cruise.

I walked into the bar out from the sun and headed straight for the bartender. She was a blonde gal, a little older, with tight jeans and a wrinkled tan that said Bar Fly. She had a cute smile and an even cuter ass.

I ordered a double rum and coke then turned while she was pouring my drink to check out the scene on the inside. Basically, I was seeing if there were any hot girls worth talking too. And there was. Standing in front of a pool table was a girl my age maybe a little younger. She had cut-off jeans tight on her body riding high on her thigh. She had a nice tan against her blonde hair. Her top was yellow and she had all the features I was attracted too. We definitely needed to talk.

I pounded a drink than ordered another. When I was confident in starting a conversation, I strolled in her direction. As I approached, I smiled at her as she looked into my eyes. She smiled back.

Sitting in a stool closest to her, I watched as she and a friend shot their game of pool. Her friend was attractive as well, but I had my eyes on yellow shirt.

When yellow shirt finished shooting, she walked towards me picking up a beer from a counter a couple feet from where I was sitting. After a couple of swigs from her drink, she turned in my direction. We both smiled at each other once again before I asked, "So what's fun around here."

She looked over the rim of her glass and said, "You're looking at it, drinking and the beach."

I liked her sense of humor. We were going to get along great.

She introduced herself as Lucy. We shook hands before it was her turn on the pool table. As she shot her game, I watched her. She was beautiful.

Lucy and I got along great. I even shot a game of pool with her as her friend watched. We joked around and laughed with one-another. We ordered shots and beers, more shots and more beers. It couldn't have worked out better. She was perfect.

When it was time to go, Lucy gave me a hug. We exchanged numbers and decided to meet up later in the night around 10:00. I was excited she gave me her number, and even more excited to know I was going to see her again.

I left the bar shortly after Lucy then drove back to the hotel. I showered and slept till 9:00. When I got up, I went straight for the bottle. When I had enough alcohol in me, I smoked a joint. I was feeling good.

I was ready to head out the door by ten. I sent Lucy a text and she gave me directions where to meet up. I was anxious to see her and all I could think about was spending time with her. She was one of a kind and the girl I wanted to be with.

I rolled into the bar shortly after leaving my hotel room. The bar was packed upon my entry as I walked around in search of Lucy. She was sitting at a table with a couple of her friends drinking from a pitcher of beer. There was an open chair next to her, so I sat down beside her while she talked to one of the other girls. She smiled at my arrival.

When she was finished with her conversation, she introduced me to her friends. They were a lot like her, so I found it easy to carry on a conversation. They were a fun crowd and exactly what I needed to enjoy myself.

Lucy and I played darts and drank from pitchers of beer. We spent most of the night together as her friends disappeared one by one saying their good-byes. I was surprised because it seemed she was happy spending her time with me and nothing else really mattered.

After the bar we walked along the beach as the ocean crashed spraying its mist into the air. Sitting on a rock wall by the pier, we gazed out into the darkness absorbing whatever thoughts came to mind. She cuddled in next to me with her head against my chest. I wrapped my arm around her to keep her warm. Then we kissed.

I spent the rest of the week hanging out with Lucy. We partied at night and hit the beach when she had time. I spent the night at her place a couple of nights and on other nights she came to the hotel. The only problem, I had to leave.

On my last night in San Diego, Lucy and I sat on the beach as the sun dropped over the horizon. We had become so close it seemed we had known each other our entire lives. She was sad to see me leave and I was sad to see her go, but I promised I would be back for her someday. I decided to move to San Diego when the semester ended.

We had sex one last time and I was on my way home to Tucson.

*

I was back in school full force. My grades were close to a 4.0 and I couldn't complain. I continued to think about Lucy and she kept the dream of moving to San Diego alive. I wanted to go back to be with her.

Halfway through the second part of the semester, I lost contact with Lucy because I was brainwashed, drunk and high on drugs. I was getting drunk every night and the neighbors were selling me drugs left and right. The drugs kept me paranoid and the Elite kept up with their brainwash. I was on a ride I couldn't get off of. The brainwash made me drink. The drink made me do drugs. The drugs made me paranoid. And I would freak the fuck out. I couldn't find a happy medium.

Halfway through the second semester, the Elite told me the neighbors were trying to kill me. The neighbors were tweaking while sneaking around my house one night when the decision was made. While the neighbors were in the back of my home, the Elite used their key system to mess with them. They left bird noises on the neighbor's toes as they haunted the back yard. The neighbors became suspicious and they decided I was a threat to their lab, so they decided to off me.

I heard the commander's wife say, "Does he know yet?"

"*Know what*," I thought?

I knew there was something suspicious going on, but I didn't know what. My brain got me thinking and I said, "What are the neighbors trying to do, kill me?"

I knew the neighbors were pissed because I heard them outside talking one night. They were talking of their business and how it was no good for a guy like me living next door. I was able to hear this conversation directly from my screen door. They kept talking of the loud beeps the Elite were putting on them as they crept around the back yard. Personally, I think it scared them and they were ready to kill over it.

The Elite laughed when I asked if I was being threatened with death. One of them said, "They want to shoot you."

I was a fighter and I didn't care, but I was going to be damned if someone was going to kill me for no reason. I was going to put up a fight. I planned on fighting with my fists rather than a weapon.

A couple of days later, I drank from a bottle before walking out into my driveway ready to fight. I stood four feet from the fence leading to their yard and yelled, "Come out and fight fuckers. You're not going to kill me when I'm not looking."

I stood there for fifteen minutes yelling at the top of my lungs. I knew they were inside because I could hear them moving around. The only problem, they wouldn't come out. They stayed inside and waited for me to leave.

Days went by and all I could think about was walking in front of a window in my home with a gun pointed at me ready to shoot. The Elite also used the scenario as a play tactic to make me more paranoid. They wanted me scared.

I couldn't take the thought of dying without a fight. These tweekers were dirty and they never played fair. I needed to get out of my house and I needed to get out now. I needed to find a place to live until things chilled out for a bit.

I packed my truck with a sleeping bag, pillow, clothes and everything else I needed to survive in the back of my 4-Runner. I needed a place to shower, so I joined a racket club. They had weights, a swimming pool, a restaurant, a bar, cookouts on the weekends, showers and lockers to store some of my belongings. It was the ideal place to be.

During the day, I went to class. After class, I drove over to the racket club to eat, lift weights and swim in the pool. At night, I studied in the library at the University of Arizona. When I finished with my studies, I drove to a large bulk grocery store which was open twenty-four seven so I could sleep in their parking lot. I parked far away from the business hustle sitting in my truck smoking pot and drinking rum. When it was time to sleep, I crawled in the back of my truck with the sunroof open staring into the stars. When I was ready to finally go to bed, I would say goodnight to the Elite before falling asleep.

I went on like this for six weeks. I studied, I drank and I fell asleep. I was always working out. I was always at the University studying in their library and I was always at the grocery store sleeping in their parking lot. The neighbors were never going to find me and I was for sure never going to die.

At the end of the semester, I ended with a 3.25 GPA. Not the best, but good enough while undergoing the most severe brainwash ever known to man. I was proud of myself. I had done it. I had made the grades. I did it while sleeping in the back of my truck high on weed and drunk on rum.

I laughed at the thought…

The day after classes, I moved from my home. I stored all my furniture in storage and began getting ready for my trip to San Diego. I was moving and I was excited, but I had one last thing to take care of before I left. I had twenty-one days in jail to serve for a DUI I had been arrested for early in the semester, so I did my time before leaving.

CHAPTER 13

I had no idea where I was going to live in San Diego. My plan was to camp in a state park until I was able to find a place. I had my truck packed with my camping gear and I was ready to set up a site upon my arrival.

I rolled into San Diego around 6:00 pm. I had no idea which state park I would be able to camp in, so I spent two hours driving around until I found the ideal spot. It was a park set around a small fishing lake about forty miles outside of Diego. My site was surrounded by trees, a picnic area and fire ring. Just down the hill, I had a short hike to the lake.

I had to set up camp a little after the sun went down. I was tired from driving all day, so as soon as I had my campsite set up I went to sleep.

The next morning, I set up the kitchen then drove down the road to fill my coolers with food. I didn't know how long I would be staying in the park, so I only bought enough food to last a couple of days. And of course, I bought enough alcohol to last the same amount of time.

I didn't want to get too wasted, so after breakfast I smoked a little weed and drank a little from my bottle. Just enough to keep me level headed while I searched for an apartment. I didn't want my landlord thinking I was a drunk, so I figured I would deal with the brainwash for the day by staying slightly sober.

After the second day of searching for an apartment, I was becoming frustrated. A lot of the rentals near the beach were already rented for the summer and I simply couldn't find a place nice enough near the beach at a reasonable rate. Most of the rentals had fucked up kitchens and bathrooms, the two rooms in an apartment I care most about.

I drove around for two weeks in search of a place. Every day, I found myself back at the campsite frustrated. I hated apartment searching. It made me drink.

At night: I built fires in the fire ring, drank rum and smoked weed. Sometimes when I got really wasted, I would walk down to the lake and go for a swim even though the sign read, no swimming. I would swim out to the middle of the lake under the light of the moon and listen for the waters wake as fish jumped through the air. It was one of the most peaceful events in my life.

I was into my second week when I finally found a place to live. I rented a small cottage two blocks away from Ocean Beach. The bathroom was so-so and the kitchen was a bit run down, but manageable.

My father was coming down the following week, so he picked up my furniture from storage in Arizona and drove my belongings to San Diego. He was cool like that; always looking out for me.

I had my cottage set up with my furniture and I was partying on the beach in less than three weeks. I made friends with the neighbors across the street and they were fun people to be around. I enjoyed their company even though I was a bit of a mess at times. Brainwash, what could you do?

Their names were Alex, Reed and Annett. They liked to party and have a good time just like me. We had cookouts on the beach, swam in the ocean and occasionally hit the bars once in a while. I didn't have many friends while I went through these times with the Elite, but I considered the neighbors friends.

By the middle of the summer, I was a fucking mess. All day long, I would get drunk then scream at the top of my lungs toward the Elite. I would plead for them to turn off the satellite. I would scream for them to stop. I would cry and I would scream. I was venting. My brain could only handle so much. I would get drunk and fucking scream. I needed the thoughts out of my head.

I didn't know what to do. My life was a mess and these guys weren't going away. I had to call someone. I didn't want anyone to get into trouble I just wanted the satellite off my fucking head. It was tearing me apart from the inside out. It had to end.

One afternoon I was on a mission. I was on a mission to end the chaos. I jumped in front of my computer and Googled Naval Criminal

Investigation Services, NCIS. Like I said before, I really didn't know who these guys were for sure. But, I had an idea. Actually, I knew who they were I just can't say.

I was transferred to a man in his late thirties early forties. He was an agent for NCIS and he seemed fairly level headed. He had a caring voice, so I immediately put my trust in him. I didn't have a choice and I didn't have a reason not to.

I spilled my story to him. I had my phone in hand as I stood in the kitchen next to the refrigerator. I told him everything down to every last detail. I needed someone to talk too and it was a relief to have him on the phone. A quarter of the way through my story, I broke out into tears. I pleaded with him to turn off the satellite. I cried and I pleaded.

I said behind wet eyes, "Please help me. Please sir. Please help me. Just get it off my head."

I was so overtaken, I could no longer talk. My throat was bulging and my eyes were balling. I had nowhere to go. All I could do was cry into the phone pleading for it to end. I collapsed to the floor in front of the refrigerator. All I could do was cry. I cried without words.

While I sat there crying with my back against a wall, the Agent spoke. He said in a clear calm voice, "Boo, just calm down. Who's doing this to you and what's his name?"

I had to take a moment to come back to reality. I was lost with a broken heart and months of brainwash and torture. I had hope. I believed it was going to be over and this man was going to be the man to do it. He was going to be the one who stopped the insanity.

I gave him the name of the commander. I had a letter from the commander's wife. We had spoken to one another while I was living in the RV Park in Colorado. It was the letter she wrote while I accidentally called her fat. She had written down her husband's name on this same exact letter. I repeated the commander's name one last time.

The agent told me to calm down as I wiped dripping snot from my nose. He said, "I will hand this report to a Special Agent who knows more about this technology. Just give him a day or so to call you back. Try to hang in there."

He wrote down my phone number before ending the conversation. I didn't want him to leave. I was holding onto his voice in hopes of salvation.

Weeks went by, I heard nothing. I was trapped in the house going insane. The Elite just wouldn't let up. At one point, I was so fed up I grabbed the bottle of rum from the counter and started slamming the fire down the back of my throat. When I finished, I stood tall saluted the commander and began shouting at the top of my lungs, "Sir, Yes Sir."

I must have repeated myself a dozen times. Through the living room of my cottage, I could see one of the neighbors standing outside his home dumbfounded. His lips read, "He's going fucking crazy in there."

And I was. I was going fucking nuts.

I lost my marbles 100%. Shit was a fucking mess. I couldn't read anything, my thoughts made my head snap back in an attempt to control them, my memory was fading quickly, I was drunk and I was high at all times.

What was starting to eat at me the most, I was beginning to lose my memory. It started with sports teams. Then I wasn't able to spell very well. After I lost my ability to spell, my childhood memories became brainwashed. Everything I thought of in the past was overcome with rape and murder. It was fucking ridiculous. I couldn't think without somebody being tortured or killed.

Names of people went next. Then phone numbers. My math was all off. I had to guess at the right number until it was correct. Nothing was normal and I was afraid I would never be right in the head again.

"How am I going to get this shit out of my head," I thought to myself?

"Is it ever going to leave my brain?"

Before I knew it, I was being evicted from my cottage. The landlord had too many complaints from the neighbors, so I was out of there.

The entire summer, I was a wreck. Every night I would swim in the ocean around 2:30 AM, just after the bars had closed. I would body surf waves setting myself free. It freed my conscious. It freed my being. It was a ritual. Every night around the same time for the entire summer, I was in the water swimming. I was myself. I was relaxed.

I was going to miss the ocean. I was going to miss my freedom here. I wasn't going far, but far enough where I would no longer be free.

*

I moved into a nice apartment complex just across the way from the San Diego City College. I was starting classes in fall, so I actually lucked out with my location. I lived on the first floor. The kitchen and bathroom were both nice and the rooms were much larger than those of the cottage along the beach. The price was a hundred dollars more a month, but I was right downtown in the city of San Diego.

In a way, I was glad to be away from those who knew me at the beach. My insanity had gone to a whole new level and I was ashamed in the way I was acting.

With these thoughts, I decided to beat these Elite on my own. I didn't want anybody caring for me and I surely didn't want to care about them. It's just how it had to be. I could lose my mind and nobody would know who I was or what I was up too. The reason being, I looked even crazier when I told the story. Nobody believed it was true. Who was going to believe a kid could hear and communicate through an advanced spy satellite system?

I wouldn't have believed it either...

I sat around drinking my days away continuously yelling at the Elite. This time, I made sure I wasn't so loud the neighbors would be able to hear. I didn't want another landlord kicking me out of another apartment.

Another week and a half had gone by and I still hadn't heard back from NCIS. I was shocked since I had put so much trust in the agent whom I had spoken to. He seemed like a really nice guy and I just couldn't believe he would have blown me off. I decided to call one more time.

I dialed the number for NCIS and patiently waited for the receptionist to transfer me to the agent I had spoken to before. When he answered, I kept my composure as we spoke. I asked, "Were you able to find anything out?"

I was disappointed to hear he had not. He returned, "Did the special agent give you a call?"

I informed the agent that the special agent never attempted to call.

The agent then said, "Hold on. I think he's in the office today."

I waited a few minutes on hold before a man opened the line. He had a slight California accent and I could tell through his voice how much he liked his job. He asked what was going on, so I told him my story. I told him of all the technology that was being used against me including the key system the Elite were operating. I also let him know I was a real telepathic who also had the ability to hear through radio waves. I then explained I was able to hear through the satellite and how the Elite were using it to brainwash me.

The agent took a moment to assess the situation. He then took an unexpected turn. He said with an angry tone, "Boo, I want to know how you know about this technology and I want to know now. There are only a handful of people in the world who know this gear exists. I want to know how you know about, where you got your information and I want to know now."

I was taken aback by his attitude. I couldn't believe my ears. As I listened to him through the phone, I thought, *"If this man knows this gear exists, then why doesn't he believe me?"*

I told him once again, "I'm hooked up to the satellite. I can hear through the same frequency they're using and they're brainwashing me. They want me to commit suicide."

The agent had no belief in my story whatsoever. He said, "I looked up the commander's name and there isn't a man by that name anywhere in our database."

My heart sank. I had the wrong name. On the letter the commander's wife gave me, the last names were different. She didn't write down his real name. I was broken. I couldn't believe it. Without a name, they were never going to believe me.

I said to the agent, "This is a true story and it's really happening. Please keep investigating. I want this thing off of my head."

The agent returned, "You're a civilian and we can't help you, so stop calling here."

I thanked him before hanging up the phone. I sat on the couch thinking, *"What a bitch. I have nothing to prove this is happening, absolutely nothing."*

By the looks of things, this was going to go on for a really long time.

A few days later, the voices from the satellite had changed. New guys had showed, so I figured the old members had gone home. I was now dealing with a whole new set of Elite. They weren't giving up. They were going to send unit after unit until I killed myself.

I drank in every bar throughout the city for the next week straight. I didn't talk to anyone, I just drank. I drank and I drank and I drank. When I went home, I drank some more.

CHAPTER 14

Classes at the college had begun. I sobered enough to get through my day and drank enough to keep the brainwash at bay. I studied hard, I made all my classes and I kept good grades.

I was five weeks into the semester holding a 3.8 GPA when I lost my shit. The commander and his boys were pressing me hard. I was angry and I wanted to explode. I needed a release from hate.

I bought two forties of Mickey's and headed to the bay for a swim. I crossed over the Coronado Bridge onto Coronado Island. I parked my truck in the designated parking area just over the bridge on the right side of the bay. I pounded one of the forties then walked down to the water. I took my shirt off, kicked my sandals free then jumped in the water. It was cool and relaxing.

There were a set of boats tied to buoys in the bay. They were about a hundred yards out from where I was swimming, so I decided to head out to them and mess around a bit.

As I swam between the boats, I thought how nice it would be to own one myself. I knew they were a lot of maintenance and expensive, but the thoughts had my imagination going. I wanted to sail. I wanted to travel the world. I wanted to eat in unique restaurants and have sex with random foreign women. In reality, I wanted to be free from this torture.

I swam for about an hour before I decided to head home. In the truck, I slammed the second forty before driving away. I cursed the Elite and they cursed me back. They kept saying, "We don't want you. You're poison and a monster. You're a rapist and a murderer."

They were wrong. They were putting those thoughts in my head. I was drinking too much. That's the only thing I was doing wrong. I did have a drinking problem before their arrival, but now they were making it a lot worse.

"We're leaving you here," one of them had said.

I knew he was right, but I still wanted to go with them. When I asked why, the commander spoke. He said, "Because I don't want you and I don't like you."

He was still upset I had called his wife fat and threatened his family. He just wasn't getting over it. He wanted me dead. And now, he was going to leave me behind.

I yelled at the top of my lungs, "Fuck you, you peace of shit. You're not going anywhere and you're definitely not leaving me behind."

I was pissed and I wasn't going to let him leave. I threatened to write this book to ensure his stay. He wasn't going anywhere.

*

My parents were coming to town and I knew they liked historical museums. There was an old wooden ship which held a museum on board. You could buy a ticket, check out the museum then go for a sail around the bay. Since my parents liked both sailing and history, I thought it a good idea to check out the ship and buy some tickets before their arrival. So instead of heading home after my swim in the bay, I drove down to the waterfront where the museum boat was moored.

I passed the boat on my right before deciding to turn around. I had missed the entrance and was down a little ways from where I was supposed to be. I was in a side lane protected by a concrete curb and median strip. It was an area where you could park your car while buying tickets for the various fairies and whale watching adventures.

Just as I turned into this lane, I was stopped by a small vehicle which was illegally double parked. I waited for a few moments to see if anyone was driving. The cars hazards weren't on, so I figured somebody must have been behind the wheel.

I waited a couple of minutes before I decided it was time to go around the vehicle. As I turned the steering wheel, my hand accidentally hit the horn. Just as my hand hit the horn, a Mexican guy around the age of twenty-six walked in front of my truck. He proceeded to the driver's side window.

My window was already down as he came closer. Standing two feet away, he gave an angered expression and said, "What?"

At first, I didn't know what to say. I couldn't believe this guy was standing in my window starting shit. What was more embarrassing, the Elite began to laugh. One of them even called me a pussy. My face flushed as I became angered. I wasn't one to back down, but this just didn't seem like the time for a confrontation. I had enough bullshit going on in my life and I didn't need anymore.

I turned my head to face the man and said in a calm manner, "Get back in your fucking car before I get out of mine and kick the living shit out of you."

The man's eyebrows lifted to the severity of the situation. With the look in my eyes, I meant business. He wasn't expecting a guy like me. Instead of continuing with the confrontation, he turned his body and walked back to his vehicle. Without looking back: he opened the driver's door, hopped in and began driving away.

The Elite wouldn't let up. They wanted war. They wanted a fight.

The Elite spoke, "You pussy. That's not how we do it. Fight that kid."

With his words, I became agitated. I didn't want to fight. I was raised a tough kid, but I was tired of jails and prisons. Fighting simply caused too many problems in my life.

But, the Elite wouldn't give up. They ranted and raved. They made me believe I was nothing for backing down.

I couldn't take their banter. My brain had become overloaded and I was ready to explode once again. Without thought, I yelled, "You want me to fight that bitch. I'll fight. I'm going to show your commander what it's like not to quit. I'm going to show you pussies what not quitting is all about."

I pushed the gas pedal to the floor speeding to the vehicle in front of me; speeding toward the man who made me look bad in front of the Elite. He turned left into traffic, so I turned left in chase. When he made another turn, I followed. I was right on his ass at all times. I wasn't quitting.

The man noticed me following him. He made turn after turn trying to shake me from his tail. It was of no use. I wasn't letting go. I wanted the fight. I wanted to show the Elite what I was made of. I yelled, "I'm going to beat this mother fucker just like I'm going to beat you. I'm not giving up and you're not either. Tell your commander this is what not quitting is all about."

The Elite laughed. They instigated.

I followed the man. He tried to get away, but I was not letting him. Before I knew it, we were back where we started except we were on the other side of the street. He pulled into a parking lot filled with cars. When he stopped, I said to the Elite, "I really didn't want this and I really didn't want to fight this man. But, I'm going to show you what not quitting is all about."

I opened the door of my truck and stepped out. Pulling my shirt over my head, I tossed it to the hood of my vehicle. Walking towards the man's car, I had fury in my eyes. I was pissed and ready to fight.

The man watched as I approached. When I came nearer, he reversed his vehicle. It was then I realized he wasn't there to fight. Something else was going on.

I became confused. I stopped in my tracks to access the situation. I looked around. The man just sat in his car waiting. Something was wrong.

Within seconds, a police cruiser hopped the curb. The back end of her vehicle bounced as the weight of her car settled. The tires screeched ten feet from where I was standing. My heart sank with the realization; I was going to jail. The worst part, the Elite knew the man had made the call and they had given no warning.

I was busted and the Elite let it happen...

The women officer was short with blonde hair pulled back in a ponytail. She had her hand at her side ready to draw her firearm. She yelled, "Put your hands in the air and turn around facing your vehicle."

I did as she commanded. I put my hands in the air, turned around and faced my vehicle. She then said, "Walk towards your vehicle and put your hands against the side."

Again, I did as she commanded.

When she was comfortable with my placement, she walked up behind me as I heard the familiar sound of her handcuffs being pulled from her waist. All I could do was shake my head thinking, *"Not again."*

I was asked some questions about the incident before being placed in the back of the cruiser. I was being booked on criminal charges of DUI and criminal or terroristic threat. In the state of California threatening bodily injury on another human being is a felony. This meant I was on my way back to the State Penitentiary.

I was arrested by the harbor police so I was cuffed to a bench in their main office while the proper paperwork was being filed. It was an older building, so as I sat there I decided the place could use a makeover. A black officer with a good sense of humor checked on me periodically and of course I had nothing to say. I just sat there waiting to be hauled off to the county jail.

When the paperwork was finished, I was transported to the City Jail which was a few blocks from Harbor Police Headquarters. I was booked and placed into a holding cell awaiting a bed in the main facility. Eight hours later, I was moved to general population.

Three days later, I was transferred from the City Jail to another Detention Facility. It wasn't much better than the city jail and the food was all the same; shit. I read books and slept for six weeks awaiting court procedures.

When I thought about the arrest, I was glad in a way. I figured prison would be a good place to undergo brainwash. I wouldn't have to be a responsible member in society, I could be as crazy as I wanted, I would be free from drugs and alcohol and it would give me time to challenge the brainwash on a sober basis.

My lawyer was a public defender. I didn't want a real lawyer because I didn't plan on fighting the case. When I went to court, I was offered a two year sentence in the State Correctional Institute for a criminal threat. The DUI would run concurrent, so I wasn't awarded any extra time. I wasn't mad and I wasn't sad. I just wanted to be left alone. I didn't want the Elite around anymore. I signed a deal taking my freedom away.

Two weeks later: I was cuffed, shackled and placed on a prison transportation bus heading for a Correctional Institute between LA and San Diego. The entire ride I stared out the window dreaming of a better place. Prison sucked and brainwash sucked even more.

They called this prison, The Hotel. The reason being, it originally served as a luxury hotel. After the depression, the hotel couldn't afford to stay open so it was bought by the government and served as a Naval hospital. When the Navy no longer had use for its structures, the hotel was turned into a prison.

The Hotel also staged a classic song by the Eagles called, Hotel California. It was inferred that Don Henley from the Eagles had once stretched time behind its walls. From his stay, his memoirs were set in lyric creating one of the best classic rock songs ever.

The bus turned into the prison well after 2:00 in the afternoon. Up on the hill standing tall with history was the Hotel. The site made me dream of its earlier days; days of wealth and prosperity; days of laughs and memories; the days of Don Henley, the Eagles and Hotel California.

Such a lovely place…

When the bus finally stopped from it's not so long uncomfortable journey, I took a moment to realize where I was. I was back in the state penitentiary and it wasn't such a nice place to be. It was now my home for the next two years.

We were shuffled off the bus and told to line up along the yellow lines. We were herded like cattle and that's just how prison was. We were a meat market of inmates creating civilian jobs. Most of us had our problems and belonged here, but many like me were just troubled in life. I never actually believed I belonged in prison, but here I found myself once again.

After a quick head count and name verification, we were led inside a building and placed in a steal cage. Our handcuffs and shackles were removed as I rubbed my wrists from the cuff's grip. I stared at a cinder block wall while absorbing the prison scent: disinfectant, mold and body odor. I was tired of this shit and I was tired of these places. I just wanted a normal life once again.

Two hours later: I was dressed in blue, given a bed roll and led down a long hallway. Where I was going, to the chicken coops. It was a series of wooden shelters constructed in the shape of chicken coops, long and rectangular. They were set three feet off the ground to prevent them from flooding and were primarily built to house the wounded during war when it served as a Naval Hospital. In my mind, the place should have been condemned. It was a fucking shit hole.

I was placed in dormitory 211. There were around 100 inmates in the dorm along with myself. I checked in at the front office and was assigned a bed number then pointed in the right direction. As I walked towards my bunk, I was struck with unknown faces. I was the new guy, so all eyes were upon me sizing my strength and character.

Passing the restroom and showers on my left, I was struck by the familiar smell of marijuana and cigarettes. I laughed as heads poked from beyond making sure the shift guard wasn't on his way down the aisle as inmates smoked away. Their eyes were blazed over as they giggled at one another passing a joint around their circle.

When I arrived at my rack, I made my bed and put my clothes away in a steel locker. When I finished, I crawled in bed and went to sleep.

I didn't want to be here, but this was life for now. This was the life I chose by not backing down. I shouldn't have listened to the Elite. I should have walked away. I shouldn't have been in prison right now.

*

A week went by. I made friends with a youngster they called Tunes. He was a blonde haired kid from California and one of the coolest guys I had ever met. He too had no reason to be in prison, but I guess that's life. We hung out every day, we ate our meals together, we worked out together and we smoked pot together.

I tried brainwash sober, but it just wasn't happening. I needed my fix to stay level headed. I needed my fix to keep the Elite away.

One afternoon, I was called into the Lieutenant's office for job placement. I just finished smoking a joint with Tunes when the call came through. In fact, I had the end of the joint in my mouth when one of the fellas told me the news. Tunes laughed as I handed him the roach. I had ten minutes to get to the office and I was high as a kite.

I walked into the Lieutenant's office right on time. I had marijuana breath and red eyes. To my relief, nobody noticed. I was led into a room where an assignment committee sat around a circular table. The Lieutenant was just to my right as a man pulled my file to review my work eligibility.

After a brief overview, I was asked a few questions about my work history. I was also asked about my schooling. I told the man I had gone to college and was still working on my BA hopefully to finish when I was out of prison.

He smiled in my direction before being interrupted by the Lieutenant. The LT asked, "So are you good with a computer?"

I confidently answered, "Yes."

She sat back in her chair taking a pause before saying, "Well, that's great because I could use an extra clerk in my office right now."

I didn't want to show my joy. Instead, I calmly answered, "That would be great. I'm good with computers and I'm very familiar with an office setting. My parents own a business and I have worked for them for many years."

I sat there excited. The reason, clerk work in a penitentiary is the best job I could have. I didn't have to work in the kitchen where the work can suck. I didn't have to dig holes or rake gravel and leaves. All I had to do was sit in an office and shuffle paperwork all day. It was the perfect job for me.

Satisfied, the head of the committee closed my file and said, "Well, there you have it. You will be working for the Lieutenant. She will send a work schedule for you."

I smiled thanking them before heading out of the office.

*

I worked for the Lieutenant for close to two weeks before I became bored. The work was slow and there wasn't much to do. Most of the time, the other inmates who worked for the Lieutenant and myself just sat around all day shooting the shit. It wasn't much fun, but it was an easy job.

It wasn't long before the yard discovered my telepathic abilities. At night I would play Pinochle and Poker. While playing these games, I would pick up a telepathic thought. At first I kept it to myself, but after time I began showing the guys my ability by answering some of their thoughts. Being the only telepathic in the world, rumor ran fast.

In time, word spread to the Lieutenant's office. I overheard one of the civilian secretaries speaking one day. She was a short Mexican women and a little high on herself. She spoke to the other woman in the office who was also Mexican. The other woman was a bit more down to earth holding a great sense of humor.

She said, "Did you hear Boo is Telepathic."

The girl with the sense of humor answered with shock in her voice, "No way."

The other girl then said, "That's what they say and they say it's true."

Overhearing their conversation made me blush for a moment. I was proud to be telepathic, but it didn't work very well. I only picked up thoughts here and there and most of the time when somebody tried talking to me telepathically I wasn't able to answer because I wasn't able to hear. It was a random occurrence to hear a thought. But when I did hear, I made sure to answer the person's thought just to prove I was the real deal.

Well, one day I walked into the secretary's office to ask a question about some paperwork I had in my hand. As I entered the office, the high on herself Mexican women looked up from her computer. A thought entered my head. She said, "He's hot."

I smile before answering, "So, you think I'm hot huh?"

She was a married woman and like I said, she was high on herself. It embarrassed her that she was attracted to an inmate. She was even more embarrassed I had heard her thought on the matter. She blushed. She said, "Oh my god. You really are."

I laughed as the situation became awkward for her. I could see by the expression on her face. I didn't know what else to say, so I just walked out of the office taking a seat in front of my computer.

Sitting there, I listened for her response. She was whispering to the other gal and in the end all I heard was, "I don't want a guy around me who can hear my thoughts."

My heart sank. In some odd way it made me feel unwanted. It made me feel like she had turned on me. She made me feel different from everyone else.

The next day, I was called into the Lieutenant's office. She sat me in a chair and said, "Boo, you're doing a great job here, but I'm going to have Tic take your position. The rest of the inmates in this office are Asian and I think it would be good to have another Asian working with them."

I knew Tic well. He was in my dorm and he was a great guy. We played cards at night and on occasion he lent me books to read. I had no problems with Tic however I did have a problem with losing my job over a secretary who was insecure with her thoughts around me.

With the look on my face, I was displeased. With the look on the Lieutenant's face there was hope. She said with a clever smile, "I'm going to make you a taxi driver on the yard. You're going to drive a golf cart around picking up various employees here in the facility taking them to their destinations. With your personality, it's a better place for you. I think you're going to love it."

I smiled. She smiled. It was the absolute best job you could have at the Hotel.

*

My taxi was a six man golf cart with scrapes and scratches down the right hand side do to the rumor of an Asian who rolled the fucking thing. They say he put it in neutral to go as fast as he could downhill and when he had to make a turn he cut the wheel too wide hitting the curb rolling the cart on its side. Funny shit is all I can say.

My first day was great. I drove around the prison yard picking up passengers here and there as I saw them. I had nurses, doctors, prison guards, captains, administration and drug counselors all riding in the back seat of my vehicle. The conversation was always good and I always caught the cool prison yard stories from those who filled my seats. I got the scoop on every fight, every needle and every drug bust. The stories couldn't get more entertaining and I couldn't be happier.

In the morning after chow, I was able to have two sack lunches for my days driving adventure; one of the perks of being a taxi driver. In my sack I was given two packs of meat, nuts, fruit and sometimes chips. The meat always sucked, so I fed it to my buddies.

I had two stops for seeing my buddies. The first stop was behind the gymnasium where a gray female cat roamed the yard. She had three kittens with blue eyes. I fell in love with all four of them.

Every morning, I would park my taxi next to the chain-link fence behind the gym. With the sound of my engine, the kittens would run with their little legs moving fast. They came from a wooden storage shack three feet away. As I tore pieces of meat from my sack, they would patiently wait for the ends to be thrown through the fence. Their heads would move up and down and at times I swore they were smiling at me. I loved those little guys.

After a ten minute visit, I would drive over to my next set of buddies. These guys were really cool. It was a family of raccoons who lived over by the chow hall. Around 8:00 am they would walk across the roof of the breezeway, down a tree then over to my cart. Sitting in my taxi, I would tear pieces of meat from my second sack lunch. The raccoons would come along side of me and stand on their back legs; it was the neatest thing ever.

They stood like humans. When I was ready to feed them, they would reach out with their hands and gently grab the meat from me. It was wild.

There was another taxi driver like myself. His name was Jordan. He was a chill black guy in his late forties who always smiled, always laughed and always had something funny to say. He was my buddy as well. The funniest thing about Jordan, he was missing a tooth in the front on his upper set. I thought it added to his character. It made me smile when he talked. It fit him perfectly.

Jordan and I talked shit, passed each other and lusted after the same hot nurses in the yard. It was funny because we had the same taste in women. We had similar stories and our characters weren't too far apart from one another. He was a good guy, married with children. We had great conversations and he always had me laughing hysterically.

My nights at the Hotel weren't too bad. I read books, I played chess and I played cards to make the time pass. Some nights were slower than others, but I always seemed to get through them with as little boredom as possible.

One night I was lying in bed talking to the Elite as subtly as possible. I had my head angled in a position so nobody could see or hear and whispered away. A lot of times they just told me to kill myself, but most of the time we would laugh at my stories and whatever shit I could come up with in my head.

On this particular night, something weird had happened. I was laying there when one of the Elite spoke. I don't remember what he had said, but what had happened was amazing. I felt the vibration from his voice on my chest.

I stopped talking and said, "Holly shit, do that again."

"Do what," the soldier asked.

"Talk again. I felt that shit on my chest. The vibration from your voice touched me," I continued.

The soldier spoke and I felt the same vibration.

"That's fucking cool," I returned. "Your laser is breaking the air just like the base from a speaker and I can feel it on my body. That's wild."

The Elite laughed. Moments later the vibrations came threw more distinct. I can't even explain the feeling I was getting on my chest. I figured they amplified their laser making the touch more pronounced.

Soon, I could hear them tapping on the laser sensitive computer screen they used with their technology. The base was thumping my body and the only way to explain it is to say it was actually indenting my skin where the laser was directed.

Next, they moved the laser to my stomach and began beating on my stomach. I was laughing as my body thumped. The Elite were laughing as well.

What happened next was completely uncalled for. The fun abruptly stopped when the Elite took it too far. They directed the laser on my asshole and began thumping my sphincter. My smile faded, my heart sank and I began thinking, "*Oh no, they're raping me now.*"

I pleaded for them to stop, but they wouldn't. I screamed into my pillow. They laughed and kept going. At one point, tears rolled down my cheek. I was being raped and there was nothing I could do to fight back.

That night, I cried myself to sleep...

I woke up the next morning to the thumping of my asshole. The Elite were at it again. I didn't know what to do or what to say. I silently pleaded for them to stop raping me, but they wouldn't. All I could do was take it.

After a good two hours of being raped, my mind formulated. I had to convince myself this was normal and it was my body reacting to something else. That it wasn't the Elite. I had tears and anger. I kept thinking it was going to be okay.

What made it most difficult was the fact that somebody was doing it to me. See, if I fell and hurt myself it's nobody's fault. Knowing someone is intentionally harming me makes the scenario that much worse. I can't make them stop and there is no way to retaliate. Mentally it's tougher to deal with and in time it doesn't go away.

When I yelled for them to stop, they would answer, "Just kill yourself. It's the only option you have."

Then they would all laugh...

Two days later, I was a drag. I wasn't talking to anyone, I walked around like a zombie and I was being raped every waking moment of the day. Words can't explain the emotions I went through. Psychologically, I couldn't block it out. It was both physical and mental. It was crushing me.

By the fourth day, I had enough. All I could do was act like it wasn't affecting me. Even though it was, I couldn't show my expressions or feelings. When I did, they just made it worse.

Then one day, I walked around feeling like I had to take a shit. At first I didn't realize what was happening, I just felt like I needed to have a bowl movement. I went to the bathroom and nothing came out. The Elite were hysterical. I asked, "Is that you guys?"

One of them returned, "We have it hooked up to your prostate."

This kid was new and he was cocky. The way he said it, I wanted to tear his fucking head off; fucking punk. He thought he was the coolest thing alive. He called himself a God. I laughed when he said this. I returned, "You're no fucking God, you're a fucking rapist."

The Elite over stepped their boundary by introducing rap to the situation. I figured these boys were going to do life in prison if they ever got caught. In Four days I was rapped over a thousand times by them.

The only problem is, they are who they are and they all can't go to jail. I figured I'd just go after their commander who was in charge of this mess. It was his battle and not theirs. He's the man I'm after. He's the man I'm going to punish for these crimes.

My only defense against the Elite while I was in prison was to smoke weed. I smoked every day.

I went fourteen months with the Elite yelling in my ears when I tried to sleep. When I wasn't sleeping, I was being raped and tortured. They even began making loud clapping noises in my ears with their key system. This key system made many noises. They used it directly on my ear drums. At times it was so loud my ears would ring. It sucked and I hated them for it. I wanted my revenge.

CHAPTER 15

I was released from prison after fourteen months for good behavior. My father was in the parking lot waiting as I exited the security gate. He had a smile on his face and I could tell he was happy to see me free from incarceration.

We jumped in the rental car he was driving since he flew in from Colorado. As we drove away from the prison, I looked high on the hill towards the hotel and said to myself quietly, "Well Don Henley, it wasn't such a lovely place after all."

I laughed thinking of his stay. I laughed thinking what a good story this was going to make someday...

We stopped for lunch at an Italian restaurant where I ate the best meal I've had in a long time. When I was finished, my father said, "I bet that tasted good."

I smiled nodding my head in approval.

After lunch, we drove back down to the city of San Diego where my father had a hotel room for a few nights. We spent our days looking for apartments and our nights eating fancy meals in nice restaurants around town.

On the second day, we found a nice one bedroom apartment for rent in the North Park area of San Diego. Located four miles from the city and just a short drive to the beach, it was the ideal place to be.

I signed a six month lease with the rental agency before heading over to the storage center to remove my belongings. While in prison, my brother moved my things for me so I remembered to thank him when I had a chance. My father rented a moving truck and in just few short hours we had everything moved in. By the end of the day, my pad was hooked up and I was relieved to finally have a home again.

My father flew home to Colorado the following day. I took the day to relax knowing I had to look for a job. My Schooling was on hold and I felt it best I just work while going through these chaotic times with the Elite.

The problem was, the Elite's torture made me drink. When I drank as heavily as I did, fucked up shit happened. The party never ended and I had lost so much of my brain there was no telling what could happen next, especially when I drank. Having them around was a fucking disaster.

The good news, dealing with the Elite while sober forced me to build natural defenses against the brainwash and torture. I was now able to deal with the stress on a different level.

I spent almost a week searching the internet and newspaper looking for a job. On a Sunday, I read an article in the classifieds of the paper. It said, make $500.00 to $2,500.00 a week. No prior training required. Sales.

I dialed the number and set an appointment to meet with the man in charge.

The next day was a Monday. I dressed in khakis and a tie before heading to my appointment. When I walked through the door, I was greeted by a man named Brian. He was short with brown hair wearing a great smile. Our dress was similar and I could tell by his demeanor he was an excellent salesman.

We shook hands before he led me to his office. The job was newspaper sales for the local paper. I was told I would be setting up a kiosk throughout the San Diego area in a variety of shopping centers pitching the paper. I would be on commission pay, so my salary depended on how many papers I sold. I was able to make my own hours and I was mobile. All I had to do was get people to sign up for the paper and turn in my slips twice a week.

An hour later, I was ready for work. I had order forms and a portable kiosk when I walked out the door. Brian had me scheduled at a grocery store in downtown San Diego, so my commute wasn't bad at all. The next day, I sold the paper.

In six hours, I sold seven paper subscriptions. For each person who signed up, I made thirty dollars commission. I made two-hundred and ten dollars in seven hours on my first day.

Within the first two months of working, I became one of the top ten newspaper salesman in California. The reason for this, I discovered the lead salesmen in our office made a hundred to a hundred and fifty-thousand dollars a year selling the paper. I learned how to sell a paper real fast and I was good at it.

Three months later, my boss came to me and said, "Boo, I have some great news for you. I'm teaming up with a buddy of mine and we are starting our own business north of here as well as the Los Angeles area. I'll give you forty dollars a slip and the paper will be a lot easier to sell. The promotions are insane. Sign up for the Sunday only paper for a year. It costs the customer twenty bucks and you will get forty dollars in commission for each sale. You're going to make a ton of money."

My eyes lit with dollar signs. If I sold ten papers a day, I would be bringing home four hundred dollars a day. It was perfect. The only problem was the commute. I had a two hour drive each way every day. With how much money I would be making, I didn't find it a problem. I was ready to sell.

My first month up north, I made a little over seven thousand dollars. Soon after, I was making eight to ten-thousand a month. I was killing it. I couldn't believe how much money I was making. The Elite couldn't believe it either. I even made them jealous a bit. They kept saying to each other, "I can't believe how much money this kid makes selling the fucking paper."

I laughed every time I heard them speak with jealousy. It made me happy.

Six months into it, I was living large. I moved out of my place and into a luxury apartment in the Mission Valley area of San Diego. My furniture fit nice and I was right around the corner from the pool. I drank beers at night and soaked in the hot tub shaded by palm trees. Life didn't get much better than this.

While I was working for the paper in San Diego, I met a girl named Danni. She was cute with dark hair and tanned skin. After talking with her for a bit I discovered she was a mixed race of Caucasian and black. Like me, she was from Colorado. She was cool and chill as they came and we had become good friends.

Danni had some troubles with her roommates, so she ended up staying with me for a couple of months. I was glad for her company and she always had a way of making me laugh. We got along great and I even got her a job with the paper. We partied at night and worked during the day.

*

I walked into work one day high on life. I was making great money, I had a nice pad, I was banging every hot chic that walked and I could care less what the Elite were doing to my head.

I was set up in a grocery store in Corona California. I had my fifth slip in the first two hours. That means I was making a hundred dollars and hour. I had a smile on my face knowing the customer had no idea how much money I was really making doing this shit.

The Elite couldn't believe it. One of them said to their commander, "How this kid lives, you're never going to get him to kill himself."

Four hours later, I had ten slips totaling four hundred dollars and still going. I was ecstatic. At this rate I was going to have an eight-hundred dollar day. And I almost did. I went home with 18 slips in my hand totaling seven-hundred and twenty dollars.

The Elite had been rapping me through the satellite system for over a year and a half. They even came up with new methods. I guess that's what happens when you sit in front of this kind of technology all day with nothing else to do but rape.

What they were now doing was insane. Well, I have to say the feeling was insane. They would target my genitals with one of their lasers and blow on the laser sensitive monitor screen. The effect from the air hitting the screen then sending millions of sound or air waves through the laser to the human body was intense. It gave my ball sack the weirdest chilling sensation I had ever felt in my entire life.

I was working in Corona again. I was set up in the same store as last time and I was ready to make some money. I started with my pitch to a lady pushing a grocery cart. She had a baby in a car seat on top of the cart and a four year old daughter next to her holding onto her leg. What happened next was unbelievable.

As I stood there pitching the paper to her, her hips started swirling. She grunted in a sexual desire. Her face blushed and all of a sudden she held onto her daughter as she realized what was going on. With the other hand, she turned her cart frantically trying to get away. The look on her face as she gazed over her shoulder said it all, she was being raped.

The first time it happened, I laughed. I said to the Elite, "You guys are a bunch of idiots. You can't rape the public. It's going to make all of this true."

The Elite laughed back. They didn't care. All they cared about was ruining my fucking life.

I went on with my day like nothing was happening. A lady in her seventies came over to my kiosk. She was still holding her youth with her look and if I had to judge I'd say she was a complete hotty in her day. She had her sunglasses through her blonde hair. She had a nice tan. She was witty and smart and by the looks of it she still liked having sex.

She stood in front of my table with a smile on her face. The Elite were cracking up. They were raping a senior citizen. Her hips moved. She had the look of a sexual sensation. She gave me this smile as we talked. She breathed heavily as she signed up for the paper. When she was finished, she said with lust, "You know how to treat an older woman."

I thanked her for signing up for the paper. She winked at me before grabbing her free paper. She turned her cart around and walked away as if she had the time of her life. She was happy and she didn't care how or why it happened. It felt good and she liked it.

My sales totals were down; way down. The Elite raped everything that came my way. Women were grabbing their children almost running away. Some yelled at me and some simply said, "That's not right. That's not how you sell the paper."

One lady was so pissed off she came over to my table, grabbed a stack of papers and threw them in my face. Again there was nothing I could do. I was being rapped. Society was being rapped. And by the looks of it, these guys were going to get away with it. The worst part, I was losing my business. I had high rent bills to pay and the money wasn't coming in like it used to.

I went to business after business trying to sell the paper. I went through at least three-hundred people a day. All of them were raped by the Elite. I was doing two to three slips a day. That's only because there were a few desperate house wives out there who needed a little loving.

I stressed the fuck out. I drank and did drugs. I showed up to work a fucking mess. Sometimes I was wasted and other times I was just hung over from the night before. I wasn't going to quit. I couldn't, it was my job and the only way I knew how to make good money.

At one point, I was drinking from a pint of rum I kept in my shoulder bag. I was drinking, popping pills and snorting lines in the bathroom of the department store. I was slurring my words and selling was useless. The women were being raped constantly. The Elite never gave up. They raped dude after dude and woman after woman. Selling was virtually impossible. They saw how bad the rape was affecting my business, so they rapped more and more. I had been going to work for weeks pitching the paper. And for weeks, I watched hundreds into the thousands of civilians raped.

Then, it got worse. I was sitting in a well-known department store high as a kite. I had a glaze of cocaine pouring from my nostril as my tie hung half off the collar. I had a rum and coke in front of me disguised in a paper Coca-Cola cup and a pocket full of uppers I popped repeatedly. Life was a bitch. I was losing everything.

A mother walked in with her children. I could barely hold my head up. I looked at her. She looked at me. The Elite laughed. She had two adult daughters and a boy. The daughters had to have been under twenty years of age but over eighteen. They were Mexican and I don't think the Elite gave a fuck. At the same time, the entire family gazed down toward their private areas in shock.

The mother's hand dropped to her vagina and she began holding herself. The other daughter's did the same. I was crushed. Tears boiled in my eyes. The mother took another look in my direction. My head hit the kiosk bouncing as she pulled her children away. She was pissed. She knew her family was being raped in some odd fashion. She had tears in her eyes.

Family after family, man after man and woman after woman were all raped by the Elite. The Elite were relentless. They raped everything that walked in my path. They raped me.

On one particular day, I watched as they raped a nine-teen year old little girl. She was handicapped. Her leg shot out to the side and she walked from the hip. Her left arm was twisted at her side. She had black hair and glasses. She was pretty with a cute little smile. She held onto her father's hand for support.

She looked at me. She looked at her private area. She looked at me. She looked at her private area. She looked at her father. She looked at her private area. Her hand went between her legs and she cried...

I cried...

Ten minutes later her father came back. He didn't say anything he just looked around my kiosk for anything funny. He looked at my hands and he looked at my pockets. He looked at me. He was pissed. His daughter was upset. I could do nothing once again.

On another occasion, I was standing in the parking lot of a department store waiting on the curb. A girl around the age of eighteen was standing a couple of feet away from me. She seemed happy. She twirled around her toes without a care in the world. She looked at me. I thought, "*Oh no.*"

Her face was deformed. She was a little Mexican girl. Her jaw shot out six inches from her cheeks. She had no lips. She had no teeth. She had a large circular hole for a mouth and it never closed. Her eyes were soft. She was pretty with dark hair. She was skinny. She was gentle in expression. She was deformed.

Her eyes went sad. She stopped dancing. She looked between her legs. She was frightened. She looked towards me for help. She touched between her legs to a feeling she had never felt before. She was being raped by the Elite.

I saddened. I turned my shoulder and said to the Elite, "You guys are a bunch of assholes."

The Elite laughed. They even raped her mother when she came to get her child.

One of the Elite was so distraught over the situation he said, "This isn't right. We shouldn't be doing this to him or these people."

He turned to his commander and said, "Give the order to stop doing this. You're going to get us in trouble."

The commander returned, "In trouble for what? I want that kid dead. He knows all of our secrets."

The Elite member said, "You're going to get us in trouble for rape."

The commander returned, "How's he ever going to prove it."

In three and a half weeks, I watched over three-thousand civilians here in the United States get raped in this unusual fashion by the Elite. Why? Because I called a commander's wife fat accidentally and I insulted him and his family. The man belongs in Federal Prison and I plan on sending him there. Just because he is a leader of this Elite organization doesn't give him the right to treat people in his own country in this manner.

I lost my business. I had zero sales and was now looking at moving out of my luxury apartment. I stayed drunk and high off my ass for days. I called my parents intoxicated telling of the rape. They didn't believe me. They believed I was mentally ill instead. I was told to call a psychiatrist and get on medication. I laughed thinking, *"There isn't a pill in this world that's going to cure this. These mother fuckers aren't letting up. They're trying to kill me."*

I hung up the phone and cried. I cried and I cried. When Danni came home, she found me in the corner of my back patio with a bottle of rum in my hand. Speed pills poured out of my pockets onto the concrete and I could barely move. I was in shock from the last three and a half weeks.

In my head, I watched every single victim being raped over and over again. In total, I would have to say over a hundred children were brutally raped by the Elite as well as three thousand American men and women. Some of them were deformed, some of them were pregnant and some of them were gay. They even raped the senior citizens. The scene was horrific.

One of the Elite even had the nerve to say, "Where's all your money now?"

I thought to myself, *"I may not have my money, but you lost the war. You raped the public and it's going to come back and bite you in the ass."*

I smiled...

*

I moved from my apartment into a house in Pacific Beach. I had three roommates, one owned a weed shop and the other was in the construction field. The girl who lived separately in the back of the house was a nurse who I didn't care for much.

Lance and Skip were the two roommates who I liked the most. They didn't give a fuck what I did and the first night staying in the home we laughed in the living room because I ditched the taxi driver on his fare. The reason being, I simply didn't like the way the man talked to me on the way home from the bar. I had him drop me a couple of blocks from my house then walked up to his window like I was going to pay then turned around and ran. He chased me in his car for ten minutes before I was able to lose him through an alley then a set of back yards.

When I got home, I was drunk and out of breath. The taxi cruised the streets as I looked out my front window from behind a set of curtains. Lance and Skip were cracking up when I told them the story. What can I say? The man was from another country. He was a wiseass and he didn't like Americans. I could tell by the way he spoke to me.

I lived at the home for a couple of months before I was sent back to prison on a parole violation. I got busted by the police for public intoxication and possession of a controlled substance. Since I was already on parole, the District Attorney dropped the charges and I was sent back to the penitentiary for a period of six months. I was sent to a facility they called Walley's.

Walley's wasn't as bad as I thought. The facility was in good shape and the inmates weren't horrible to deal with. I spent my time reading books and making hooch out of apple juice and sugar. I was out of there before I knew it and back on the beach where I left off.

I moved back in with Lance and Skip. In fact, I really never left. I had left all my furniture there and rented out my room to a guy for six months. The same amount of time I was going to be gone. It worked out perfectly. The guy was gone two weeks before I got home. I moved my clothing out of the back shed and was right back in my place.

I worked for a house painter during the day. It was summer again and there was plenty of work. The guy's name was Andy. He was a great dude with a great family. The Elite raped his daughter. She never told on me and in fact I let her in on the secret of what was going on. She was a cool little surfer girl, so she didn't mind. I even read her thoughts a couple of times, so she would believe in me. Every day when I showed up for work, she had a smile waiting. She wanted me to win and she wanted me to win badly.

The Elite kept on raping. Whenever we showed up for a job no matter where it was, the Elite raped everyone around me. I even heard an eighty year old woman tell her daughter one day as I was painting their back porch. The lady said, "That's the boy with powers."

The daughter laughed. I laughed. I thought, *"If only these people knew the true story."*

Soon, I had lost my job. I don't know why, but Andy was suddenly out of work. I figured it had something to do with the Elite's rape. In fact, I knew this was the reason. I went home, drank a bottle of rum and prepared to move out of my place. I was going to have to live in the ghetto to beat these fuckers. I wasn't going to let them take another thing away from me.

I sold all my furniture to my roommates for six hundred bucks, packed a bag full of clothes and moved to a seedy roach infested apartment complex downtown San Diego. It was a shit hole and the perfect place for me.

CHAPTER 16

The apartment I moved into was fucked. There was an elderly lady who lost her marbles. She stood outside the main entrance with a cigarette in her hand and a wool cap pulled tight over her head. It didn't matter if it was a hundred degrees or forty degrees outside she always wore that cap. She talked to herself and she yelled.

She yelled, "Yaba dabba. Yabba dabab cadoo."

Every time I passed her, I felt as if I was living in a mental institution. The rest of the building was filled with people just like her. It was a fucking nut house. Some seemed sane, but inside they were just as crazy as the lady on the front entrance, "Yaba dabba caddo."

I drank and I did drugs. I can say I was depressed. For a kid like me, it was hard to get me down. I loved life and I loved living. I loved people and I loved animals. I loved trees, flowers and spirits. Most of all, I loved being me.

Some days were worse than others. I would wake up with a drink in my hand and pass out in the same fashion. I didn't know what to do and my world was collapsing around me. The Elite weren't letting this one go. They were going to keep sending soldiers until I was dead.

I called NCIS numerous times only to get the same reply. They would say, "You're a civilian and we can't help you."

They didn't believe my story even though they were aware of the technology the Elite controlled. In my mind I thought, *"How could somebody be so stupid to not realize a kid was telling them of top secret classified technology which they were aware of and to still not see the truth in my story. How stupid could they be?"*

I called so many times they began speaking to my parole officer. They told him to talk to me and to have me stop calling their agency. I was given a direct order by my parole officer to no longer call NCIS. If I did, it was to be determined a parole violation and I would be sent back to prison. I had to obey and I did. I never called them again.

NCIS was aware these guys were rapping people due to my phone calls and they did absolutely nothing. If they did investigate, the Elite lied to them to cover for their actions. Total fucking bullshit.

One night, I came home from the bars completely wasted. I stepped into the elevator onto a puddle of piss. My shoes made a splash. It was the third or fourth time this happened. I looked towards the ceiling of the elevator and said out loud, "This is not happening. This can't be happening."

Then I yelled for the Elite to shut off the fucking satellite. I wobbled. I held onto the wall to gain my balance. Reaching for my zipper, I pulled out my dick and began pissing all over the walls of the elevator. I had become crazy too.

When the elevator door opened, I stepped out feeling a sense of relief. For some reason pissing in the elevator made me feel as if I was getting back at something. Getting back for the place I was living in.

Down the hall, I bumped into a man around my age. He had on a t-shirt with the sleeves cut off. His eyes were wide and I could tell he was on something. He was on exactly what I needed. I needed a pick me up. I needed some speed.

I stopped him, asked him for some shit and was granted my wish. He pulled a fifty dollar sack from his pocket and handed it to me. I gave him the money and walked away.

Back in my room, I sat on the edge of the bed. I looked around. The room was no bigger than a jail cell. The shower and toilet were right next to my bed separated only by a short wall. There were no doors except for the entrance. The bed was a single bed quilted with a fabric from a cheap hotel. The floor was linoleum and the shelf holding an old television was pink. I had one window and no place to run. I was stuck.

I grabbed a bottle of rum from a short refrigerator in front of my bed and began pounding its fuel. Alcohol poured down my cheeks as I drank thinking I couldn't get enough. It was the only escape I had and it sucked. In my hand, a white sack of speed having the power to bring me back from this drunken slumber.

I sniffed a line. I smoked a foil. I sniffed and I smoked. I smoked that shit until I was high in the clouds. Then, then I freaked out.

Speed made me paranoid. I don't know why I kept doing the shit because every time I did it was a fucking disaster. Thoughts raced through my head. The Elite knew the program so they added to them.

Soon, I was looking around the room with weird feelings and emotions. I would get stories stuck in my head. My imagination would get the best of me. I would think people were invading our country. I would think I had a bomb secretly planted in my mist and the Elite were here watching. North Koreans, Chinese and Aliens were all stuck dead center in my fucking head. The worst one, people were out to kill me.

The next thing I knew, I was walking down the center of the highway next to a median. Cars were passing at sixty miles per hour. It was raining and I was soaked. Everywhere I looked, North Koreans were hiding in the bushes. They were in the shrubs and on the other side of the over-pass. I didn't know which way to turn.

The Elite used their key system to tap on my body. They used it to make the sounds of bullets whistling past my ears. My brain on the drugs and brainwash made me believe the scenario a reality. We were under attack and I was going to die.

Two Navy helicopters flew overhead. They were loud and with the rain brought on a sense of war. My imagination ran wild. My heart thumped as my legs kept on walking.

I ended up in North Park not trusting a single soul. Everywhere I looked seemed unfamiliar. Everyone I saw was the enemy. Everyone was out to get me.

I walked in a daze for blocks. When somebody was on my side of the street, I would quickly cross to the other side. I didn't want to die and I definitely didn't want to die like this. I was freaking the fuck out.

When the drugs finally wore off, I found myself down by the San Diego Zoo. The sun was coming up and I was drenched from the night's rain. I felt like I had nowhere to go. I had made it and I was still alive. I needed to go home. I needed to get sober.

I went weeks like this. I would get drunk and get high. When I got high, I flipped out. For some reason my brain wasn't letting me get away from the drugs. I knew what they were doing to my head and I kept doing them. The brainwash was too much for my imagination and the drugs were making it even worse.

The brainwash was killing me...

The drugs were killing me...

*

I was in my room at the apartment complex when a moment changed everything. It was around eight o'clock in the evening as it began to get dark. I wanted to smoke a cigarette, so I traveled the elevator to the first floor. I walked out of the elevator and towards the patio area where a set of metal tables and chairs were set around an array of planters. It was my favorite place in the complex.

Through the double doors, I headed for my favorite spot back in the left hand corner secluded from the crazies and riff-raft. On my way, I stepped in something with my sandals. It was mushy making my sandal slide to the side. It was hard to see and a bit dark. It oozed a bit between my big toe; a piece of fruit perhaps.

Moving to the side, I let light from the food court window enter the concrete walk. There, on the ground, lay a human turd. To the right of the turd a couple feet away lay a pair of woman's panties. I was completely grossed out.

"*Yabba Dabba*," I thought. It had to be Yabba Dabba Cadoo.

The Elite were laughing hysterically. I had nothing to say. Instead, I walked over to the water hose used for watering the planters and washed off my sandal and toe. When I finished, I sat in one of the chairs, lit a cigarette and smoked while looking up to the stars. It was a beautiful night.

I was embarrassed. I was embarrassed for living in this shit hole. I was embarrassed for drinking and doing drugs. Most of all, I was embarrassed I had just stepped on a pile of human shit.

I walked out of the court yard and back into the elevator. When the door closed, I pulled out my dick and pissed all over the floor once again. I smiled.

The Elite said, "We're taking this kid with us."

Opening my room door, I walked to the edge of the bed sitting down. I grabbed my bottle from the counter and began drinking. When the bottle left my lips, I found myself gazing at the television. I didn't realize what I was staring at until my vision came to focus. I had an epiphany. I needed to get my story out to the News. I needed help from the public.

I scrambled my brain. I needed a plan. But, who was going to trust this story? Surely the News wouldn't believe. Why would they? I had no evidence. I needed to be creative. I needed them to believe.

Three days later, I called an old friend who was into broadcasting. His name was Arron. He had connections and he also had the gear I needed to achieve my goal. If I wanted to get in touch with the News, I had to blow them off their feet.

I let Arron in on the plan. I told him of my story and he believed me. He knew me as a person and he trusted me.

Two days later, Arron arrived from Los Angeles. I met him in a parking garage right around the corner from my complex. As we stood at the rear of his car, he opened the trunk. Inside, plastic cases filled with all the gear needed to create an open line to every major News channel in California. He had a smile on his face as he popped open one of the cases.

I was excited. I shook his hand thanking him. We hopped in his car, did a line of cocaine and reminisced for a bit before we decided to head back to my place to set up the gear.

We carried the cases through the front office and into the elevator. Arron took a look around and said, "This place is a real shit hole. What are you doing here?"

I explained to him how the Elite were rapping people making it difficult to work. I explained the situation. He gave me this look, half from disbelief and half to say, what the fuck. I looked at him before saying, "If you only knew what was really going on."

We set the cases on my bed and got to work. Arron had to leave pretty much as soon as he arrived. He was due back in LA by the end of the night.

Within an hour my room was filled with antennas and laptops. I was channeled into every major News network I could possibly imagine. The monitors streamed with live broadcasts and in the center of all the gear stood a small microphone. This was how I was going to talk to the News.

Arron said, "Just click on a network when you see someone you want to talk too. Turn up the volume on the microphone here and start talking."

I was amazed with how well he set me up.

"The News will be able to hear me," I asked?

He answered with excitement, "It will go right on the floor as they speak. They will hear you and it's the channel they use to communicate with one another."

I was stoked. I couldn't wait to see it in action. I asked, "Should we try it?"

He answered excited, "Watch this!"

He clicked onto MSNBC, turned up the volume on the microphone, laughed before speaking and said, "This is a test. We are talking to you live and we have some great News awaiting you."

Every single News anchor in the room looked around in surprise. They had an expression of confusion and disbelief on their faces. It stopped them in mid-sentence. It worked and it worked really well.

We laughed for a moment as Arron covered the microphone grunting through his nose. He turned down the volume and said, "You're all set. Let me know when you're finished with this stuff and I'll come down and get it."

He gave me some more direction on the gear and said if I had any questions to give him a call. I thanked him one more time. We celebrated with a rum and coke followed by a couple of lines of cocaine.

Before we knew it, we were at the bar drinking shots. We took turns in the bathroom of the bar doing bumps from what was left of an eight-ball. We drank our asses off. He kept saying, "I'm so late. I have to get the fuck home."

We would laugh.

I woke up the next morning in a hotel room a few blocks from where we were partying. The sun was peeking through the curtains and I had a headache like no other. Arron was passed out on the bed next to me and all I could think about was having a drink to cure the hangover.

I rolled out of bed and headed for the bathroom. When I passed the dresser on my left, I noticed a few empty shot bottles and a couple cans of killed beers. On the desk, a bag of cocaine bigger than the one I started the night with. I laughed thinking, "*I must have met the coke man last night.*"

I took a leak then headed for the bag of cocaine. I snorted a line then reached into the wet bar grabbing a Budweiser and a shot of Vodka. I pounded the shot then drank from the can.

I was on my second beer when Arron woke up. He looked at me and began laughing. He held his head, looked at the beer in my hand and said, "Throw me one of those beers you fucker."

I walked over to the small refrigerator, grabbed a beer then tossed it too him. He cracked it open and began drinking. I smiled thinking it was good to see him.

Arron and I drank while snorting lines for most of the morning. Around noon, he decided it was time to hit the road. He jumped into the shower as I straightened out the room a bit. When he finished, we drank what was left in the refrigerator. We snorted more lines.

At about 1:00 in the afternoon, we headed for the parking garage. The cocaine had Arron somewhat stabilized from the alcohol, so I decided he was okay to drive. He gave me one last run-down on the gear and I thanked him for coming down. We shook hands one last time as he said, "It's always good to see you fucker. I'll talk to you soon. Let me know how it goes for you."

"I'll do that," I returned.

When he was out from his parking spot, I walked back to my complex. On the way home, I stopped by the liquor store to grab a bottle of rum. *"The drink of champions,"* I thought to myself.

*

When I arrived at the complex, I was greeted by Yabba Dabba Cadoo. She had a cigarette in her hand and she was talking to nothing. When I passed, she yelled, "Yabba Dabba Caddo."

I laughed thinking, *"I gotta get the fuck out of here."*

In my room, I jumped in the shower before changing into some fresh cloths. The gear spread throughout my room was impressive. I giggled at its power, the power that was going to set me free.

I drank from the bottle while surfing the channels waiting for somebody worthy of talking too. My plan was to speak to a government official, an official with connections high enough to get this satellite off my fucking head.

I drank for three days straight and found not one single person worthy of my cause. I didn't want to speak to the News directly because I didn't want to wear out my plan of attack. I wanted the element of surprise.

On the fourth day, I had become frustrated. I found nobody. I drank and I drank; purely out of frustration. By eight o'clock in the evening I was wasted. I passed out.

When I woke in the morning, I lay in bed. Every News channel on television streamed through the monitors. The anchor's voices reported all the latest breaking stories. The only problem, they had not heard mine.

A bug crawled across my face. I swatted it off. I was angered. This place was gross and I needed to get away. I needed my normal life back.

I hopped out of bed and poured myself a drink. I gazed upon the female News Anchors thinking, *"I need a girl just like that."*

They were beautiful and I longed for a good woman in my life.

I thought of how crazy this satellite had made me. I wasn't normal in any way. Even though the outside world could not hear my thoughts, I knew they were there. They were making me insane.

I pounded a full glass of rum poured another then walked over to the sink. I turned on the light. What I saw next completely freaked me out. I had red dots all over my face. I looked closer. My arms itched. I gazed upon them. They were covered in red markings. My legs, back and stomach were the same. I had fucking bed bugs.

I shivered. I cursed. I threw my cup across the room. Rum splattered the wall. I took a cold shower. I cursed the Elite.

I spent the rest of the day drinking my life away. I watched the News and still nothing. I wasn't giving up hope.

That night, I bought a fifty dollar sack of speed from the guy downstairs.

By 11:00 pm I was spun out of my mind. I smoked from a speed pipe cursing with a bottle in my hand. I freaked out.

By 2:00 in the morning, the Elite were telling of killers in the building and they were looking for me. I had all the lights off seeking any noise for their whereabouts. The Elite would make noises outside my door with their key system.

With a noise, I jumped on the floor thinking someone was going to shoot me through the door. I was going nuts. Between the Elite and the drugs I was off my rocker. I was on a sick one.

By 5:30 am, the Elite had switched the brainwash making me believe there was a killer in the building killing my neighbors. They made me believe the cops thought the killer was me. Sounds of radios pierced my walls. It sounded just like the police.

It was not. It was the Elite using their key system to imitate cops talking over their radios. With the drugs in my system, it made my brain think it was reality; it made me believe it was all true. They thought I was a killer.

"What's going on guys," I asked? "Who's out there?"

The Elite responded, "It's the police and they think you're a killer."

My heart dropped and I didn't know what to do. I was back on my feet standing there listening.

I then thought to look out the window to see if the complex was surrounded by police. I opened the shade then sat at the edge of my bed. Outside there was nothing to see with the naked eye. I figured the police were hiding in case I had a gun.

Ten minutes later, I had my hands in the air yelling out the window. I didn't want the police coming into my room shooting. I didn't want to die. And once again, I didn't want to die like this.

I yelled with my hands still in the air, "I'm unarmed don't shoot."

There was no response. I went on like this for almost forty-five minutes. The police never appeared. No swat no nothing. Just me in the window shocked thinking the police were after me for murder. When I thought about it I thought, I've never killed anything on purpose in my life. I ran over a few dear with my jeep in Colorado, but I never killed anything on purpose. Just a few bugs and spiders along with a couple of deer in the road and that's it.

With my hands in the air, I yelled through the window to the city of San Diego, "I'm unarmed. Don't shoot."

I stopped yelling. The drugs were wearing off. I called 911. They told me there was nothing wrong. I gave them the address to the complex and asked, "Are their police outside of this address looking for somebody?"

The lady took a moment to check her screens before reassuring me there was not. It was all built in my head. The drugs made me paranoid and the Elite put the thoughts in my head. They made me look like an idiot once again.

I jumped in the shower to cool off. I grabbed my wallet from the dresser then headed out the door. I was on my way to the liquor store for a bottle of rum. When I stepped off the curb to cross the street in front of my complex, a black women came up to me and said, "Hey Boo."

I didn't know what she meant. She was calling me Boo. I walked around the corner and another woman called me Boo. I began to think, *"Why are these people calling me Boo?"*

I purchased my bottle of rum and headed back to the complex. I kept thinking about the Boo comments and it was beginning to piss me off. Then, it hit me. These fuckers put my night's adventure with speed and paranoia on YouTube. I said, "Did you mother fuckers put me on YouTube?"

The Elite busted out laughing as one of them said, "Buy your tickets now. They're cheap."

I reddened in the cheeks. I had chills up my spine. They were putting me on the fucking internet. Dirty I tell you. Dirty mother fuckers.

I went back to my room, opened the bottle, poured myself a drink, and sat in front of the computer monitors. I wanted my revenge and I wanted it bad.

An hour later, I had finished my bottle. I was still amped from the speed and I was on a roll. The only problem, I drank close to a fifth and I had not slept from the night before. I was losing motor functions and crashing fast. My head was drooping and I could have sworn I was drooling from the mouth.

I reached for my bottle cursing. I said to the Elite, "This is bullshit. I'm not quitting."

Then the man I wanted to see appeared before my eyes. He was giving a speech on the News. The headline read the name of the News Agency. I couldn't believe what I was seeing. I had hit the jackpot. The dude of all dudes to speak to was now on the News. I turned the volume up on the microphone and said, "Mr. O, you're just the man I'm looking for."

My words were slurred. Mr. O froze with his speech. A smile appeared at the corner of his lips. He continued talking to the public.

I said, "Mr. O, do I have a story for you. I'm a real telepth and I'm being brainwashed through one of your satellites in a very unique way."

I gave him the name of the Elite crew responsible. He put his hand in the air to gesture both he heard me and also to wait a second. He wanted to finish his speech. So, I waited.

When Mr. O finished, I said with slur, "Mr. O, I'm a real telepath and I have been hooked up to a spy satellite system used by the Elite. I've been on it for over four years now and it's brainwashing the shit out of me. This Elite crew is also using their key system to torture me. I want it off my head."

When I began talking of the Elite's technology, Mr. O put his hands in the air and said, "Hold on. This is something we should talk about in person."

What he meant was this is classified information that shouldn't be revealed to the public. But, I had his attention. He was aware of the technology.

I said, "I can't wait to talk in person because everyone I call blows me off. Nobody wants to talk about this situation, so you and I are going to talk about it now in front of the News."

Mr. O, being the man of the United States of America was caught off guard. He was kind and he was going to listen.

He walked to another News room as the camera's followed him. He sat next to the News anchors in an open chair. Everyone was silent including Mr. O. The public could not hear my voice, but the News anchors could and Mr. O could. It was a live broadcast. The world could see and hear them, but they could not see and hear me. I said to the president, "I'm drunk. I'm drinking every day. I'm doing drugs. I've been up on speed and cocaine for three days. I just drank a fifth of rum and I'm drunker than shit. I got this fucking satellite on my head and I want it off."

Mr. O was trying not to laugh. It wasn't because the situation wasn't serious. It was because I was so wasted I could barely talk. I looked down at my arms. They were covered in bed bug bites. I didn't have a shirt on and I was sweating profusely. I was drunk, coming down from a speed high and talking to the man of the United States of America. I laughed. I said, "Mr. O, I'm a fucking mess. This shit sucks."

I went on telling of the story from the last four years to Mr. O. What I didn't tell him, I didn't tell him the Elite were rapping people through the satellite. I felt it best to be left un-said in front of the public for the time being. I really didn't want Mr. O mixed up with the Elite's rape. I just wanted him to look into what was going on.

Mr. O was concerned as I spoke. He was still serious, but he smiled. When I gave him the commander's name, his thought was this, "*He even knows their names.*"

I didn't repeat his thought, I just smiled. When the News broke for a commercial break, Mr. O was gone. I wasn't sad or mad. He listened to my story. I was sure he was going to look into it. I laughed thinking, "*He's my favorite next to Bill Clinton.*"

Since Mr. O was gone, I began speaking to the News about random shit mainly because I was wasted and I felt we had a moment in time together. The girls were funny. I said my name one more time. The women anchor feeling sad for me then said, "We are here on a live feed with Boo Marx."

She was sweet and I could tell that after the News heard the story they had mixed feelings about the situation. I spent the next three hours talking with them. They no longer spoke of the News to the public. We were having conversations with one another. In fact, in three hours I hadn't heard one single word of News. We were just bullshitting through the television and my microphone.

At one point, I heard the ladies thought. I repeated it back to her. Her face froze and she said, "Oh my God, a real telepath."

I said, "Yes mam, a real telepath."

She and two others began laughing.

The Elite were in shock. They couldn't believe what had just happened. They were busted. I heard the commander say, "Get that fucking kid off the News.

What happened next was unreal. These guys from the Elite were so cocky they began rapping the News anchors. Moments later, the women said, "We are feeling some things over here that are inappropriate. Stop doing that."

I felt her concern and said, "It's not me mam. There is more to this story that has yet to be revealed."

I think she figured it out. They continued talking to me.

For the next three weeks I spoke with the News Anchors while being brainwashed and tortured by the Elite. I didn't talk about my story much, I just drank and bullshitted with them. We had fun.

The Elite were pissed off, so they continued raping the News anchors as I spoke to them. All I could say to the News was, "It's not me, its' part of the story and you will have to wait and see what happens."

They understood.

In four weeks, I had spoken too many through the News. I covered every major News network in the United States. They were all aware of my telepathic capabilities as I showed them by answering many of their thoughts. They were in both shock and disbelief. I had succeeded. I had stunned News networking throughout the nation.

I partied, I drank, I snorted drugs and I acted like an idiot. I was out of my mind.

A couple of days later, I was walking down by the beach. I was in constant communication with the News and the Elite didn't like what was happening. The story was leaking out to the Nations News Industry and the Elite's technology was going to be next. If this shit didn't stop soon, I was going to leak more than the Elites key system and rape of the public. I was going to release the secret of all secrets. A secret I had discovered eighteen years ago on my own. This is a secret about humanity and this is something I can prove. It's insane what I had discovered being a real telepath.

As I walked, I was beat down by the sun. It was hot and I was drunk as usual. I looked out to the ocean thinking how nice it would be to take a swim. With the thought, a loud high frequency entered my ears and it kept getting louder.

It was intense. I stopped walking. I held my ears trying to block out the noise. Since it was coming through a laser it went straight through my hands to my eardrums. I yelled, "Stop that. That shit hurts my ears."

The Elite said with anger, "We don't want you talking to the News anymore and we don't want you reading their thoughts. And keep our technology out of your mouth you fuck."

I was bent over harmed by the noise and holding my ears. I tried walking but the sound was so intense it began knocking me off balance. I stumbled trying to keep myself upright. But, I couldn't. Before I knew it, I was tripping sideways. I crashed, landing on a concrete driveway in front of a home. I kicked with my legs as my ears rang with the rage. I violently turned my head from side to side as the noise pierced through. I felt like I was going to vomit and I did.

When the noise stopped, the Elite yelled, "Now stay off the News."

I got up from the pavement, walked to my truck and drove home. When I got home, I talked to the News.

For the next three days, the Elite ran the frequency through my ears. All I could do was drink. I lost a portion of my hearing in both ears. I'm partially deaf now and sometimes it's hard to hear. There is more damage in my left, but both have been harmed. I don't hear so well telepathically anymore, but I do hear thoughts on occasion. It still works just not as well as it used too. The worst part, I can still hear the Elite.

I called NCIS to let them know what was going on. I called to tell of the rape. I called to tell of the children and the disabled. I called to tell of the women who were pregnant. I called to let them know I had spoken to the president.

In return, they told me to stop calling. They told me I was a civilian. They told me there was nothing they could do. They told me I was crazy.

They called my Parole officer. My parole officer wasn't happy...

CHAPTER 17

I was standing on the side walkway of the complex late at night. I had a black man with me who I was purchasing crack cocaine from. He was a bigger man with a lot of comedy to his character. Right before we were about to make the deal, a police officer rolled by stopping at the traffic light on the corner. I gazed upon him thinking nothing of it.

Five minutes later, another police officer pulled around the corner in his cruiser. This one stopped along the curb in front of us. He got out of his car and asked if either of us was on parole. Both of us were. According to the fourth amendment waver, police officers were allowed to search parolees at any given time they wanted to.

I had a crack pipe and a speed pipe in my back pocket along with some pills. I was busted. It was a matter of time before the officer searched my person.

Within minutes I was searched. I was caught with both pipes and the pills. I was arrested for the possession of drugs and drug paraphernalia. I was handcuffed and placed in the back seat of the cruiser. I was on my way to jail.

I wasn't disappointed I was under arrest. It seemed to be part of the brainwash program. I was fucked up all the time and my brain was such a mess I was getting arrested all the time. I couldn't stay out of jail or prison for the life of me.

I was booked, processed and given a bed for the night. When I went to court, the District Attorney cut me a break. She sent me back to prison on a parole violation instead of charging me with the possession of a controlled substance.

Days later, I was sent to the nearest Correctional Facility. I went in front of the parole board and was offered a six month inpatient drug and alcohol treatment program. I accepted the offer.

Two weeks later, I was released from prison and placed on a transportation van. Where I was heading, to a Rehabilitation Center in Downtown San Diego.

We arrived a little after noon. I was anxious to be out of prison and back into society. It was a rehab, but it was better than incarceration.

The first two hours, I went through an orientation process. I was assigned a room and a bed. I was given hygiene products and bedding. I was handed a rules packet then given some free time to set up my room. My clothes were still down the street in my apartment, so I was given a ride over to get them.

The first two weeks, I went through a series of daily treatment classes. It was always funny to hear the stories behind those walls. This guy, Gary, was a black man. Whenever he told a story at the end of the sentence he would say, "You dig."

Gary had a great story and Gary was funnier than shit.

Gary was telling of one of his crack adventures. He had been on crack for many days. He had also been roaming the streets fiending for another hit.

Gary said, "I was high. You dig? I had been running the streets, looking in people's windows trying to steal shit. You Dig? Well as I was walking around, it was like two o'clock in the afternoon and I was high as shit. You dig? Well, well I shit my pants. You Dig?"

Everyone in the room was hysterical. Gary had me laughing my ass off. He continued, "After I shit my pants, I had to go. You dig? At one point I was running down the street because I had flies buzzing me. They smelled the shit. You dig? I swatted at them, I was running, I took my shirt off and twirled it around my body. I couldn't get those mother fuckers to leave me alone. You dig?"

The room was in tears. Gary finally said, "It was then I decided I needed to change my life. I was so fucked up I had flies chasing me because I shit my pants. You dig?"

The way this man told his story, it was the funniest story I'd ever heard. I laughed for days.

I went through that program for months. I battled the Elite and they battled back. They mainly told me I was a monster, a rapist, a murder and a terrorist. They used the brainwash for their excuse. They were going to tell everyone I was some fucked up kid, but I wasn't. I was a nice kid with addiction issues.

One of the guys said to the commander, "What are we going to do if we get caught?"

The commander returned, "We'll just tell everyone we thought he was a terrorist."

I laughed knowing it would never hold value. I didn't even own a BB-Gun. I wasn't a rapist or a murderer either.

At the end of the program, I said good-bye to the many counselors who helped me through my stay. They heard my story and even though they did not believe, they stayed supportive. They were loving, caring, honest and fun. The Lighthouse had a way of making you want to stay sober and it had to do with the counselors working there. They were the true backbone of the program. Hands down my favorite rehabilitation center so far.

I moved out of the Lighthouse on my last day and into a sober living complex in North Park. The place was old and rundown, but the rent was cheap. I just needed a place to rest my head until I transferred my parole back home. I wanted my family back in my life.

During my stay in the sober living, I began writing this book. In return, it began changing my life. I was free in a way as I wrote these words on paper. In some odd way, it made me feel like everything was going to be okay.

CHAPTER 18

Two months later, I was on a plane heading home. As I soared the cloudy skies, I felt as if I was leaving my troubles behind. It was a relief to be on my way home.

The stewardesses were nice. They were raped by the Elite as well. They liked me and would always laugh when they walked by. One of them even called me a pervert. It came in her thoughts. I just smiled knowing it felt good for them, but it was still rape. The sensation was like no other on earth.

I arrived home late in the evening. My parents were at the airport waiting to pick me up. They had smiles on their faces and as I smelled the desert air. I thought, *"It's good to be home."*

My parents had since moved into a new home. It was nice and spacious with plenty of land and a swimming pool. It was high in the mountains of the Colorado National Monument surrounded by Juniper trees. I loved it.

My room was cozy and I had plenty of space with a nice view of the canyons. The sun was still shining and I thought of how good it was to finally be home in a nice place. I had been living in hell holes because of the Elite. I smiled thinking, *"You can't hurt me here."*

My brother owned a Philadelphia Cheese Steak restaurant in town. My father had taken over the restaurant since the construction business was slow due to the crash in the economy. He wasn't much of a cook, but he was definitely a good business man.

The name of the restaurant is T's Steaks located right on campus of a University. It's the best cheese steak in Colorado and my favorite place to eat. If you're in Colorado, go get yourself a T's steak. My father no longer owns the place, but my old roommate does and he's one hell of a guy. He's an islander from Hawaii.

I moved to town working at T's during the day and at night during the weekends. I tried to stay sober, but it just wasn't happening with the Elite around. They were rapping people again. Every girl and guy who walked through those doors was raped.

I got weird looks and funny looks. I got perverted looks. I even had girls think they were in love. Their googly eyes gave them away. Most of the people who were rapped here were enrolled in classes at University. They weren't very old and they were all college students. They are now victims of rape by the Elite.

I couldn't handle what was going on around me. I started drinking again to get away. I went months just working and drinking. I started going to the bars hoping to meet a good girl to bring into my life. Most of all, I wanted to be normal.

I went to the bar one night. I was heavily intoxicated. I wanted to get sober and the only way I knew how was by doing drugs.

I met a guy who wore a shirt symbolizing the British Flag. He had on eyeliner and he had the look of a tweeker. I asked him if he could get me some drugs. His eyes lit up as he said he could. We went back to his place where I purchased a fifty dollar bag of crystal meth. I smoked a couple of bowls before walking home.

When I got home, the nightmare began. I became paranoid. It's what the drug did to me. The Elite saw my paranoia and acted upon it. They began saying, "Give him the gas."

My eyes searched the windows. My brain began thinking. I began to freak out. With the drugs in my system, I began to hallucinate. I began thinking somebody was inside my house. I began thinking somebody was outside my house. I freaked out.

When I looked towards my window, I began to see gas. In reality it wasn't there, but in my mind it was. I was hallucinating and I began to believe I was under attack. I opened my bedroom door stopping by the basement stairs. The Elite made a noise which sounded like a bullet being chambered into a gun. They made this noise several times.

In my bare feet, I ran out the front door. As soon as I hit the sidewalk, I heard a noise. It sounded as if a bullet was whistling past my ears. I freaked out and ran. I ran across the street into a neighbor's yard a couple of blocks over. I hopped the fence and began knocking on the back door.

Another whistle…

Another bullet missed…

It wasn't real it was just their key system making these noises. They wanted me to panic and it was working.

I was afraid and desperate. I turned the knob of the back door and ran in. I yelled, "Call 911 I'm being attacked. I was delusional and out of my mind. The drugs and the Elite had me freaking out once again.

Noticing a light coming from the crack under a door, I opened it. It led down to a basement where I heard a woman's voice. She said, "What the fuck is going on."

I answered, "Call 911 please."

I was down in the basement standing next to her. She was as freaked out as I was. She had a phone in her hand dialing the emergency number. She gave her address to the dispatcher then she went to a cabinet and grabbed a gun.

We went upstairs where I sat on the stairs in a complete panic. She was standing behind me with a 357 Snub Nose pointed directly at the back of my head. She told me not to move or she would shoot. I didn't care she had a gun pointed at my head. I just felt safer with somebody else around.

The police arrived and I was arrested for felony trespassing. I was locked up at the Mesa county jail where I spent the night in a cell letting the drugs wear off. The Elite laughed calling me an idiot. They were right. I needed to stop doing that drug.

I had to wonder if doing drugs had anything to do with them. I realized it was partially them and partially me. They were at fault for causing me to drink so heavily and I was at fault for doing the drugs.

I concluded it was their fault since there was no telling if I would even be drinking if it wasn't for them torturing, brainwashing and rapping me. I may have decided to get sober a long time ago. There was no way to tell.

I spent six months in the county jail going through court proceedings. I was released on parole and sent home to my parents.

A month later, my parents decided to move to Minot North Dakota. My father took a job with a company that was doing a large construction project. I was moving with them. In my mind, it was just another town for the Elite to rape in.

CHAPTER 19

We packed our house and got ready for the movers. My father had headed to Minot a month ahead of my mother and I. He was going to rent a home for us to live in while our house was being sold.

When the movers finished packing our house, my mother and I drove with my father who had arrived back in Colorado the night before. We began our drive to Minot North Dakota.

It took us twenty-two hours. We made the trip in two days. My ass hurt and I was ready for a new change. When I stepped out of the vehicle for the first time in many hours, I stretched taking a look around. We would be living in an apartment complex until my parents figured out what they were going to do. It was nice, but it wasn't home.

We unpacked the car and moved in. The Movers weren't showing up for a few more days, so I slept on a cot. I lay awake at night talking to the Elite. They were my only friends. I hate to say it, but I had gotten so used them I was no longer upset with what they were doing. They had become a part of my life. They had become a part of my head.

*

I found a job down the street from where I lived. They made the best pizza in town. I worked and I stayed sober. I was doing much better with my life.

The Elite… The Elite rapped everyone who came through the door including my coworkers. The girls I worked with gave me funny stares. The guys didn't know what to say. I had to live with the Elite and I had no other choice. I was going to have to live with them rapping everyone around me.

I spoke to my bosses Son-In-Law. I told him what I was going through and who was behind the charade. He didn't believe me at first, but he soon felt the feeling on his nuts. Now, he just smiles at me and shakes his head. He's a great guy and a good friend.

*

My life was anything but normal. I lived with lasers on my asshole and scrotum. I was threatened. My family was threatened. I was told to kill myself. I drank, did drugs and kept getting into trouble with the law. I lost my head and my natural thoughts. My memory had gone. I was delirious and out of touch with society.

I wanted to be normal. I wanted a normal life. I'm currently writing this sentence you are reading right now with seven years of brainwash, rape and torture under my belt. It all started June 25th 2007. I didn't ask for this in life and I definitely didn't deserve it. I've had my problems, but nobody deserves this type of treatment.

I needed to find love in my life. I had been ill treated for so many years by the Elite. I hadn't had a girlfriend for thirteen years, six because of prison and seven due to the Elites treatment.

I decided the human is not capable of normal survival without love. I needed and longed for the love of a woman. I wanted conversation. I wanted to cuddle on the couch and watch movies. I wanted to cook and laugh. I wanted to fulfill sexual desires. I wanted my girl.

I stood in front of the Pizza oven at work one day and told myself, "*I want a girl.*"

I thought about it for a minute. I laughed thinking, "*This is going to be a bad idea. If I go looking for a girl, I'm going to get the emotions stuck in my head.*"

I didn't care. I just wanted a girl.

Two days later, the perfect girl walked through the doors of the Restaurant. She was pretty with blonde hair. She had a smile of love. She had these teeth like the singer Jewel which made her appear even sexier. She had tattoos on her arms and she was quiet and caring.

When I walked around the corner seeing her for the first time, my heart melted. I said to the Elite, "This is the one."

I made as much conversation as I could with her without overdoing it. When it was time to give her the bill, I wrote my number at the top of the paper. She smiled as she read. I was a little shy. It had been a very long time since I asked a girl out. I turned around and walked away.

Ten minutes later, she stood by the front counter. I walked over and said, "Hi."

She gave me the softest smile and said, "Do you have a pen? I'm going to give you my number as well."

I handed her the pen and she wrote down her number. At the top of the paper it read her name, Kylee. Her name was one of my favorites. She was perfect.

We said our good-byes as I watched her walk out the door.

I waited three days before calling Kylee. I actually sent a text. I asked if she was interested in meeting up for a drink. She wrote back, "I'm actually trying to make things work with my ex- right now. It was bad news, but not the worse."

I wrote, "Would you be interested in keeping a friendship until you see what's going on."

She wrote, "I would."

A week later, I tried again. I wrote asking her if she wanted to meet up for a drink. She wrote back saying she had to work. I was sad, but I wasn't giving up.

Two weeks later I tried again. This time there was no response. Since the Elite were with me and they had a satellite on her, I asked, "What's her deal."

One of the Elite said, "We rape her every time you send a text. She doesn't like you."

I was devastated. I didn't know what to do. For weeks I dreamed of being with her. I thought of her smile and her cuteness. I loved everything about her.

I got pissed real fast. These guys were fucking off everything in my life. I walked over to the beer tap and poured myself a drink. It was the drink that ruined my life once again.

I drank for weeks on end. I went to the bars in search of the perfect girl. With the town I was living in, I was limited on selection. Every time I found a good girl, the Elite would rape her steering her away. They knew it was affecting my heart and causing me to drink more heavily. They used it as a strategy hoping I would kill myself.

I went through girl after girl. My selection was diminished. I had to resort to the internet hoping to find the right girl. The drunker I got, the more fucked up my messages became. I was frustrated writing nonsense on the computer screen. I was ruining girl after girl.

After a while, I decided I just wanted to get laid. I said, "Fuck love. I just need to get laid."

I came home from the bar late one night. I was drunk off of rum and still on a mission to get laid. I got a phone call from a girl. She lived two hours away and was willing to meet up. I was happy. I didn't know what she looked like and I didn't care. I just wanted to get laid. It was stuck in my fucking head and I couldn't get it out.

I told her I was on my way. I said, "I have to jump in the shower and I'll be right over."

She agreed giving me directions to her place. I was excited.

I was on the road twenty minutes later. I did 90mph the entire way. When I arrived, she came out to my car. She had a blanket and pillow in her hand. She was big and ugly. It was dark and I didn't care. She said, "We can't hang out here, but there is a campground down the road."

She opened the passenger door and jumped in. She looked at me and said, "You're wasted. I can smell alcohol all over you."

I laughed. I was wasted. She opened her purse and pulled out a bag of Crystal Meth. She asked, "This will help you out."

It was only a line, but I was in need of its strength. She crushed up the rock. I rolled a bill. She handed me the bag. I stuck the straw in the open end and snorted.

It burned my nostril...

We drove down a couple of side streets. The girls thought, "*Oh my God, this kid is making me so horny.*"

The Elite were rapping her. It was an amazing feeling, but it was still wrong.

The girls name was Megan. We were both high and on our way to the campsite to get naked. I didn't care what she looked like I just needed a woman with me. The drug made the sexual desire even more intense.

We pulled out onto the main road and headed west at the normal rate of speed. We talked and got to know one another along the way. She was a nice girl, just not the typical person I normally hung out with.

It wasn't long before she had me turn down a country road. I was still drunk and the drug hadn't taken on its full affect. It was early in the AM hours and I was excited for a good time.

We arrived in the campsite. There was nobody else around. It was cold and into the mid-winter temperatures. There was a little snow on the ground. I parked the ride along a site on the river and hopped out to put the back seats down. Then I made a bed.

Megan climbed in the back. She was wearing spandex. I pulled them over her hips, around her ankles and tossed them into the corner. I put my head between her legs and worked my tongue around her vagina. She wasn't attractive in any sense, but like my father always said, "Big girls need loving too."

The Elite were cracking up. I wasn't giving up. I drove all the way the fuck down here, so I was getting laid no matter what.

Megan was on top of me. With the drugs, I couldn't get a boner. She wrapped her lips around my cock and proceeded in giving me a blow-job. It felt good, but I still couldn't get hard.

An hour went by then two more. Megan was still going at it. She kept her mouth wrapped around me the entire time. I still couldn't get it up.

The sun started coming up. The alcohol wore off and I was feeling the intensity of the drug. My mind started playing tricks on me like they always did from the Elite's brainwash. I wanted to get the fuck out of there.

I called it quits on busting a nut. I grabbed my pants and threw them on. Megan got herself situated. Within minutes, we were back on the road. I was beginning to become paranoid.

When I pulled out of the campground, I passed a red pickup truck. The man behind the wheel looked at me strangely. One of the Elite said, "He just spotted Vince."

My heart dropped to the floor. The Elite finally sent somebody to kill me. I cut the wheel turning in the opposite direction of the red truck. I sped down the road. I turned the windy path hopping the man wouldn't catch up. Megan had an expression on her face. She was becoming scared.

I didn't want her to panic, so I slowed down a bit. It wasn't long before my brain had me believing every vehicle on the road was after me.

I headed out to the main road making a right hand turn in the direction of Minot. All I wanted to do was get home. I wanted to be in a familiar place. I sped down the road at 80mph. I dodged cars and trucks. Each time I passed a vehicle, I waited the devastating blow. I waited for the bullet that was going to shatter my skull.

Megan was beginning to panic. We came upon her town. She said, "Turn here into Ray. That's where I live."

With killers on our tail, I wasn't stopping for anyone. I went straight through the green light without turning. Megan was beginning to panic even more. She said with scare in her voice, "Dude, that's where I live. You have to turn around."

What sounded like a bullet piercing metal struck my vehicle. One of the Elite said, "That was a miss."

I was frightened, but I was giving up. Megan was just going to have to come along for the ride. I pushed the gas pedal to the floor taking off. I didn't want to tell her, her life was at risk. I knew if we stopped the car we were both dead. We had to keep going.

Bullet after bullet hit the car. Each time it was considered a miss. The windshield had not broken and the engine was still running. Fuck the damage we were on the run.

We were doing 90mph with what seemed like bullets racking the car. With each sound, Megan looked around. She was curious to the noise. I wouldn't tell her. I was scared for our lives. I told her to call 911 and tell them I'm having a panic attack. I said, "Tell them to send an ambulance as well."

Megan looked at me and called 911. She was on the phone with a dispatcher. She gave them our direction along with the color and make of the vehicle. She said, "This kids having a panic attack and he won't stop the car."

Ten minutes later, a police cruiser was on our tail. I didn't see him at first because the windows of the vehicle were fogged over. I didn't have the heat on and I wasn't stopping the truck. The cruiser pulled in front of us pressing his breaks. I was forced to stop the car.

The officer stepped out of his vehicle drawing his gun. I was told to place my hands in the air. Once my hands were in the air, I was told to step out of the vehicle. I did as he commanded. I was handcuffed and placed under arrest. I was charged with a DUI even though I was no longer drunk. I just had alcohol on my body.

Megan was placed in a separate cruiser. The officers drove us to the Police station where I was asked a series of questions. I knew they would never believe my story, so I kept my mouth shut. I even had the Elite saying, "Don't tell. Just don't tell."

In the end, the Elite had used their key system to make me believe I was under attack. When I was on drugs, they got me every time.

When it was all over and the drugs wore off, I had to laugh at myself. Even though I was undergoing severe brainwash, the drugs made it that much worse. Sometimes I would say to myself, "What the fuck was I thinking."

And that's just it. When you're brainwashed you lose your entire brain and you're never thinking clearly. It's a bitch.

CHAPTER 20

W ell, I finished my book. This story is 100% true and there is a lot more left from these pages. I was raped and tortured the entire time while writing this book. This Elite crew didn't want these words published.

This is the best I could write while under duress. I know it's not perfect and it hasn't been edited properly. I just needed to get it out to the public.

For the public, since many of us were raped by the Elite. I have a secret which I'm still holding. This secret was discovered by me many years ago. It is a secret of humanity and it affects every single one of our lives. It's a great secret. It's actually the best secret you could possibly imagine. It is a secret the Elite have been aware of for some time. I've just known longer than they have, that's all.

Since I'm pretty certain this story is going to get covered up, I'm asking the News to put me live on air for the entire world to learn about this secret. I'm giving the Elite a choice. They can either give up their commander who is responsible for all of this, or they can lose their secret. I'm willing to bet this secret is more important than the commander.

The News is for the people by the people. So let's show our concern for all of those who were raped by the Elite in our country. Let's find the man responsible together. Let's bring this story to all of our homes in hopes of justice.

First, I would like to forewarn the News and the public. The Elite are going to try and cover for themselves by sending satellite footage of me while losing my mind. They are going to try and use this tactic to discredit this book. They are going to try and make me look crazy.

The question is why is there satellite footage of me in the first place? If any of this footage floats around, all I can say is, "I was a fucking mess."

I don't do drugs anymore and haven't for some time. I only drink a few times a month and my life is starting to come around. I'm still under attack by the Elite, but I don't let them get to my head as much.

So now I have to ask, "Is everybody out there ready to see who the number one serial rapist is in the world? Or, do you want to know the coolest secret in the history of mankind."

Let's find out!

Before we get started, I have one last thing to say to all the News agencies of our nation. I was respectful in keeping my secret of how I actually broke into your live broadcasting system. I'm asking of you to do the same by respecting me and my story. Don't let the Elite cover for themselves on any of your networks. They raped some of you as well. Naval Criminal Investigative Services needs to know the truth, so let's make sure they get the proper story.

I hope everyone enjoyed my story and I want all to know it is not over. I'm tortured daily for these words and it has not yet stopped. Today is July 16, 2014.

CHAPTER 21

Today is October 30th 2016. I'm writing this chapter to let all those who have read my book the secret I have kept from these pages. The reason I am revealing this secret now is due to the Elites constant improper treatment towards me. They are running high frequencies through my ears severely damaging my hearing trying to destroy my telepathic abilities. Telepathy is a radio wave and can be built.

In the human brain between 10 and 50 mega-hertz is an electromagnetic frequency. An electromagnetic frequency is a radio wave. If we build a laser that recreates the wave pattern, amplify the wave and build a fiber optic receiver we will be able to hear human thoughts.

The secret I am about to reveal has been discovered by me in 2001. I have discovered as a real telepath human spirits communicate on the telepathic frequency. We are still alive after death. Everyone is alive and well; just without body. They talk normal, travel the streets, ride on boats and walk through our walls and homes. Everyone is normal and exactly the same as the day they died.

The Elite has tried killing me to protect this secret. With my knowledge in building telepathy and it's capabilities creates a big problem. They can't keep spirits out of our secret facilities. Spirits communicate with us now and they can move freely through buildings. I believe this discovery to be the natural evolution of the human race as well as the animal kingdom as whole; it's science and we should all be aware.

We are alive after death!!

Awesome!!

Printed in the United States
By Bookmasters